for

PEGGY McCORMACK

and

MARY SUE MORROW

CONTENTS

ACNOWLEDGMENTS

A sabbatical semester provided by the Grants and Leaves Committee of Loyola University enabled me to begin work on this project. My colleagues Mary McCay, Peggy McCormack, Melanie McKay, and Nancy Anderson graciously answered my many questions about American literature, American history, and feminist theory. Alice Templeton helped me to revise and edit the manuscript. And, as always when I write, Loyola University's interlibrary loan officer, Pat Doran, provided me with every book and article I needed. I appreciate their assistance as well as the daily support of my husband, Vick Adams. I also very much appreciate and wish to acknowledge the positive spirit and fine judgment of SUNY Press's director, Priscilla Ross, and production editor Laurie Searl.

INTRODUCTION

Much of what literary scholars assume about women's entrance into professional writing at the beginning of the twentieth century comes not from history but from the fictionalized example powerfully rendered in Virginia Woolf's *A Room of One's Own*, published in 1929. Woolf's characterization of Judith Shakespeare, situated in the Renaissance but applied to women's situations from that time forward, focuses on a group that even a very gifted woman could not join, a public door she could not enter beyond which men learned their craft and performed. Shakespeare's hypothetical sister is described as an outsider, unable to study acting or to learn playwriting:

> She stood at the stage door; she wanted to act, she said. Men laughed in her face. The manager—a fat, loose-lipped man—guffawed. He bellowed something about poodles dancing and women acting—no woman, he said, could possibly be an actress. He hinted—you can imagine what. She could get no training in her craft. (83)

Woolf emphatically concludes that such a gifted woman, barred from the world of art, would have "dashed her brains out on the moor or mopped and mowed about the highways crazed with the torture that her gift had put her to" (85).

Although Woolf's title focuses on women's need of a secure living and a separate space for work, this characterization of Judith Shakespeare clearly also concerns women's separation from professional training and interaction with colleagues. For young men of the 1920s, Woolf asserts, college provided the best locus for studying the craft of writing. Since few women could venture there, however, they did not learn their craft as well, and thus they rarely created truly artistic renderings of their frustrations and dreams. Woolf substantiates her belief "that poetical genius bloweth where it listeth, and equally in poor and rich, holds little truth" by examining the lives of Coleridge, Wordsworth, Byron,

Shelley, and other famous writers: nine of twelve were university men, and they all had groups of colleagues available to them—for criticism, support, and entrance into professional publication (186). In discussing Oxbridge, her combination of Cambridge and Oxford, Woolf mentions professors that her fictional "Mary" cannot talk to, libraries she cannot use, seminar rooms she cannot enter, community dinners she cannot attend. Woolf even considers "the admirable smoke and drink and the deep armchairs and the pleasant carpets . . . the urbanity, the geniality, the dignity which are the offspring of luxury and privacy and space" (39). This passage may seem to concern nonessentials of the better funded men's college, the accouterments of a club, but instead it describes a rare and important privilege, a site where men could comfortably share their work, respond to their reading, and seek literary advice.

Women's isolation from such groups of writers, Woolf contends, also leads to isolation from the larger community of readers. Although all artists have a difficult time establishing themselves with an appreciative audience, the general public believed that the woman writer, not supported by a creative tradition or part of any influential network, had no right to even make the attempt:

> The indifference of the world which Keats and Flaubert and other men of
> genius have found so hard to bear was in her case not indifference but hos-
> tility. The world did not say to her as it said to them, Write if you choose;
> it makes no difference to me. The world said with a guffaw, Write? What's
> the good of your writing? (91)

This sarcastic "What's the good of your writing?" stemmed from two sets of doors that constrained women: the doors of their homes, behind which their lives should occur, and the doors to public sites, like the theatre or the college, behind which experience and training were available only to men. Judith was meant to stay within the doors of her home as the wife of a wool-stapler and never to seek entrance to school or theatre doors.

As a result of this isolation and restriction, most women confined their literary efforts to letters or short poems shared among friends. When they tried to create professional products, Woolf argues, their lack of training generally rendered them unable to move beyond plainly stated anger or fear. As Woolf moves along imagined library shelves, she finds very few products by women and almost none that mine the potential of Judith Shakespeare and so many of her sisters.

Twenty years later, in 1949, this depiction of the hypothetical Judith was given a powerful theoretical overlay in Simone de Beauvoir's *The Second Sex*.

De Beauvoir asserts that as men envisioned themselves as the powerful Subject, they did so by casting woman as the Other—the dependent, the inessential, the care-giver, the object: "[S]he is taught that to please she must try to please, she must make herself object; she should therefore renounce her autonomy. She is treated like a live doll and is refused liberty" (295). As a result of these narrow definitions and expectations, de Beauvoir contends, women did not become the authors whose works shaped an era, or even the audience of such works; they lived within a dominant culture not of their own mental creation:

> Women do not set themselves up as Subject and hence erected no virile myth in which their projects are reflected; they have no religion or poetry of their own; they still dream through the dreams of men. Gods made by males are the gods they worship. Men have shaped for their own exaltation great virile figures: Hercules, Prometheus, Parsifal; woman has only a secondary part to play in the destiny of these heroes. . . . Representation of the world, like the world itself, is the work of men; they describe it from their own point of view, which they confuse with absolute truth. (150–51)

In a social system defined by Self/Other, women's writing would be no essential act, but perhaps a mode of self-expression or a means of wiling away the time. Even within these limited genres and purposes, de Beauvoir argues echoing Woolf, women's efforts suffered because of their lack of training in writing and lack of experience with disciplined work:

> Even if she begins fairly early, she seldom envisages art as serious work; accustomed to idleness, having never felt in her mode of life the austere necessity of discipline, she will not be capable of sustained and persistent effort, she will never succeed in gaining a solid technique. (739)

Both *A Room of One's Own* and *The Second Sex* describe a European intellectual life from which women were kept separate, as untrained and unworthy. This influential description and analysis, from 1929 and 1949, would certainly also apply to American cultural life of the nineteenth century. In America as in Europe, that century ended as it began, with Writer firmly inscribed as a role of Man. In nineteenth-century America, the Man/Writer had the cultural role of telling meaningful stories—about life and death, man and nature, the struggle to build America, the role of the individual—to other male intellectuals, an audience located entirely, as in a Venn diagram, within the larger circle of Man. Among authors in this category, however different their goals and allegiances, were Howells, Norris, Twain, Emerson, Thoreau, Hawthorne, Poe, Melville, and Cooper. Similarly, influential newspaper editors such as Amos Kendall and Horace Greeley aimed their political and business news at an audience of men; infrequent gossip and feature columns would suffice for the few women readers. The culturally influential Writer, and even the intellectual Reader, were thus key roles of a striving male Self.

At this time, within the circle of Woman defined as Other was a smaller circle representative of another category of writer that I will discuss as Non-Writer. She could only function within the appropriate roles for women, thus as a moral beacon, as a representative of the home, as a mother. Her audience would be other literate middle-class wives and mothers, and her messages would be meant not to form a culture, but to help women adjust to and excel at their established domestic roles within a society defined by men (Coultrap-McQuin 15–16). Since both "writer" and "author" seemed to be terms appropriate only for men, representatives of this group, including Lydia Maria Child, Susan Warner, Maria Cummins, and Harriet Beecher Stowe, were frequently identified by less respectful names: bluestockings, poetizers, authorlings, or a "d—d mob of scribbling women." At newspapers by the end of the century, a few women worked part-time as women's page or society editors, but they were kept separated from the real, hard-bitten "newspapermen." The very limited identity available to female poets, novelists, and journalists—that of Non-Writers—did allow them to write but severely constrained their opportunities, subject matter, and audience. Although women's writing proliferated in nineteenth-century America, it existed within narrow definitions, with strict penalties for treacheries against the Non-Writer code.

However applicable Woolf and de Beauvoir's depictions may be to nineteenth-century America and however compelling a portrait they create by which to measure recent gains and goals, they do not accurately depict intellectual life of 1929 or 1949 in the United States. The difference for American writers was college education. For ironically although Virginia Woolf advocates a room of one's own, what American women did was to leave their private spaces and move into dorms and classrooms—in much greater numbers and much larger percentages than in England and France. In England from 1925–1926, only seven in every 10,000 male and female high school or academy students, or .0007 percent, attended college (Mowat 210). The 8,376 women then enrolled constituted only 29 percent of the very small student group. In the United States in 1929, however, where the number of colleges and universities was then 1,377, a larger percentage of college-age people attended college, 6.6 percent of that population in comparison to .0007 percent in England. Although this trend had at first primarily involved white middle-class women from the Northeast, the large number of schools functioning by 1929, both state and private, helped to extend it to African American women, women from lower income families, and women in all states. Because of the varied sorts of opportunities, the percentage of women students was much greater in 1929 than in England, 40 percent of the student population instead of 29 percent, and so were the numbers: of approximately 1,100,000 American college students, more than 40 percent, or 440,000, were women (*Historical Statistics* 383). Even by 1949, the year that *The Second Sex* was published, only 20 percent of French college students, or 26,400 students, were women. The percentage of women students there did not reach forty until 1967 (Duchen 154).

At schools across the United States, especially after 1880, large numbers of female college students entered into the habits and environments of "learned discourse," a privilege reserved in England, in Woolf's depiction, for just a few affluent men. In the college setting, as Woolf would have predicted, they encountered a redefining opportunity, described vividly by Lucy Martin Donnelly, a teacher at Bryn Mawr, in 1908:

> A strange passion for a lady! To forswear gardens and parlors for mere grassy quads and academic porticoes; to exchange silks for the never-changing fashion of a scholar's rusty serge, and trinkets for goose-quills and inkpots; to prefer the bookish scent of libraries to roses, perhaps; to devote her days to learned discourse, and her evenings to the solitary meditation recommended the student; this, in a word, is the discipline to which the Lady Collegiate vows herself. (537)

This new "discipline"—of classes, extracurricular activities, and dorm life—did seem in the first years to be a "strange passion for a lady" and many families, such as Eleanor Roosevelt's, thought the experience too extreme and unnatural for their daughters. But after 1900, as numbers grew, as families had a wider choice of public and private institutions, and as education and home economics departments provided more comfortable settings for some women, college attendance became more acceptable as an appropriate training for motherhood—and for careers.

As American women went to private and state universities in ever increasing numbers, adopting more freely the role of "Lady Collegiate," many began participating there in an innovative writing curriculum that did not exist in Europe at all. In late nineteenth-century America, following the Morrill Act and a reexamination of the university's role in an industrializing nation, pressure was placed on even liberal arts departments to offer practical specialties. With new departments of education taking over the role of training teachers,

English departments looked at advanced curricula in writing as another form of specialization and career training that could bolster their student numbers and funding. Older professors and younger hires began offering courses in poetry, fiction, drama, pageants, advertisements, newspaper articles, and magazine features as well as on English and American literature. In the new writing courses, teachers often used a workshop format to imitate a newspaper office or a publishing house, and they focused on training professional novelists, poets, and journalists as well as extending general reading and writing skills. In the literature classes, before the creation of large college libraries for research and before the critical apparatus of New Criticism, teachers often allowed students to experiment with the genres studied in class, thus to write fiction and poetry as well as analytical essays. In all of these classes, at least in part because of the development of new male college specialties, such as business and engineering, women often made up the majority of students, even in universities in which they were a small minority of the total student population. While taking literature and writing classes, women also participated in college magazines and newspaper offices, literary clubs, and theatre groups. At women's colleges, these activities might not be geared to enabling women to become professionals; at coeducational schools, women's participation might be accepted with great reluctance. But in these classes and organizations, along with serious prejudices against them, women such as Elizabeth Bishop, Ruby Black, Pearl Buck, Emma Bugbee, Fanny Butcher, Willa Cather, Jessie Fauset, Zona Gale, Mildred Gilman, Zora Neale Hurston, Mary McCarthy, Marianne Moore, Pauli Murray, Elizabeth Spencer, Milicent Shinn, Ruth Suckow, Dorothy Thompson, Eudora Welty, Margaret Walker, and Leane Zugsmith found a place to learn fundamentals of technique and enter professional groups. In journals, letters, college papers, school magazine articles, yearbook entries, and then later in their published novels, newspaper stories, and autobiographies, hundreds of American women analyzed the impact of these college experiences on their writing skills and on their paradigm of professional life.

This experience of college, both in the course work and extracurricular opportunities, caused the numbers of women in the United States who worked for at least part of their adult lives as professional writers to increase dramatically. After 1890, in fact, women entered writing careers at a much faster rate than they chose any other career that had not begun to assume a "women-only" definition. Although the way was certainly hard for those who made the commitment, by Woolf's publication year of 1929 more than 40 percent of American literary authors and 25 percent of the journalists and editors were women. Acccording to literary critic Elizabeth Ammons, this trend involved black as well as white writers: "From the 1890s to the 1920s, African American women published fiction at an unprecedented rate" while also working as reporters and editors at magazines, such as *Colored American Magazine* and the *Crisis* (22). By de Beauvoir's publication year of 1949, one-third of editors and reporters were women (Newcomer 179). Half of the Pulitzer Prizes given for fiction between the award's inauguration in 1918 and World War II went to women. The large number of black and white writers began not only to address the traditional audience of middle-class women in more varied and challenging manners, but also to write for women of all classes as well as for audiences of men and women. They moved out from manners and childrearing into news and editorial writing, magazine feature writing, textbook writing, scholarship, historical studies, poetry, and fiction, making a Male/Writer definition no longer really possible and the male grip on culture formation harder to maintain. As Ammons asserted in her study of works written by American women between 1892 and 1929, this early-twentieth-century group was the first to "invade the territory of high art traditionally posted in western culture as the exclusive property of privileged white men" (5).

What enabled this change, beginning well before 1929, was not just the training secured in college but the encounter there with a model for professional endeavor, a working routine and support mechanism that these women carried with them from college into careers. Immediately after graduating, they began participating in clubs, workshops, political parties, and government agencies where they could continue working within groups as they had done in college. Although they might not be wanted in existing groups where men had dominated, and forming new ones could be an all-consuming endeavor, these women proceeded doggedly, creating a pattern of collaboration as well as possibilities for women writers that had never existed before. With the support of this lifelong commitment to the group, many women faced the realities awaiting them—claims made by parents, husbands, social and racial conventions, editors, the public, the bank account, and the work itself—and entered the previously closed circle of Writer.

As these women, with group support behind them, became influential at newspapers and at publishing houses, they did not just conform to what they found there but, working from the security of their own group structures, they introduced new subjects and prose styles to American writing. And so ultimately their model of collaboration, so carefully nurtured in college and after, created not just the possibility of career but a redefinition of writing itself. Writer could no longer be situated within the circle of Man, and thus the writing produced could no longer be simply the topics, logic, and style that a man might produce for an all-male audience. Along with women's substantial number of varied publications before World War II came influential new styles of journalism and fiction that redefined these genres for both women and men.

The elements of women's experience discussed here—their education, their incorporation of a learning model into their working lives, and the texts they produced—have been central to a theoretical debate in recent decades. In 1975, in "The Laugh of the Medusa," which appeared in a special issue of *L'Arc* devoted to Simone de Beauvoir, Hèléne Cixous recognized that the domination of man as Self and the designation of woman as Other had occurred through writing and that "woman must put herself into the text—as into the world and into history—by her own movement" (276). Of the resulting *écriture féminine*, she refuses to provide a limiting definition since "this practice can never be theorized, enclosed, coded" (287). By moving beyond traditional modes of performance, she asserts, these products can "surpass the discourse that regulates the phallocentric system" (287). Many other feminist theorists who question Cixous's emphasis on the individual body and voice, such as Toril Moi, Ann Rosalind Jones, and Domna C. Stanton, have also recognized the relationship between limitations placed on women's prose and the restrictiveness of dominant social codes. At the same time, writing teachers have speculated on the types of instruction that will help young women find their own voices and influence others. Cynthia L. Caywood and Gillian R. Overing, in their collection on writing and gender, claim that the "less-structured, less rigidly hierarchical" collaborative-workshop model of learning is "compatible with feminism, if not feminist in and of itself" (198); Frances Maher discusses it as the best pedagogy for "voicing and exploring the hitherto unexpressed perspectives of women and others" (30); Patricia Bizzell claims that such curricular reform will "promote more equitable relations" (486); Pamela Annas calls the collaborative classroom a "nurturing but rigorous/tough space" (14; Ashton-Jones 7–11). Lisa Ede and Andrea Lunsford in *Singular Texts/Plural Authors*, as well as Ann Ruggles Gere in *Writing Groups: History, Theory, and Implications*, view this writing model as involving women in the best traditions of literary and corporate authoring, territories once limited to men.

As scholars add to the picture of women's creativity begun by Woolf and de Beauvoir and as they investigate new models of instruction, they should also look carefully at the experiences of the first generations of women who sought collaborative training and then began professional careers writing poetry and prose. From 1880 to 1940, American women came to college to learn to be writers, they took advantage there of every opportunity to form groups of colleagues, and they continued to rely on this model after they left college, creating new types of personal/professional groups. And, from this home base, they crafted very influential texts that helped shape their era. The real choices made by the generations of women who shattered the definitions of Writer/Non-Writer, both in their college classes and then in their careers, can enable us to truly examine *écriture féminine* and the learning environment needed to nurture it: these writers reveal to us not new theoretical possibilities but specific models of work that nurture creativity and transform lives.

CHAPTER ONE

BEFORE 1880,
THROUGH EXCUSES ONLY

She is in the swim, but not of it.

—*Journalist* magazine

In 1890, only 4 percent of American journalists were women, and percentages in other writing fields were even lower. Those few who made a serious commitment to writing found their course severely constrained—by their education, family responsibilities, social codes, and isolation from other writers. Because of these limited freedoms and connections, American women in the eighteenth and nineteenth centuries wrote by relying on some form of justification or rationalization, which varied with the decades, and they usually wrote professionally for only part of their adulthood. Cast in the insubstantial role of Non-Writer, a subset of the care-giving Woman, these writers were meant to address only women readers on narrowly defined women's topics such as homemaking while the genres and pronouncements of male Writers were shaping American intellectual culture. Although their choices were few, for women working within a patriarchal system without supportive networks or groups, these excuses and restrictive definitions did provide some space for writing.

DURING THE COLONIAL PERIOD

In the colonial period, women's labor was frequently needed, in towns and certainly on the frontier, and it provided their means of securing a living when left without father or husband. Some better educated single women and widows worked in journalism—writing, editing, printing, and distributing newspapers while also taking on contract printing jobs. Elizabeth Glover of Cambridge, whose husband, the Reverend Jose Glover, died on the boat to America, operated the first printing press in North America (Marzolf 2). She supported her five children by printing colonial pamphlets and bulletins until she married Harvard's president, Henry Dunster, in 1641. The first reason or justification that could propel American women to authorship was this necessity to earn a living when left without a male provider, an acceptable excuse that enabled a few white middle-class women to write and publish both political and literary pieces.

Ann Smith Franklin, widow of Benjamin Franklin's brother James who had been publisher of Boston's *New England Courant*, inherited his printing business in 1735 when his death left her without other means of supporting her children, and she ran the newspaper for thirteen years aided by her daughters Elizabeth and Mary. In 1736, she also became official printer for the Rhode Island General Assembly, issuing 500 copies of its *Acts and Laws* in 1745, a folio volume of more than 300 pages. She also printed almanacs, religious tracts, and local literary efforts, along with her own almanacs published under her husband's pseudonym of "Poor Robin." She continued working with her son James Jr., who finished his apprenticeship with Benjamin Franklin in Philadelphia and returned to Newport in 1748. In 1762, when her son died, she took over his newspaper, the *Newport Mercury*, and assumed sole control of the printing business, running both until her death the following year.

Anne Catherine Hoof Green, who bore fourteen children, took over her husband Jonas's newspaper and printing business at his death in 1767, aided by two of her sons. She continued his *Maryland Gazette*, the only newspaper in Maryland, without a break and regained her husband's contract as official colony printer. An important chronicle of pre-Revolutionary fervor, her paper published news of colonial reaction to the Townsend Act and accounts of the Boston Tea Party as well as John Dickinson's *Letters from a Pennsylvania Farmer*, a series of tracts against British taxation policy that stirred opposition to Parliament, both in the colonies and in England.

Clementina Rind, whose husband had been Jonas Green's partner on the *Maryland Gazette*, took over his *Virginia Gazette* at his death in 1773. She expanded his regular fare of reports on foreign and domestic politics, shipping news, and advertisements by including essays and poems from local contributors and from London newspapers and magazines. To improve her region, she also published news of scientific developments, philanthropic efforts, and plans for improving education, especially at the College of William and Mary. To attract and keep a female audience, she regularly included poems concerning women, news with a women's slant, and vignettes of European high society and of home life in other colonies. In 1774, she purchased a new set of types from London and began to serve, until her death later that year, as the official Virginia colony printer (James I 662–63; II 80–81; III 161–62).

For these white women who had the requisite literacy skills, writing provided a means of supporting themselves and arranging careers for sons and unmarried daughters. Shielded by this justification, they could aggressively seek private and governmental contracts for printing books and pamphlets, purchase new equipment, and run newspapers that combined political news, essays on women's issues, and literary works. Since most colonies had only one newspaper and few printing presses and since the husband had already assumed the role of printer, they might not be competing with any established businessmen and thus their efforts might appear all the more acceptable to men. But, although ambition during a family crisis was generally deemed appropriate, ongoing careers were not; women were expected to turn their operations over to adult sons or to discontinue working if they married.

Because journalism and printing could offer immediate and ongoing income, very few women ventured into other genres to earn a living. Those few who chose scholarship and textbook publishing encountered great difficulties in entering these male-dominated domains. Hannah Adams, born in Massachusetts in 1755, was perhaps the first American woman to make scholarly writing her profession, "as the last resort, to attend to my manuscript, with the faint hope that it might be printed, and afford me some little advantage," she wrote in her autobiography, a step she took after her father's bookstore failed and she had tried to support her family by weaving bobbin lace and tutoring college students (*Memoirs* 12). With poverty providing the exigency, she could pursue the love of research and writing that had begun in her childhood. Even with her acceptable justification well known, however, she encountered great difficulties when her works challenged the money-making projects of established male authors. Her second book, *A Summary History of New-England* (1799), embroiled her in a ten-year controversy when her abridgment intended for the schools, and thus as a moneymaker, conflicted with the Reverend Jedidah Morse and Elijah Parish's attempt to reach the same readers. Morse moved quickly to forestall her, an act that he defended in several derogatory tracts concerning her ambitions and writing skills. In response, she wrote an account of the conflict and sent it to many influential people, a few of whom, such as politician Josiah Quincy, offered her financial help. In reviews of the two books published in the *Monthly Anthology* in July 1805, Reverend William Emerson, Ralph Waldo Emerson's father, praised her work for being more clear and correct and even accused Morse and Parish of copying some of her information.

Reviewing this case in a 1993 article, literary scholar Michael W. Vella criticized Adams for the contrasting tones that she adopted, but he did not consider the connection between her public declarations and a woman writer's need to position herself as a Non-Writer seeking income during a crisis. In Adams's letters to politicians and lawyers concerning this case, Vella finds "a false self-effacement, a posturing of a helpless female, something of a martyr." To provide an example, he notes her tabulation of the difficulties she faced: "my being entirely destitute of pecuniary recourse, my retired situation, ignorance of the world, incapability of conducting business myself, and the want of friends who were able and willing to assist me." Vella judges such declarations as hypocritical since Adams pursued her rights as an author aggressively and could speak persuasively, as she did privately to her lawyers about injustices wrought against women: "To the curiosity of the idle, and the envy of the malicious their sex affords a peculiar excitement; arraigned not merely as writers, but as women, their characters, their conduct, even their personal endowments become the objects of severe inquisition" (30–32). Adams's "posturing," which Vella labels as a "fundamental ambiguity" in her character, was perhaps her only means of negotiating her way through a world in which frank public declarations of her strengths and rights would have left her without the support she needed, support that would only be accorded to the meek female Non-Writer. After succeeding at her quest to gain recognition for her talents and financial needs, Adams next published *The Truth and Excellence of the Christian Religion Exhibited* (1804) and then *History of the Jews* (1812), choosing the latter subject because fewer of her contemporaries had written on Judaism and thus it offered the chance for greater profit with less opposition.

During the colonial period, women also wrote poetry and fiction although generally as a private commitment and not as a means of earning a living. Since poetry could offer little hope of profit, it seemed especially immodest and unwomanly to seek its publication beyond broadsheets aimed for ladies' clubs or recital hours. Anne Bradstreet's brother-in-law secretly published her poetry in London in 1650 under the immodest title of *The Tenth Muse Lately Sprung Up in America*, surprising and shaming her, as she recorded in a poem printed in a second edition of her work, *Several Poems Compiled with Great Variety of Wit and Learning, Full of Delight* (1678):

At thy return my blushing was not small,
My rambling brat (in print) should mother call,
I cast thee by as one unfit for light,
Thy Visage was so irksome in my sight.

("The Author to Her Book" 7–10)

Although she continued to revise her poems and choose others for publication, this second edition did not appear until six years after her death. Like Bradstreet, Ann Eliza Bleecker (1752–1783) showed her work to only her family and friends. Her poems and stories, on idyllic rural life as well as the atrocities of the French and Indian wars, were sent after her death to *New-York Magazine* by her daughter Margaretta V. Faugeres, who also published *Posthumous Works of Ann Eliza Bleecker* in 1793.

Other writers had more contact with the larger public, but not ongoing careers. Sarah Wentworth Apthorp Morton (1759–1846) and Judith Sargent Murray (1751–1820), for example, secured magazine publication for their poems and essays, but not as a means of financial independence. By hiding her identity and thus maintaining her modesty through the pseudonyms "Constantia" and "Philenia," Morton contributed her poetry to the column "Seat of the Muses" in the monthly *Massachusetts Magazine*. She also published three longer poems, on Indian life and New England patriotism. Murray, who also used the pseudonym "Constantia" to publish her poetry in the *Massachusetts Magazine*, wrote a column, "The Gleaner," for that magazine from 1792 to 1794 for which, like Addison and Steele in *The Spectator*, she created various characters and anecdotes to discuss contemporary education, politics, and manners. Two of Murray's plays were performed in Boston at the Federal Street Theatre in 1795 and 1796—her play *The Medium*, published as *Virtue Triumphant*, was the first to be written and performed in America.

In the eighteenth century, publication occurred even more rarely for an African American woman. Lucy Terry of Deerfield, Massachusetts, wrote many poems, but the first publication of her work did not occur until 1895, seventy-four years after her death, when her "Bars Fight, August 28, 1746," a poem about a successful Indian raid, appeared in a history of Deerfield (Stetson 3). Having been sold from a slave ship in Boston at age eight, Phillis Wheatley began writing poetry at age fourteen; her *Poems on Various Subjects, Religious and Moral* was published in England in 1773, where she had been sent to improve her health. A poem published in 1776, dedicated to George Washington, brought her further acclaim but, like Morton and Murray, she never secured financial independence through writing. Her attempts to publish a second volume of her poetry in America met with failure (Robinson 98).

IN THE EARLY NINETEENTH CENTURY

In the colonial period, the boundaries were firmly inscribed: women could acceptably seek publication to solve financial problems—if their efforts did not rob any men of their livings and if they maintained a self-effacing presence. The early nineteenth century would bring changes not in these definitions but in the opportunities available to the few women attempting to work within these constraints. After 1820, a better possibility of earning a living by literary production and scholarship, for both men and women, resulted from new methods of producing and selling writing. Before then, publishing houses were undercapitalized, unstable businesses with no efficient means of distribution; they generally sold books in a small area, with publicity coming from short reviews in newspapers. Since books from England could be reprinted without copyright infringement, publishers had little incentive to contract with native authors. However, during the 1800s, developments in press technology and paper production, better organization of booksellers, and more sophisticated publicity techniques combined with a drastic rise in literacy rates among men and women to greatly increase opportunities for American writers. In 1820, book sales in the United States totaled $2.5 million; by 1850, the figure rose to $12.5 million (Wroth and Silver 123). In 1891, the passage of the Chace Act extended copyright protection to foreign authors, taking away the monetary incentive for privileging foreign works. As magazine and book publishing developed, this expanded industry involved small but growing numbers of women, who primarily addressed the expanding female audience. As the century progressed, new educational opportunities for women were leading to growing numbers of readers to buy books. By 1850, more than 50 percent of white women could read and write; by 1880, one-third of African American women were receiving some elementary and secondary training. In New England, where settled towns made for the greatest number of opportunities, more than 75 percent of girls between the ages of five and nineteen were in school by the 1860s (*Historical Statistics* 370; Coultrap-McQuin 22; Kelley 8–9).

Between 1820 and 1850, a few popular authors such as Catharine Maria Sedgwick, Caroline Howard Gilman, Lydia Howard Huntley Sigourney, and Maria McIntosh began making their livings from writing prose and poetry for the enlarging group of readers, with their frequent short productions appearing in periodicals, newspapers, and books. As critic Susan Coultrap-McQuin has noted, this choice was generally available only to white, middle-class women, most often from New England (21). Sisters Alice Cary and Phoebe

Cary earned enough from newspaper, magazine, and book publication of their poetry to move from Ohio to New York in 1850 and "by 1856, through stringent economies buttressed by their literary productions, the sisters had earned enough money to afford a pleasant house on 20th Street" (E. James 1: 296). When David Child's earnings from his Boston newspaper dwindled, his wife Lydia Maria Child published a guide on homemaking, *The Frugal Housewife* (1829), which went through seven editions by 1832, when it was renamed *The American Frugal Housewife* for distribution in England and Germany. Maria McIntosh, having sold her Georgia property after her mother's death and moved to New York to live with a half brother, wrote children's stories that were gathered into a volume issued in America and England. Her first novel, *Conquest and Self-Conquest* (1839), sold 100,000 copies. Susan Warner's novel *The Wide, Wide World* (1851) was the first book by an American to achieve a million sales. She began the novel when her father's failing law practice necessitated another source of family income.

As they strove to achieve success, these writers frequently reminded readers of their financial necessities, and thus of their excuse or justification for writing and publishing. Editor of the very successful *Godey's Lady's Book* Sara Josepha Hale, left penniless with four children when her husband died, maintained that she engaged in literary and editorial work "foreign to the usual character and occupations of her sex" only to "obtain the means of supporting and educating her children in some measure as their father would have done" (Douglas 93). Emma Dorothy Eliza Nevitte (who wrote as Mrs. E.D.E.N.) Southworth entered the writing profession only after her husband deserted her and refused to support their three children; she also frequently reminded her readers and publishers that she had entered the literary arena only out of necessity.

Using financial exigency as a form of protection and legitimacy, these few women writers of the nineteenth century began to occupy an accepted place in society, as modest souls supporting themselves and their families, as "literary domestics," a label suggested by literary scholar Mary Kelley in *Private Woman, Public Stage*. Etiquette book writers even formulated practical and specific rules for their appropriate conduct and for conduct toward them. Eliza Leslie, who at sixteen had opened a boarding house with her mother to meet the expenses of a large family, authored one of the earliest cookbooks by an American, *Seventy-five Receipts for Pastry, Cakes and Sweetmeats* (1827), as well as books for children, stories for women's magazines, and etiquette books. Her *The Behaviour Book: A Manual for Ladies* (1853) describes common activities in the lady's life and rules thereof: for tea visitors, introductions, conduct on the street, shopping, traveling, conversation, and decorum in church—and for socializing with literary women and joining their ranks. In "Conduct to Literary Women," she provides suggestions for visits to the serious working writer, attempting valiantly to meet her deadlines and earn her living while also finding time to entertain friends and help neighbors. While making her subject seem like a normal member of the community, Leslie also emphasizes the writer's dedication and asks readers to treat this hard worker with respect. For visits and for larger parties, she suggests several rules: don't ask the writer's opinions of contemporary and thus competing writers; don't expect her to divulge her research sources or the real identities of her characters; don't ask to borrow copies of her books since publishers do not provide her with many; don't make a pun on "littery" if her desk is messy; don't discuss her income; at large gatherings don't ask her to entertain your children, pit her against other writers, or introduce her to every dull guest; and speak to her only in private about her work and then do so thoughtfully: "Take care not to speak of her first work as being her best; for if it is really so, she must have been retrograding from that time; a falling off that she will not like to hear of" (256). Leslie also cautions against expecting busy writers to critique manuscripts since "the least talented of the numerous females pretending to authorship, are generally the most conceited and the most obtrusive" (269); usually the established author's emendations just give offense. In her characterizations and advice, Leslie aims to protect her colleagues from censure: writers are kind and generous—"normal"—women who should be welcomed in society; they should not be stereotyped or abused because of their occupation, one they took up only out of necessity.

In a chapter on "Suggestions to Inexperienced Authors," Leslie gives advice for young women who might try to become writers if a financial exigency should arise. She surveys the serious work ahead and offers specific advice on choosing subject matter, marketing manuscripts, managing correspondence, and handling proof-sheets. She stresses the long hours of labor, especially in the revision stage, made more taxing by women's poor preparation: "Few women can write well enough for publication, without going twice over the subject; first in what is called the rough copy, and then making a fair copy with all the original errors corrected, and all proper alterations inserted" (280). In this chapter, Leslie presents new writers, like those with established careers, as women who should be respected for supporting themselves and their families through such a difficult means.

IN THE LATE NINETEENTH CENTURY:
THE "TRUE WOMAN" AS WRITER

By 1853, when Eliza Leslie was attempting to increase social acceptance of writing as a means of earning a living, changes in American business and culture had begun to obviate against this choice. As industrialization brought a higher standard of living to the middle and upper classes, it created a separate world of professional work. After 1830, commercial farming began replacing family farming. Manufacture of wool moved from the home to the factory, with management jobs developing there for middle-class men and line jobs for lower-class men and women. Physicians replaced midwives; engineers replaced or supervised mechanics. Men worked as clerks, bookkeepers, lawyers, and bankers in growing cities.

As more families moved to urban centers where work occurred in the male-dominated world of offices, as standards of living rose, and as time-saving household inventions altered home life, most middle-class women were freed from the need to work outside the home or to toil so diligently inside it. They thus began to lose their identity as midwives, home weavers, or endlessly busy mothers, and gradually a new role, a new reason for being, emerged: the ideal of the lady. In this changing climate, women found a new identity and importance, not as laborers but as moral beacons, overseers of a family and of society's best values, an antidote to the growing power of big-city capitalism. Women created the attractive home space out of which public men and their sons could operate, one where happiness and prosperity served as both reward and emblem of the economic competition for success.

After 1850, therefore, women writers had to have some other justification, besides economic necessity, since even women in financial difficulties were expected to adhere to this image of the true woman, demonstrating the appropriate virtues of piety, purity, submission, and domesticity (Welter 152). In this climate, women's writing took on a new power as reinforcement of the mythology of the lady: writing could raise the moral standards of women and help them become truth's embodiment; it could improve their housework and child rearing; and it could greatly expand the influence of all their domestic virtues. Like women in earlier decades who frequently reminded the public of their financial crises, these writers often emphasized their moral calling. Novelist Sarah Edgerton Mayo wrote that she wished to accomplish in her writing "the same amount of good to one individual that I received from a single sermon" (Douglas 109). Harriet Beecher Stowe claimed that she served as an "instrument" of God: He had written *Uncle Tom's Cabin* to improve public morality. Thus, after 1850, the justification for women's writing evolved from economic self-preservation to social and moral didacticism. With this redefinition, the appropriate topic for women's writing narrowed to moral betterment and the appropriate audience narrowed to other women seeking that betterment (Douglas 80–117).

At the beginning of their careers, many women made their domestic and moral allegiances clear by publishing advice for a happy, well-ordered home. As author Thomas Wentworth Higginson commented, "[I]t seemed to be held necessary for American women to work their passage into literature by first compiling a cookery-book" (Cone 113). Jane Cunningham Croly ("Jennie June"), for example, began with *Jennie June's American Cookery Book* in 1866. While publicly establishing a moral purpose, these domestic projects could provide a good living: Marion Harland's *Common Sense in the Household: A Manual of Practical Housewifery* (1871), one of her twenty-five books concerned with home life, became a best seller; the various translations of Lydia Maria Child's *The Frugal Housewife* went through thirty-five editions.

Another women's genre, the sentimental domestic novel, dominated popular publishing from the 1850s to the 1880s, pressing upon women their duty to be the moral corrective of capitalism. As historian Ann Douglas notes in *The Feminization of American Culture*, these stories often concerned heroines who were morally strong yet physically dependent and weak: they would sacrifice all for the family and home, but they were ultimately too delicate and saintly to thrive without protection in this cruel world. Susan Warner claimed to have written *The Wide, Wide World* (1851), one of the most popular of these novels, "on her knees" in supplication to God (Douglas 109). In this story, the heroine Ellen is victimized by her father's economic woes and his neglect of wife and family. When he finally takes her severely ill mother to Europe for a rest cure, he leaves Ellen with a cruel aunt, with whom she must remain after both her parents die abroad. Then for several years she must work as a servant for her cruel relatives in Scotland. Through these trials, she remains steadfast and kind—a separate being who deserves protection from the capitalist world and who is morally superior to it. And she is finally rewarded for her virtues: by marrying a minister's son from home who will honor her and care for her. Maria Cummins's *The Lamplighter*, published in 1854, concerns little Gerty, an orphan mistreated by her foster mother but rescued by a kindly lamplighter, aptly named Trueman Flint, and then taught by a wealthy blind woman, Emily Graham. When her boyfriend Willie goes abroad, she spends her life doing good for others, "weeping at sick beds and funerals." By the novel's end, Gerty has found her long-lost father, who turns out to be Emily's stepbrother, and she is reunited with Willie in a cemetery where both are mourning over lost friends: both men vow to protect her and enable her to help others. Such novels create a vision of a purer world, one in which benign power and justice radiate out from the "true woman," who offers fine values for the home and family and who thus, in her small world, can perhaps ameliorate the worst effects of capitalism.

Like Warner and Cummins, Harriet Beecher Stowe also gained popularity with tales of women's limited but saintly influence. In *My Wife and I* (1861) and *We and Our Neighbors* (1873), her heroine Eva van Arsdel is worshipped by her husband for her purity and refined appearance. Through her noble thinking and example, she returns lost animals, redeems drunkards, and generally improves the character of those around her. In *Uncle Tom's Cabin*, pure women and children obviate against the cruel world of men: Mrs. Shelby detains the slave trackers, Eliza flees with young Harry, Eva protects Uncle Tom, and Miss Ophelia raises Topsy. In their love and sacrifice, these heroines temporarily relocate power from the marketplace to the home and church and offer a vision of woman as an assuagor of man's cruelest acts and institutions (Tompkins).

While creating a vision of moral womanhood, many short stories and novels also explicitly concentrated on the evils of men that necessitated this role for women—their message is not to turn against men but to become their gentle reformers. Lydia Huntley Sigourney's 1848 pro-temperance collection of stories and poems, *Water-Drops*, depicts the drunken brutality that was often unleashed against women. In the preface, she speaks of the need to redeem men through kindly "home-influences" and thus to rescue the family from violence:

> Are the female sex fully aware of their duties in this matter? Too many of them have, indeed, felt the miseries of the desecrated fireside, and the transformation of the natural protector of themselves and their children into a frenzied foe. Peopled prisons, and blood upon the hearth-stone, have brought into prominence before the public eye, that fearful intemperance from which such sufferings flow.
>
> It has been repeatedly asked, if females are prepared to render all the aid in their power for the suppression of a crime which peculiarly threatens their own sacred interests. What is the nature of the power that they may command? Does it not consist principally in home-influences? (iii–iv)

In Fanny Fern's "The Widow's Trials," a man refuses to offer a job at his newspaper to his widowed niece ("Can't afford to pay contributors, specially new beginners. Don't think you have any talent that way, either. Better take in

sewing, or something.") and then brags about her and steals her work for publication in his newspaper when she succeeds without his help (*Fern Leaves* 20).
The niece forgives him, however, and prays that he can learn to inject a concern for honesty and family into his capitalistic enterprises. Since almost all the
readers of these redemption stories were women, what they provided was an
opportunity for women to understand and even valorize their own situations—
not for men to examine their treacheries and reform themselves.

The few published novels by African American women in the late nineteenth century also concentrated on women's necessity to be strong, moral
forces in a world that they could not tranform. These writers, however, rarely
give their characters an easy or happy ending (Foster 29; Watson 9). In *Our Nig;
or Sketches from the Life of a Free Black* (1859), the first novel known to be published by an African American, Harriet E. Wilson's Frado is abandoned by her
white mother after the death of her black father. Frado works as an indentured
servant: she is treated hatefully by Mrs. Bellmont and her cruel daughter Mary,
but protected and given religious instruction by the son Jack and his Aunt
Abby. When Frado's indenture, a torture she bore with kindness, is finally over,
she is too weak to work steadily. She finally marries, but, unlike many heroines
of sentimental novels, she is abandoned by her husband and left to find her way
alone. In Emma Dunham Kelly's *Megda* (1891), the main character becomes
isolated from her high school friends and the Reverend Stanley because of her
lack of religious faith. When her rival for the Reverend's affections, Ethel Lawton, dies on the night before their wedding, Megda is inspired by her rival's
calm acceptance of death and begins a life of Christian teaching. Four years
later she marries Stanley but at the end of the novel they cannot ease the suf-
fering of their friend Maude, who has drifted through life seeking ease and
entertainment and who meets death in a state of terror. They agree to raise
Maude's child, but they see that Christianity and their good intentions cannot
save black women in an America that does not offer them a clear social purpose and moral stature.

As domestic stories and novels became popular in the second half of the
nineteenth century, many women's magazines regularly published serialized
sections of the novels as well as shorter instructional fiction and moralistic
poetry. One of the first and most successful of these magazines was *Godey's
Lady's Book* of Philadelphia, publishing fiction and poetry along with articles
on fashion, household furnishings, and domestic ideals. Sara Josepha Hale
served as editor from 1837 to 1877, when she was eighty-eight (Marzolf 12).
With its large audience of women who sought moral instruction and entertainment, *Godey's* easily outdistanced most of the magazines for men: in 1860

it claimed 150,000 subscribers to *Harper's* 110,000 (Mott, *A History of American Magazines* 11). Its competitors, like *Patterson's* and *Graham's*, also enjoyed a wide readership. After the Civil War, magazines for African American women also combined short fiction with household advice: *Our Women and Children* began publication in Louisville in 1888 with support from local Baptist preachers to offer instructive stories and articles on education, temperance, and the home; *Ringwood's Afro-American Journal of Fashion*, published in Cleveland beginning in 1892, included love stories along with fashion advice (Bullock 167–69).

Like household manuals and domestic novels, women's magazines celebrated women in the home. Edward A. Bok, editor of the best-selling *Ladies' Home Journal* from 1889 to 1919, looked for fiction that was not overly realistic and that portrayed women as noble creatures who deserved protection. He also included articles on homemaking and child care and many antisuffrage pieces. In editorials, he opposed women's clubs, especially if they were not intended to promote philanthropy, since they would draw women out of their homes and away from their true calling as mothers. He began by opposing all women's employment, but by 1911 his articles featured a few positions, such as minister's assistant and social worker, for which women, as moral beacons and nurturers, might be suited.

Bok asserted his own editorial control, but he did feel that the goal of forming women into steadfast wives and mothers could be furthered by having women address each other in the magazine. He provided opportunities for women to write professionally but only on prescribed topics: Jane Addams wrote on social welfare issues but not suffrage; Esther Lape, one of the first professors at Barnard, wrote on immigration and the Americanization of foreigners, but not on women's education. Inspirational fiction by Kate Douglas Wiggin, Jean Webster, Elizabeth Stuart Phelps, and Mary E. Wilkins also appeared regularly. Bok's staff included Isabel A. Mallon, who as Ruth Ashmore answered letters and dispensed advice in "Side Talks with Girls," extending a column that Bok began himself, as well as Margaret Bottome, who addressed the spiritual needs of older women in "Heart to Heart Talks." Bok introduced each writer as a courageous crusader who chose to temporarily enter the working world, or preferably to send in writing from home, only for the purpose of extending the morality of other women (Bok 166–80; Steinberg 34–74).

African American women's magazines offered women the opportunity to write—within the acceptable genres. For *Our Women and Children*, for example, Baptist minister and editor William J. Simmons secured school administrator

Mary Virginia Cook as education editor and Greek teacher Ione E. Wood as temperance editor; Ida B. Wells-Barnett, who was then teaching in Memphis, was made editor of the home department but was discouraged from submitting any pieces on racial injustice (Bullock 168).

As in book and magazine writing, women entered newspaper reporting ostensibly to help other women fulfill their God-given moral roles while also providing harmless entertainment that could enliven days spent at home. Since nineteenth-century newspapers primarily reached an audience of men, they rarely had women's pages or sections, but most did include some women's features, society news, and advice columns "with the female slant." A few women found jobs in general reporting: during the Spanish-American War of 1898, Anna Benjamin worked as a war reporter for *Leslie's Illustrated Newspaper*, and she next covered the Philippine insurrection and the political situation in Japan, China, and Russia. But writing "bright articles, travel impressions or essays on society and manners" that would entertain and improve women readers was the only common means of entering daily journalism (Marzolf 19). Positions were most often part-time and free-lance because newspapers did not need full-time employees for such limited work. Journalism historian Frederic Hudson wrote in 1873 that "These female journalists, pure and bright, are the growth of the last fifteen years in America. They are now to be seen everywhere—in every large city where influential papers are printed" (504). In his choice of "pure and bright" as descriptive adjectives, words he would never have used to describe the cynical newspaperman, Hudson recognized that a woman in journalism was expected to be a separate entity, a moral beacon and sentimentalist.

As they dealt with the narrow confines of their assigned work, these few women reporters found themselves separated from the rest of the staff—in professional purpose, status, and physical space. The trade magazine *Journalist* reported in a January 1889 issue about women in the profession: "[H]er sex makes her solitary . . . her existence is generously tolerated rather than desired, and the most she knows of the satisfaction of being wanted anywhere is the consciousness of not being wanted" (13). The magazine even viewed the struggling young woman writer as being woefully separate from the social world given her to report: "She is in the swim, but not of it, and, recording the flops and flounders of the big fish, she in time descends to a state of mental and moral petrification that is simply awful" (13). In this issue ostensibly focusing on women's achievements, a poem by newspaperman Sam Wilkeson Wistrom illustrated, through a phallic joke, the common belief that women could never truly be journalists:

Why flatter the ladies to enter the field
Of tripod, brain, muscle and pen?
No matter how potent a Dixon they wield,
They'll never make "newspaper men."

Such a poem reflects the definition of Writer that kept women journalists within the confines of moral justifications and a few acceptable genres, in enclosed circles apart from the real writing domain, of "newspaper men."

Although women generally worked part-time or only until they married, some did secure full careers within the appropriate journalistic genres for women. Jane Cunningham Croly ("Jennie June") experienced success by producing a ladies' column for several newspapers, with articles on clothes, parties, and beauty as well as marriage and childcare, which the New York *Dispatch* began syndicating in 1859. In 1856, she married David Goodman Croly, on the *Herald* staff, and three years later they bought and began publishing the *Rockford* (Illinois) *Daily News* where she wrote a column called "Gossip With and For Ladies." In 1860, the Crolys returned to New York to begin working for the *World*; that year Jane also helped found *Demorest's Illustrated Magazine of Fashions*, which she edited for twenty-seven years while still writing on fashion, food, and home decoration for New York newspapers. She was one of the first women to teach college-level journalism, at New Rutgers Institute for Young Ladies, opened by Columbia University.

While most women didn't move beyond the accepted moralistic and entertainment genres, some managed to include realistic advice and social critique within these confines. From the genres open to women, Elizabeth Meriwether Gilmer chose advice-column writing, creating the persona of Dorothy Dix, a world-wise moralist who responded to readers' individual needs. Raised in rural poverty on the Tennessee/Kentucky border, she left a bleak home life by marrying her stepmother's brother, but he was financially unstable for all the years of their marriage. After meeting Eliza Jane Poitevent Nicholson, who became publisher of the New Orleans *Picayune* after her husband's death, Gilmer moved to New Orleans and began writing birth and death notices, recipes, and then in 1895 a Sunday column as Dorothy Dix. One of her early columns realistically addressed options available to single women:

> It is foolish for girls to think that they have the same chance of marrying that their mothers and grandmothers had. Now, for the girl who is sitting around waiting for some man to come along and marry her, it is a catastrophe to be passed by. She becomes the sour and disgruntled old maid, eating the bitter bread of dependence, the fringe on some family that

doesn't want her. Or else she has to take any sort of a poor stick of a man as a prop to lean upon. . . . Learn a trade girls. Being able to make a living sets you free. Economic independence is the only independence in the world. (Rose D-9)

Her format rapidly developed into responses to letters that poured in. Besides offering traditional advice on courtship, child rearing, and family conflicts, she forthrightly advised soldiers not to marry before they left their hometowns, suggested that women obtain "trial divorces" from violent spouses who could not be reformed, and urged wives to make their own choices throughout their married lives. When Gilmer's popularity grew, William Randolph Hearst invited her to work for him at his New York *Journal*, but after she moved there she soon returned to New Orleans to write a syndicated column until 1950, a year before her death.

Although most women journalists wrote on marriage, home management, and childcare, a few had the opportunity to investigate larger social issues, such as abortion and temperance, that seemed clearly connected to family morality and social reform. Like Dorothy Dix, they used the general umbrella of moral suasion to defend their activism. Jane G. Swisshelm began working in the Senate press gallery in 1850, but she did not stay there long because she caused a scandal by reporting that Daniel Webster, who was then arguing for the strict enforcement of laws concerning the return of runaway slaves, had fathered a mulatto family. This story appeared first in her Pittsburgh *Sunday Visiter*, which she started as a Liberty Party organ in 1848 and wrote for until 1857 when she bought the St. Cloud *Democrat*, another platform for her abolitionist views. She launched the *Reconstructionist* in Washington in 1865 to oppose President Johnson's abandonment of civil rights priorities.

Like Swisshelm, other women founded specialized newspapers to provide a site for their crusades, with their key moral issues changing along with readers' interests and the political climate. As they pursued more rigorous critiques of the status quo, however, they lost readers and encountered public criticism even though they attempted to rely on the familiar cloak of woman as moral reformer. In 1841, Lydia Maria Child had to leave her editorial post at *Juvenile Miscellany*, one of the first children's magazines, because subscriptions dropped after she published an essay against slavery, "Appeal in Favor of That Class of Americans Called Africans," in William Lloyd Garrison's *National Anti-Slavery Standard*. Child claimed publicly that she had written the abolitionist piece only because a wrong had to be righted for the future of all children, but her decision alienated her from her editors and usual audience. Elizabeth Cady Stanton and Susan B. Anthony began their 1868–1869 *Revolution* to protest the

Fourteenth Amendment, the first specific mention in the Constitution of voting as a male perogative, but soon they also discussed problems of working women, jury service for women, and divorce laws. Stanton and Anthony sent out ten thousand copies of the first issue, but circulation of this increasingly radical journal quickly fell to between two thousand and three thousand. Clara Bewick Colby, valedictorian of the first class of women at the University of Wisconsin, published the *Woman's Tribune* from 1883 to 1909, to chronicle the events of the suffrage movement, but she soon added poetry and fiction to gain a wider audience and stay in business. Her more traditional women's magazine had 12,900 subscribers in 1891 (Marzolf 233). Although losing readership, jobs, and public stature could be painful, for some writers the penalty for activism went much further. Ida B. Wells-Barnett used her salary as a teacher to buy a half interest in the *Memphis Free Speech and Headlight;* she then bought out her partner so that she could write freely about inequality of education, the treatment of minorities by social service agencies, and the opportunities for black men and women in the West. In May 1882, when her paper revealed the identities of members of a Memphis lynch mob, her office and printing press were burned. She then went to New York where she wrote for the *New York Age* and continued her campaign against lynching.

To attempt to gain public acceptance as morality's humble servants and fend off personal attacks, many women hid their own names and instead chose first names or alliterative double names as pseudonyms; they thus indicated that they did not seek fame but just an opportunity to deliver right thinking through an anonymous good-woman's voice. Ida B. Wells-Barnett wrote as "Iola" for newspapers and magazines in Ohio, New York, and Chicago. Sarah Jane Lippincott Clark wrote as "Grace Greenwood" for the *Home Journal, Saturday Evening Post, Saturday Gazette*, and *National Press.* Emily P. Edson Briggs, as "Olivia," became a successful Washington reporter. Mary Abigail Dodge frequently denied that she was "Gail Hamilton," a name she had formed from her middle name and her hometown when she began to write for two abolitionist journals, Washington's *National Era* and Boston's *Congregationalist.*

Since the only publicly declared aim of these writers and editors was to improve other women and to increase public morality, most of them eschewed, whether disingenuously or not, any trappings of a literary career. They tried to efface themselves, to avoid fame and notoriety, because they knew the dangers inherent in being publicly recognized and discussed. When poet Caroline Howard's work appeared in a newspaper without her permission, she wanted it known that she had not sought the fame of publication, a naturally male attribute like wearing pants: "When I learned that my verses

had been surreptitiously printed in a newspaper, I wept bitterly, and was as
alarmed as if I had been detected in men's apparel" (James I 110). Mary Clem-
mer Ames, pressed for funds during her marriage and divorced in 1874,
worked for papers in Utica, New York, and Springfield, Massachusetts, and
then began writing a "Woman's Letter from Washington" for the *Independent*,
an influential New York weekly. Only a few weeks after she took this job, she
declared in print that fame did not appeal to a virtuous woman like herself:
"That fame is a curse which soils the loveliness of the womanly name by
thrusting it into the grimy highway, where it is wondered at, sneered at, lied
about, by the vulgar, the worldly, and the wicked." She scorned women who
sought admission into the Capitol press galleries and assured her readers that
she would not venture there:

> Because a woman is a public correspondent it does not make it at all nec-
> essary that she as an individual should be conspicuously public—that she
> should run about with pencils in her mouth and pens in her ears; that she
> should invade the Reporters' Galleries, crowded with men; that she
> should go anywhere as a mere reporter where she would not be received
> as a lady.

Ames argued that women journalists should enter the fray of politics and writing only to improve public morality: "It is her work to exalt the standards of
journalism, and in the midst of an arduous profession to preserve intact the dignity and sweetness of individual womanhood" (Beasley, *The First Women* 11).

As they spoke against fame and ambition, and even avoided naming
themselves, these women were seeking the safe definition not as artist, but
instead as humble and simple do-gooder, and they described their products as
anonymous types of reform documents, like religious tracts, in which the doc-
trine, not the quality of the prose or the personality of the writer, would matter. "Mine is a story for the table and arm-chair under the reading-lamp in the
living-room, and not for the library shelves," novelist Marion Harland
announced in the foreword to her autobiography, while in an introductory
note Fanny Fern dedicated her *Rose Clark* to the same limited uses:

> When the frost curtains the windows, when the wind whistles fiercely at
> the key-hole, when the bright fire glows, and the tea-tray is removed, and
> father in his slippered feet lolls in his arm-chair; and mother with her nim-
> ble needle "makes auld claes look amaist as weel as new," and grand-
> mamma draws closer to the chimney-corner, and Tommy with his plate of
> chestnuts nestles contentedly at her feet; then let my unpretending story
> be read. For such an hour, for such an audience, was it written. (n.p.)

Self-effacement and disdain for their own products furthered the picture of women as anonymous moralists of little talent, as Non-Writers who could never challenge the artistic status of male Writers.

Embued in these appropriate definitions, women writers were also quick to state their limitations as logical thinkers or analysts, and thus to lessen fears that they were taking over that special province of men. Emily P. Edson Briggs, who as "Olivia" covered women's suffrage, political meetings, inaugurations, and Congressional debates, did not hesitate to remind readers of her limited female sphere and abilities:

> This article is not written with the attempt to portray that which makes Charles Sumner the central figure of the American Senate. No woman possesses the gift to explore his mind. Yet there may be those who read *The Press* who feel an interest in the material part of his nature, and who would like to know something about his every-day life—how he looks, how he appears, and the impression he makes upon the womanhood of the day. (Beasley, *The First Women* 13)

Sarah Jane Clark Lippincott, as "Grace Greenwood," adopted the pose of a clever woman at the dinner table, reporting on the personal style of leaders and repeatedly stating her inability to judge their policies. When she began an article series on Millard Fillmore, she carefully described her work as "purely womanly":

> I will not, of course, presume to pronounce upon the political principles or executive abilities of the new President, but if I may be allowed a purely womanly observation, I would say that, in some respects, he is certainly peculiarly fitted to his new position. He will wear gracefully the honors and dignities of that high station. (Beasley, *The First Women* 15)

In 1871, she started writing a column for the *New York Times*, first during a western trip and then from Washington, claiming that she only "hovered" near the press galleries although she did watch the inauguration of Rutherford B. Hayes from there, seated with the rest of the press corps.

Although Lippincott supported herself through a long and successful career, she defined "true feminine genius" as "ever timid, doubtful and clingingly dependent; a perpetual childhood." She admired the woman who risked the "vulgarity of unfemininity" and dared "to live up to her own capacity" in the service of a moral cause, but she advised aspiring poets to "never unsex yourself for greatness" (Solomon 37). Lippincott had learned firsthand the necessity of these contradictions. She had succeeded well at writing poetry and articles on scenery, books, and famous people for *Home Journal* and *Godey's Lady's Book*. But, like Lydia Maria Child at *Juvenile Miscellany*, she lost her editorial position at *Godey's* in 1850 when she began freelancing as an investigative reporter for the *National Era*, an abolitionist journal.

To stem criticisms of their precarious role as moral beacon/working author, women often wrote about the anxiety of being judged as bad wives and mothers since their credibility emanated from the home. Harriet Beecher Stowe circulated an anecdote concerning her ability to give directions to a cook, tend a child, and write at the same time. In Fanny Fern's stories "A Practical Blue-Stocking" and "A Chapter on Literary Women," the surprise endings reveal that women writers can be loving homemakers, with perfect clothes, housekeeping, food, and children. In "A Practical Blue-Stocking," the husband's visiting friend imagines that he will find "inky fingers, frazzled hair, rumpled dress, and slip-shod heels have come between me and my old friend—not to mention thoughts of a disorderly house, smoky puddings, and dirty-faced children"; he is instead amazed to meet a model wife (*Fern Leaves* 100). The Colonel in "A Chapter on Literary Women" seeks a bride but not a literary woman because "I should desire my wife's thoughts and feelings to centre on me,—to be content in the little kingdom where I reign supreme,—to have the capacity to appreciate me, but not the brilliancy to outshine me, or to attract 'outsiders'" (*Fern Leaves* 176). When a female friend tricks him into courting a writer, however, he finds her bright but acquiescent: not all the tribe are "vain and ambitious female writers," he realizes, a type that even his friend would shun (*Fern Leaves* 177). Eliza Leslie includes this axiom in *The Behaviour Book*: "When in company with literary women, make no allusions to 'learned ladies' or 'blue stockings,' or express surprise that they should have any knowledge of housewifery, or needle-work, or dress" since the best writers will be humble in front of men and fully dedicated to the home (259). In fact, Leslie claims, it is more likely that posturing "authorlings and poetizers are apt to affect eccentricity" (263). The real woman writer, appropriately situated as Non-Writer within the accepted definitions of Woman, would never be slatternly or egotistical, a defense these authors created for their literary heroines that they hoped would extend to themselves.

When, for the January 1889 issue, *Journalist* sent an interviewer to the home of Louisa Knapp, who had then edited the *Ladies Home Journal* for six years, his greatest curiosity concerned her keeping of the house, and whether she was a "stern female who doubtless ignored aesthetic possibilities, was indifferent to her husband's comfort and, did genius burn, would hang the baby out of the window in his tall hat, while she wrote of impressive leaders" (2). He was thoroughly relieved to find Knapp not "Minerva-like" but instead part of a perfectly acceptable world that included a contented husband, well-behaved child, happy dog, grand furniture, sumptuous food, and weekly church work, with only a perfectly ordered roll top desk as evidence of her editing duties. Published in a special issue on women's contributions to journalism, such an interview could lessen fears concerning women's entrance to the profession and thus help them to find employment.

THE CRITICAL RESPONSE TO TRUE-WOMAN TEXTS

Regardless of genre, as we have seen, women writers gave repeated assurances of their own morality and limited role: to pursue a career, they had to appear as fervent mothers who loved the home, who cared only for moral crusades and not for ongoing professional success, and who excelled at personality sketches but would not undertake critical analysis. A more aggressive posture could lead to lost jobs and no readers. And, ever since that time, these women's purposes and literary products have been judged through the lens of this initial identification, with few critics looking beyond survival tactics to real intentions and achievements. Although the ongoing condemnation may seem harsh, it in fact recreated the women's own Non-Writer portrayals of themselves.

Scorn for women's moralistic prose and verse was voiced most influentially by Nathaniel Hawthorne, writing from Liverpool in January 1855 to his publisher William D. Ticknor, at a time when the continuation of his job as consul there seemed uncertain:

> America is now wholly given over to a d—d mob of scribbling women, and I should have no chance of success while the public taste is occupied with their trash—and should be ashamed of myself if I did succeed. What is the mystery of these innumerable editions of the "Lamplighter," and other books neither better or worse?—worse they could not be, and better they need not be, when they sell by the 100,000. (Ticknor 141–42)

Hawthorne had been especially enraged in 1852 when Harriet Beecher Stowe's *Uncle Tom's Cabin* sold more than 300,000 copies whereas in 1851 he had made only $1,800 from *The Scarlet Letter*. His rancor only increased when in 1854 Maria Cummins sold 70,000 copies of *The Lamplighter*, a year when women were writing more than half of the novels published, a figure that would grow to two-thirds by 1870 (Coutrap-McQuin 2). Certainly these writers would not have referred to their own work as "trash," but they might have agreed—publicly—that it was no better than was necessary for expressing a moral message.

Echoing the writers themselves, many literary historians and critics have argued that the moral purposes of these texts, their focus on good and evil, wrongdoer and victim, subsumed any other artistic goals. An 1851 reviewer in *Holden's Dollar Magazine*, for example, found Susan Warner's *The Wide, Wide World* "wholly and unmistakably good in the moral instruction" but too sentimental in its plot: "It is a pity, however, that the author has such a taste for crying. The frequent outbursts of tears are really too harrowing to one's sympathies. We never knew such incessant blubbering" (Review 332). Writing in 1853, Caroline Kirkland, who had published stories of frontier life and two books of moral essays, praised Warner's religious content, but criticized the exaggerated portraits of men, scenes of poverty, and use of dialect. In 1891, New York City Normal College Professor Helen Grey Cone echoed these judgments and asserted that women's poetry also portrayed mawkish, sentimental values: "a general fashion of feminine singing-robes, of rather cheap material, verses entitled *Tokens* or *Keepsakes* or *Magnolias*. One of them early wrote about the Genius of Oblivion; most of them wrote for it" (110).

Since the beginning of the twentieth century, this denunciation has persevered through generations of critics who viewed these writers as moral crusaders telling exaggerated stories awkwardly. In 1940, Fred Lewis Pattee in *The Feminine Fifties* found the fiction overbearing in its sentimentality: "Instead of action, descriptions of feeling; instead of dramatic sensation, emotion" (57). Susan Warner's *Queechy*, he pointed out, had 245 tear flows in its 574 pages. In *American Women: A Story of Social Change*, from 1970, Robert E. Riegel called the heroine of Warner's *The Wide, Wide World* "one of the most priggishly nauseous little girls in all literature." He found *Uncle Tom's Cabin* "mawkishly sentimental and badly overwritten; the characters tend to be caricatures; the writing is sloppy." The poetry of Lydia Sigourney and others he judged as wildly sentimental and morbid, on topics such as "children, commonly called angels or cherubs or rosebuds" and "mothers, and especially their graves" (163–67). In *Woman's Fiction: A Guide to Novels by and about Women in America, 1820–1870*, published in 1978, Nina Baym also pointed to the inartistic excesses of these moral fables: "[F]oiled villainesses gnash their teeth and tear out hair by the handfuls; triumphant heroines roll their eyes and point heavenward; villains indulge in demonic laughs, sneering asides, and Machiavellian monologues" (34). In *The Feminization of American Culture* (1978), Ann Douglas explained that these inartistic genres furthered the goals of an embattled Protestant clergy, its power waning in an industrializing nation in which the fittest and most competitive, not the most saintly, were gaining admiration and success.

Not until 1985 did a critic move out from these nineteenth-century writers' definitions of themselves and attempt to analyze their work more thoughtfully. In *Sensational Designs*, Jane Tompkins praised Douglas for having written about this long-neglected body of work but concluded that, like other critics, she had concentrated on didactic intentions and had not fully evaluated the literature itself. All of these earlier critics had not understood, Tompkins claimed, that these writers were creating not poorly crafted realism but a heightened form of allegory—an affective, revolutionary prose that posited a society morally re-formed by women. To provide an example, she analyzed *Uncle Tom's Cabin* as a topological narrative of religious sacrifice: "By giving Topsy her love, Eva initiates a process of redemption whose power, transmitted from heart to heart, can change the entire world" (131). She discussed *The Wide, Wide World* as an apotheosis of women "who bind themselves to one another and to God in a holy alliance against the men who control their material destinies" (163). Written more than one hundred years after the works themselves, Tompkins's study was perhaps the first to move beyond Non-Writer definitions to a consideration of artistic purpose and achievement.

Until recently, women's contributions to journalism have received even less attention than their fiction. As women took advantage of a limited space by writing about fashion, gossip, and moral advice, they were thus, like female fiction writers, defined as Non-Writers unworthy of critical study. In his *Journalism in the United States, 1690–1872*, published in 1873, Frederic Hudson made fun of the odd combination of subject matters in Stanton and Anthony's *Revolution* and other women's reform journals by labeling the writers as "Communists in crinoline against the Versaillists" and summarizing their arguments as "Woman is a wretched slave, with nothing to wear" (499, 501). In the 518 pages of Frank Luther Mott's historical study *American Journalism* (1941), five pages mentioned women writers; short notes concerning women journalists appeared on five pages out of 196 in Edwin Emery and Michael Emery's *The Press and America* (1954). When Marion Marzolf chose to title her 1977 history of women journalists *Up from the Footnote*, she was pointing to this lack of coverage. Although her emphasis was on the twentieth century, she did consider the lives of a few earlier journalists, including Sara Josepha Hale and Jane Swisshelm. Barbara Belford's *Brilliant Bylines* (1979) and Medelon Schilpp and Sharon M. Murphy's *Great Women of the Press* (1983) provided short biographical treatments as well as short excerpts, but neither text attempted a thorough analysis of any journalist's style and influence.

In journalism as in fiction and poetry, the necessary assumption of the Non-Writer stance led to the writers' being treated as just that: as Non-Writers, scribblers whose success had depended on the many uneducated women readers seeking sentimental drivel, readers who could profit from inarticulate renderings of home values, but whose inexperience and poor taste made anything more complex inappropriate for them. These writers' successes were thus devalued—both the genres they wrote in and the readers they addressed were judged as "less than" and "outside of." Attempts to experiment with new genres or redefine their readership or goals, however, also brought on intense criticism. Few writers had their offices burned, as did Ida B. Wells-Barnett, but many found that any departure from their delineated spaces of audience and genre was deemed acceptable.

ENVISIONING NEW DEFINITIONS THROUGH EDUCATION

Whatever their perspective or judgment, whether they denigrated or applauded the efforts, critics of nineteenth-century women writers have acknowledged that they faced severe restrictions, on subject matter, audiences, and career paths. Ann Douglas, in fact, labeled these literary women as "professionals masquerading as amateurs" because they had to continually place moral fervor before career development (85). By dismissing the regular goals and claims of literature, as Nina Baym recognized, these women "foreclosed certain possibilities for themselves and others" (33). A greater range of work could only occur if writing became a true choice for women, redefined as a profession and not just as a temporary extension of family responsibilities or church work. And that change, many women asserted, had to begin with education in the liberal arts and especially in writing—with professional training for a career. When Margaret Fuller took over the editorship of the *Dial* in 1840, she bemoaned her own poor education and the resultant gap between her speaking and writing abilities: "I have served a long apprenticeship to the one, none to the other" (Capper 339). In 1845 in *Woman in the Nineteenth Century*, she argued that "[w]oman can express publicly the fullness of thought and creation, without losing any of the peculiar beauty of her sex" (35) because "the sounding lyre requires not muscular strength, but energy of soul to animate the hand which would control it" (80). And she asserted that women would begin to sound that lyre only when they could avail themselves of a then revolutionary type of education: college study. While teaching at the Greene Street School in Providence and conducting conversation groups for adults, she urged her students to learn persuasive rhetorical devices and practice their writing, to pursue every possible adult education opportunity, and to fight for college admission (Kolodny).

For the 1848 women's rights convention in Seneca Falls that she sponsored with Lucretia Mott, Elizabeth Cady Stanton wrote her "Declarations of

Sentiments and Resolutions" focusing on the equality of men and women and enumerating severe injustices. One of the grievances against man, stated in the form of the colonists' denunciation of George III in "The Declaration of Independence," was that "he has denied her the facilities for obtaining a thorough education, all colleges being closed against her" (14). In her conference address, Stanton argued that only with access to college education would women enter into fulfilling careers and achieve real equality:

> When we shall have had our freedom to find out our own sphere, when we shall have had our colleges, our professions, our trades, for a century, a comparison then may be justly instituted. When woman, instead of being taxed to endow colleges where she is forbidden to enter—instead of forming sewing circles to educate "poor, but pious," young men, shall first educate herself, when she shall be just to herself before she is generous to others, improving the talents God has given her, and leaving her neighbor to do the same for himself, we shall not hear so much about this boasted superiority. ("Address Delivered at Seneca Falls" 29)

At the convention, she urged participants to pursue every educational opportunity, and she argued that those who chose to seek training as writers could improve American society as well as their own lives.

In *What Can a Woman Do; Or, Her Position in the Business and Literary World* (1886), Martha Louise Rayne, a novelist and journalist who had written for the Chicago *Tribune* and the Detroit *Free Press*, employed a dramatic rhetorical device to object to women's limited education, especially their lack of training in writing. To illustrate this poor preparation, she created a poorly educated housewife whose letter to a magazine editor is reprinted with Rayne's caustic commentary:

> dear Mr editur
>
> "I stop my moping"—, she was washing the floor at the time and meant mopping—"to Inform yure reeders how to keap yung Children from geting into Hot water." She then tells them to have the water "torpit;" she probably meant "tepid," and if the child falls in, it will not be "scalt." For this very valuable information she demanded the modest sum of five dollars!

In 1886, Rayne set up a private school in Detroit to give practical training in writing to women. The course of study—including reporting, essay writing, reviews, sketches, short stories, poetry, and novel writing—made professional instruction available to women who had no access to traditional higher education (Beasley, *The First Women* 11).

In 1891 in *Woman's Work in America*, Helen Grey Cone blamed the "desultory and aimless education of girls" for the past failure of women to write well, finding in the attention that they had given to embroidery instead of to travel and study the reason for "dramatic characters as lifelike as those figures in floss silk" (112). Using Hannah Adams as her example, she noted the impact of a poor education on both a writer's capabilities and her professional status:

> This, then, is our starting point: evident character and ability, at a disadvantage both in production and in the disposal of the product; imperfect educational equipment; and a hopeless consciousness of inferiority, almost amounting to an inability to stand upright mentally. (109)

Cone concluded that women's writing and their confidence as writers would improve dramatically only with college education.

As Cone foresaw, women's participation in professional writing did increase dramatically as they began to attend college. In 1840, only 1 percent of women over the age of ten worked as teachers and writers (Kessler-Harris, *Out to Work* 47). In 1870, only 14 percent of women over age sixteen held any job, a figure going to 16.9 percent in 1890 when most of these women were certainly not employed as writers but as seamstresses, textile and other factory workers, farm workers, and clerks; the largest group of these working women, 42.6 percent, held domestic service positions (*Compendium of the Eleventh Census* 381). Working as journalists in 1890, along with 20,961 males, were only 888 women, or 4 percent of the total (*Compendium of the Eleventh Census* 396). In 1910, by which time 23.4 percent of women over the age of ten were gainfully employed, there were 4,181 women journalists as compared to 30,201 men, or 12 percent of the total. But by 1920, in a new census category of authors, editors, and reporters, the number of women was 8,736 or 21.3 percent of the total; in 1930, 17,371 or 37 percent, with 43 percent of those in the category of author ("authors and other literary persons who do not follow journalism as a distinct profession") and 23 percent in the category of editor and journalist. Thus, in the twenty years between 1910 and 1930, the percentage of women's participation in writing careers tripled and the actual numbers of women writers quadrupled (*Abstract of the Fourteenth Census* 494).

This tremendous increase came from education, a new career requirement for professional workers by 1920, but especially for women who needed more and better credentials than men. College, and especially college literature and writing courses, would ultimately put an end to the presumption that women writers were unprofessional aspirants—Non-Writers—just temporarily supporting their families or inartistically speaking out to seek moral reform. By the end of the nineteenth century, American colleges were beginning to provide women with the professional training and the supportive groups that would enable them to address a variety of audiences, shattering the traditional demarcations of Non-Writer and thus of Writer as a firmly ensconced circle within the territory of Man.

CHAPTER TWO

THE COLLEGE LITERATURE
AND WRITING CLASS

> If possible a verse-writing course should meet out-of-
> doors, or at least in a private study and around a table.
> Stiffness and conventionality must be dispelled. So far
> as may be, the class should be like a club of friends
> gathered for common enjoyment and helpful sugges-
> tion and criticism.
>
> —William Carruth, *Verse Writing*

Even though many feminist leaders advocated full equality for women and higher education as the means of achieving it, their goals did not persuade the general public to accept this new extension of educational opportunity; instead, women's entrance into college occurred through some of the same justifications that had enabled American women to write—to improve their parenting and homes and to initiate them into true moral rightness. Because they were not at first envisioned as regular college students, women experienced many means of separation: in single-sex seminaries and colleges, in separate departments at coeducational universities, and in sex-segregated clubs and associations. In the period between 1880 and 1920, as the definitions of the woman student shifted and her horizons enlarged, the notion of college for women went through various public assessments: it was judged as an aberration or a natural formative period before marriage; as a place to study "feminine" courses such as music or to pursue the classical curriculum of men's colleges; as a path to the home or to the more revolutionary choice of a career.

And, in accordance with these judgments, the women themselves might be looked upon as highly accomplished wives—or as unwomanly and selfish careerists. Initially, women were expected to enter English departments to become more literate mothers and readers; then this major became an acceptable form of preparation for elementary school teaching. Those women who envisioned themselves as becoming well-educated and influential writers by choosing this major, however, did not seem so benign: their incursions threatened a sacrosanct territory of patrician males whose proclamations shaped American intellectual life.

These rebellious and determined women entered college at a glorious time for advanced writing instruction. This curriculum in flux, influenced by Progressive theories of education as well as by the huge increase of career-minded students, offered new ties to professional life. For prospective creative writers and journalists, the newly conceived classroom community stretched from authors of the past, to contemporary authors, to publishers, to teachers, to workshop groupings of students. Although the collaborative "lab" environment would be judged by later generations of educators as too practical, haphazard, and untheoretical, it was just what women students needed to gain entrance into writing careers. At colleges and universities across the country, even at sites where women were not welcomed or where the goals set for them were severely restricted, women greatly profited from the aura of experimentation and the new purpose found in both literature and writing classes.

HIGHER EDUCATION FOR WOMEN

The first form of higher education for women occurred before the Civil War in seminaries across the country that stressed religious training, domestic work, and a classical education, as at Troy, Hartford, and Mount Holyoke: an education intended to create rationally educated wives and mothers. At the best of these schools, women studied writing, reading, grammar, French, Latin, math, history, geography, and the Bible as well as drawing and needlework. Women usually went to nearby seminaries for a year or two and then returned to their parents' homes and to marriage. After the Civil War, some seminaries also opened for African American women, with the emphasis generally on the liberal arts as well as household skills. Scotia Seminary, founded in Concord, North Carolina, in 1867, for example, offered such a combination of subjects.

The first opportunities to attend four-year colleges came at evangelical schools that enrolled women to improve their moral life and influence in the home. Most of these schools first offered separate classes for women. In the

Oberlin College *Circular* of 1834, founder John Jay Shipherd announced that one of the primary objects of the school would be "elevation of female character, bringing within the reach of the misjudged and neglected sex, all the instructive privileges which hitherto have unreasonably distinguished the leading sex from theirs" (Fletcher 373). Shipherd made available to women a less demanding curriculum in a separate Female Department. Also following this model were Knox College in Illinois, founded in 1837 by abolitionist missionaries; Antioch College in Ohio, opening in 1852 with education reformer and abolitionist Horace Mann as its first president; and Bates College in Maine, founded in 1855 by Freewill Baptists as the first coeducational college in New England. Grinnell College in Grinnell, Iowa, founded in 1846 by Congregationalists and granting in 1854 the first college degrees west of the Mississippi River, began admitting women as degree candidates in a separate "Ladies Course" after the Civil War (Zimmerman 156–57). Boston University, established in 1873 to fulfill the ideals of its Methodist founders, was one of the very few that rejected this belief in separation. The school admitted women to every department, as the first announcement for its College of Liberal Arts stated: "Ladies will be admitted to all the privileges of the College on the same conditions as gentlemen." The first entering class was one-third women, seven out of eighteen (Ault 8). Like many other colleges, Boston University also had a preparatory school for male and female students who were not ready for college-level work. Although the numbers were quite small, these schools enrolled some African American as well as white women. From 1865 to 1895, seventy-five black students graduated from Oberlin College, a fourth of whom were women. Journalist and women's rights activist Mary Church Terrell graduated there in 1884, followed by Effie Lee Newsome, Octavia Beatrice Wynbush, and other writers. During those thirty years, another 119 black students graduated from all other Northern colleges, often in isolation from other students and the campus life. The 1919 yearbook designation for Esther A. B. Popel, a day student who was the first black woman to attend Dickinson College, indicated this all too common separation from the campus "we": "[I]f not in class she is tucked away in some far remote corner, her mind intensely concentrated on the subject matter before her, usually Browning. We do not know very much about her, as she comes from Harrisburg each day" (Roses and Randolph 268).

In very small numbers before the Civil War and larger numbers thereafter, African American women also attended college at historically black private schools, which began by offering secondary instruction to prepare students for college. Before the Civil War, church groups initiated these schools. The Methodist Episcopal Church opened Wilberforce University in Ohio in 1843;

post-secondary instruction began there in 1856. Founded by the Presbyterian Church, Lincoln University in Pennsylvania offered post-secondary instruction in the year that it opened, 1854, along with preparatory classes. In the postbellum period, the Freedman's Bureau aided church groups in establishing additional private colleges for black men and women. From 1865 to 1890, hundreds of these schools were established, with many including the name "normal" in their titles to indicate their primary mission of training teachers. The American Missionary Association founded seven coeducational black colleges, including Atlanta University, Fisk University, Talladega College, Tougaloo Institute, and Hampton University, while also opening thirteen normal schools and giving financial support to another 170 colleges (Roebuck and Murty 24–27; Bowles and DeCosta 20–30).

By the end of the century, separate private colleges also developed to educate women, initially, as at seminaries and evangelical colleges, to make them better wives and mothers. By 1907, this group included Mills, Trinity, Rockford, Woman's College of Baltimore, Simmons, Smith, Mount Holyoke, Wellesley, Wells, Elmira, Vassar, Bryn Mawr, Randolph-Macon, and the coordinate Newcomb and Radcliffe colleges, extensions for women of Tulane and Harvard. At Wellesley, students entered a unique women's community; many members of the entirely female faculty lived on campus and thus interacted regularly with students both in and out of class. These teachers "fashioned their professional and private lives around the college and each other," providing students with "a sense of belonging to an all-purposive, all embracing whole . . . a local, particularistic, face-to-face community" (Palmieri 234, 251). Even this supportive women's community, however, could seem less than accepting to the few African American students. Clarissa Scott Delany, who graduated from Wellesley in 1923, described "the anguish of her days" there in her poem "The Mask":

> My life is fevered
> and a restlessness at times
> An agony—again a vague
> and baffling discontent
> Possesses me.
>
> (Roses and Randolph 81)

Poet Pauli Murray found at then all-female Hunter College, where she graduated in 1933 as one of four black students in a group of 247, a complete lack of regard for black history and culture; her friends attempted to form an organization of black students to end their isolation and influence the curriculum

(85–92). Instead of subjecting themselves to this isolation and struggle, African American women could choose to enroll in the few private black women's colleges. Bennett College in Greensboro, North Carolina, was founded in 1873 as a coeducational liberal arts college but reorganized as a women's college in 1926 with the same curriculum. Spelman College, originally the Atlanta Baptist Female Seminary, opened in 1881. Barber-Scotia College, which began as the Scotia Seminary, developed a full undergraduate curriculum from its older regimen of preparatory and basic courses.

Many women's colleges followed the liberal arts curriculum of the men's schools, proclaiming that its special purpose for this student population would be to create the enlightened mothers who could raise children well. Mary Sharp College announced in 1853 that their sole innovation would be to offer a classical education, extending to women the educational privilege that had been reserved for men. Radcliffe, at first called the Harvard annex, had a considerable variety of liberal arts courses provided by Harvard professors, with twenty-nine classes offered for twenty-five students in the first year (Newcomer 72–88). Smith College chose to require Greek for entrance and opened in 1875 with courses in Greek, Latin, English, Biblical literature, French, German, mathematics, and chemistry. M. Carey Thomas, president of Bryn Mawr from 1894 to 1922, advocated the "old fashioned college curriculum" as providing "in a much higher degree than certain other subjects training in thinking straight and in reasoning clearly" ("The Curriculum of" 586, 588). Bryn Mawr's list of requirements included Latin and Greek, higher mathematics, philosophy, literature, economics and politics, and English composition. Women's colleges, she believed, should hire the best qualified teachers of both genders and avoid women's subjects such as domestic science, painting, music, and acting; otherwise these schools would dwindle into "a while-life-lasts asylum for the physically young and vigorous, but mentally incompetent" ("The Curriculum of" 590). She frequently disparaged "Japanese geisha schools," seminaries that had classes in music and painting but didn't offer Latin, Greek, and higher mathematics.

In contrast to Bryn Mawr, and to M. Carey Thomas's dismay, other women's schools combined parts of the classical curriculum with subjects deemed especially appropriate for women, holdovers from the seminaries. Such schools tended to offer more art and music and more modern language study, especially of French, as well as more lab science, a practical requirement for future homemakers. Elmira College opened in 1857 with a curriculum of three and a half years of French, introductory courses in every science field, and music, drawing, and painting. Vassar opened in 1865, offering classical and modern languages, history, philosophy, and abstract sciences as well as health training, music, and painting. Baylor University had no Greek courses in its Female Department, but offered women chemistry and anatomy courses as well as drawing, painting, and embroidery. Newcomb College in New Orleans, which grew out of art classes for women created by Tulane professors for the Cotton Exposition of 1884, began with embroidery, brass work, jewelry, ceramics, and bookbinding as well as vocal music, chemistry, modern languages, and Latin.

While educational leaders experimented with the appropriate definitions and curricula for a women's college, the states were also being pressured to admit women to public universities. In fact, by 1900, more than twice as many women attended coeducational schools than women's colleges, with opportunities especially arising at state schools that received funding from the Morrill Act of 1862, through which the federal government authorized the selling of federal lands to support practical and technical education for both men and women, and the Morrill Act of 1890, which led to the creation of historically black public colleges in the South—and to the end of the Reconstruction practice of admitting some black men and women to other Southern state schools. In 1923, more than 165,000 women were enrolled at coeducational colleges and universities, compared with 30,000 at the ninety-seven colleges for women; in 1909, there had been a combined total of fewer than 65,000 women students (Blake 5). Because of the growing number and size of coeducational schools, the female proportion of the total college population went from 21 percent in 1870 (.7 percent of women ages eighteen to twenty-one) to 39.6 percent in 1910 to 47.3 percent in 1920 (7.6 percent of women ages eighteen to twenty one) (Solomon 62). Especially for the first enrollees, this coeducational route could seem terrifying. M. Carey Thomas reflected on this experience in her journal written while she was an undergraduate at Cornell in 1877 and applying to Johns Hopkins as its first woman graduate student: she found it a "fiery ordeal to educate a lady by coeducation—it is impossible to make one, who has not felt it, understand the living on a volcano or on a house top." But she felt that "learning is *worth* it" ("From *The Making*" 182).

Like Cornell, some state schools plunged fully into the "fiery ordeal" by allowing their first women students to enroll in all classes, not just in separate female departments. In 1870, the University of Michigan admitted women, without any special sections, with the full support of President James B. Angell. Many legislators had preferred separate education for women, away from the men on another campus or in their own classes on campus, but the state could not afford either of these plans. In the first year, there was one woman student and 429 men; by 1898, there were 588 women and 745 men (Rudolph 323). In 1882, Angell stated that although male students had not welcomed the women's presence and his faculty had predicted doom, women "have done every kind of work successfully and without injury to character or health," making the same impact as the "addition of the same number of earnest, intelligent young men" (Woody I 129, 245). Like the evangelical colleges, however, most state schools first chose to keep women separated in curricula that focused on their future in the home and in the elementary school classroom. The University of Wisconsin allowed some local women to attend all types of classes during the Civil War because of the lower numbers of male enrollees, but its first thirty full-time women students entered a separate Female College in 1863. Although the University of Chicago's incorporation resolutions of 1890 had guaranteed opportunities in all departments furnished to "persons of both sexes on equal terms" and the entering group of 750 in 1892 had been more than one-fourth women, by 1900 the school had established separate classes for men and women in the freshmen and sophomore years because the men did not like competing with women (Gordon 43–44; Storr 41, 109).

At most universities, however, these duplicate departments soon proved too costly, and women began enrolling in the same courses as the men. Common in 1900, separate sections were disappearing by 1910. Then another separation occurred through the installation of new units at the upper division that were intended to serve just one sex. At Grinnell College, President John Hanson Thomas Main abandoned his preference for a liberal arts curriculum and instituted majors in business, engineering, mechanical drawing, and public affairs to provide separate majors for male students who felt pressured by the women sitting by them in English and history classes. Another segregation effort occurred through the development of new curricula and departments for women only. Ellen Richards Swallow, a chemist trained at Vassar and the first woman professor at MIT, coined the term "home economics" at an 1899 conference to denote the training in nutrition, sanitation, and hygiene, and the household arts that she thought proper for women to receive in high schools, colleges, and seminars for adults (Kenne). Many land-grant universities that African American women attended, such as Delaware State College, South Carolina State University, Tennessee State University, and North Carolina Agricultural and State University, quickly developed home economics curricula. At these and other land-grant schools, such as South Dakota State University, Washington State University, and New Mexico State University, home economics programs were inaugurated along with schools of agriculture as administrators put emphasis on improving the quality of life in the rural communities from which their students came. The home economics major offered women the practical training stipulated by the Morrill Act while keeping them separate from men and from male career paths and responsibilities.

Colleges also experimented with another separate space for women that fulfilled Morrill Act requirements: departments of education. In the nineteenth century, normal schools offered some secondary education and training in classroom management to prospective teachers. After 1890, as universal education requirements created more teaching jobs and America embarked on a commitment to career training, these normal schools developed into teachers' colleges, whose two-year curricula soon expanded into four-year degree programs. Northern Illinois State Normal School, for example, chartered in 1895 with a two-year curriculum, began offering a four-year program in 1921 with general education requirements and pedagogy courses (Biggs 14). Many normal schools that opened during Reconstruction to train African American teachers also developed quickly into four-year schools: Huntsville Normal School (Alabama A&M University) opened in 1875; the State Normal College for Colored Students (Florida A&M University) opened in Tallahassee in 1887; Elizabeth Colored Normal School (Elizabeth City State University) opened in North Carolina in 1891. State and private universities also began to incorporate teacher training programs, extending them, as the University of Wisconsin did, from separate two-year curricula to majors within the regular college program. Because women's colleges did not claim to be vocational institutions and because they had no need to segregate women students, they generally didn't include education, or home economics, within their selection of majors.

WOMEN AND THE ENGLISH MAJOR

Although college administrators viewed education and home economics programs as providing the separate spheres appropriate for their women students, many chose liberal arts courses of study. At coeducational universities by the beginning of the twentieth century, enrolled as English majors, English education majors, or as non-majors seeking elective credit, women were regular members of courses on literature and writing and often the majority. English was also a popular choice of major at women's colleges. At both school types, women might choose the major for general enrichment or as preparation for a teaching career, but, following goals for education set by Margaret Fuller and Elizabeth Cady Stanton, many also ventured there with the goal of becoming writers. Some became fully aware of this real choice only after they entered college. Florence Finch Kelly, for example, who was born in 1858, had decided in early childhood to become a writer but, because her father disapproved of this goal, had attended a county high school for six months to qualify for a teaching certificate. After two years of teaching, she had saved enough to leave a job she had come to hate and enter the University of Kansas, where she studied literature with Professor James Canfield. In her junior year there, she realized that she did not have to return to teaching; college had placed before her the choice of writing:

> My head dropped into my hands and my heart filled with the bitterness of revolt and despair. I did not want to teach, anywhere! I wanted to write! Presently a light broke through the blackness as the thought flashed into my mind—newspaper work! (121)

Others, and more with each decade, came to college already determined to seek the training they would need to be professional writers. Zona Gale entered the University of Wisconsin in 1891 because she had cherished the goal of "writer" since childhood and she knew that her state university could prepare her well. Edna St. Vincent Millay went to Barnard for preparatory courses and then on to Vassar in 1913 "to learn the ABC's of my art" (Brittin 27).

As these students entered literature and writing classes offered by English departments, some male intellectual leaders documented and attempted to reverse this trend because, like Virginia Woolf although with different priorities, they understood the importance of a secure college environment to a writer's development and thus to a literary tradition: they thought that as women enrolled in English courses, men would lose the creative enclave that had fostered the nation's literature. The numbers painted a stark picture as reported in 1924 in *Harper's Magazine* by Rollo Walter Brown, a Harvard graduate who had taught at all-male Wabash College and coeducational Carleton College. To first prove that men would major in English if no women interfered, Brown provided data from private schools for men. At Harvard in 1923, he reported, 41.7 percent of the senior class studied languages and literature; at Washington and Lee, 60 percent; at Hamilton, 35 percent; at Kenyon, 30 percent; at Haverford, 26.7 percent; and at Princeton, 24.3 percent. He found a decidedly different picture, however, at coeducational colleges and universities. At Grinnell College in 1923, where President Main had initiated the new male domains of business, engineering, and public affairs, in a senior class of forty-three men and sixty-two women, only four men, or 9.3 percent of the men in the class, were majoring in literature and language. At Brown's Carleton College during that same year, no senior male had chosen the English major. At the University of Oregon, thirty-seven women and only five men were majoring in literature or language; at Indiana University eighty-eight women and only sixteen men were pursuing these majors. Wherever coeducation goes, Brown concluded, "the humane subjects come to be looked upon as women's subjects, 'ladylike' subjects and the men flee" ("Coeducation" 790).

Although Brown did not provide data on any universities with large education or home economics departments, even at those schools by World War I nearly half of the students in English classes were women. In 1915 at the University of Iowa, according to the lists of students provided in the catalog, one-third of the English majors were women, but they may have constituted a majority in most classes because the education department required eighteen semester hours of English for students in English education and foreign-language education. By 1925, only 36 percent of graduates in the College of Liberal Arts were men. English was also a very popular major at women's colleges. In Brown's year of comparison, 1923, the percentage of seniors majoring in languages and literature there varied from thirty-five to fifty-four, numbers similar to those at liberal arts colleges for men.

For Rollo Brown, this steady attack on all-male literature classes, such as he had participated in at Harvard, could only lead to a lapse in literary production, "a loss which, it must be borne in mind, is absolute" ("Coeducation" 788). Without this intellectual sanctuary, this "privilege of solitude to reflect with one another on intimate and sublime matters," men would no longer be "linguistically self-expressive": "[T]hey are not going to lay bare their hearts, or give expression to convictions that are very sacred, if women are sitting promiscuously about in the classroom" (790). And then, Western civilization itself would begin to decline. Since the effect on men's rhetorical training and powers, and on American intellectual life, would be so severe, men had the responsibility to question "the divine right of coeducation":

> But if we can see that infinite difference between a drab race of men who arrive at the age of prosperous rotundity in perfect content to "let Marry enjoy the poetry and pictures and all that bric-a-brac," and that other race of men who carry the spirit of poetic prophecy into every enterprise they undertake, then we can know that a man might question the divine right of coeducation and still be neither a woman-hater nor a malcontent. (790)

Brown's fellow Harvard alumnus, Chicago English professor Robert Herrick, also viewed the impact of coeducation on American literature as potentially cataclysmic. In his university novel, *Chimes* (1926), he argued that male students often became silent members of coeducational English classes, moving to the back of the room as the numbers of women increased:

"Gen. Lit." was popular, especially with women. The women took by pre-scriptive right all the front benches in the room, while the minority of men slunk into the rear, as if ashamed of exposing their cruder mentality before women in mass. It was difficult to evoke more than a monosyllabic response from the men, even by direct question: they seemed obsessed by a mental diffidence before the other sex, with single members of whom they had just been on such familiar terms. And they felt themselves out-numbered. (57–58)

Although women might appropriately enroll in history or science classes, Her-rick argued, they should not enter this private domain where men should be responding spontaneously to new ideas, discussing their personal values, and planning their own influential texts.

For Brown and Herrick, the American trend toward coeducation—as well as writing instruction in the women's colleges—was threatening the secure circle of Writer within the territory of Man. Since many women were study-ing journalism as well as creative writing, they were infiltrating another enclave where influential writers would be trained. Women's colleges generally offered only a few journalism courses within the English major since these schools rarely established separate technical or job-training programs. But at state schools, journalism was a common choice for women: in departments and schools of journalism across the country in 1925, 30 percent to 60 percent of seniors in journalism were women. According to student lists in catalogs for that year, at the University of Wisconsin, the bachelor's degree in journalism was awarded to twenty-nine women and seventeen men; at Syracuse Univer-sity, seven women and seven men; at the University of Illinois, nine women and fifteen men; at Columbia, twenty-seven women and forty-one men. Even Kansas State's bachelor's program in industrial journalism, which focused on printing and business management as well as writing and editing, enrolled nine women and twelve men that year. From 1909 to 1918 in the school of jour-nalism at the University of Missouri, women graduated in numbers of thirty-six to 128, or as 28 percent of the class, and by 1928, thirty-nine of the ninety-six graduates, or 41 percent, were women (Williams 148–50).

Emulating Brown and Herrick, many journalism professors found these women's presence inappropriate in this crucial site for training skilled writ-ers, the tough investigative reporters who would influence political decision making. In 1927, for example, Grant Milnor Hyde of the University of Wis-consin bemoaned their effect on male camaraderie and creativity and sup-ported separate curricula in society or feature writing ("a broadening of the field") as a means of preserving the city room for his clearly demarcated male "us": "Such a broadening of the field has saved us from the embarrassment incidental to the persistent influx of women students into journalism courses" ("Raising the Quality" 21).

THE WRITING CURRICULUM

Brown, Herrick, and Hyde would turn out to be right: women's entrance into the sites where professional writers sought training would have far-reaching results. This impact would come not only from the fact of their enrollment but from the types of writing and literature classes in which they enrolled. From 1880 to 1940, college education changed tremendously as a new emphasis on career training, the development of new departments and graduate study, the larger college population as well as the enrollment of women conflicted with accepted traditions. In English departments, these new trends helped to foster an expanded list of literature and writing classes that offered exactly what critics feared: the opportunity for women to envision themselves as influential writers as well as the tools with which to achieve this vision.

Creating Literature in Literature Classes

Throughout the nineteenth century, literary study had primarily occurred in courses on Greek and Latin, where grammatical analysis and etymologies often received more attention than the discourse itself. Such linguistic training provided a form of mental discipline intended to develop the brain's general powers of concentration and analysis. Following the recitation method, one student might read a passage, another translate it, and another answer questions about its constructions (Graff 32).

Although classical studies reigned supreme, a few courses dealing with English and then American literature began during the early nineteenth century. Like Greek and Latin poetry, this literature provided a means of studying language development and history, a philological approach derived from scholars at German universities where many American professors received graduate degrees. With the availability of texts such as Francis March's *Method of Philological Study of the English Language*, this methodology spread from undergraduate instruction to the lower schools. At Leicester Academy in 1845, for example, students reviewed grammar and then studied Milton in the following way:

> The rest of the hour [was spent] reading Milton as if it were Homer, calling for the meaning of words, their etymology when interesting, the relations of words, parsing when it would help, the connection of clauses, the mythology, the biography and other illustrative matter, suited to the class. (Graff 38)

In 1904, in the University of Illinois' summer school for new high school teachers, MIT professor Arlo Bates warned his students that they would soon be spending their time on "drill in the history of authors, the study of conundrums concerning the sources of plots, the meaning of obsolete words" (31).

By the 1880s, when "English" was becoming an established specialty, college major, and high school course, scholars were beginning to chafe at the subjugation of literature to language study. Theodore W. Hunt of Princeton argued in a paper for the 1883 meeting of the Modern Language Association that classes instead should emphasize

> the study of the great forms of poetry, of the principles of poetic art, of the leading canons of style as illustrated in English classics, of the life and times of an author as related to his literary productions, of the influence of other literatures upon the English. (45)

James Morgan Hart argued in *PMLA* in 1884 that students could use English literature to study "the great movement of English life and feeling, as it is reflected in the *purest* prose of representative men" (35). Such new historical and thematic approaches to literature quickly gained approval and led to courses covering chronological periods first of English and then of American literature, along with study of creative genres (Berlin, *Rhetoric and Reality* 22–24). By 1905, the University of Missouri's curriculum, as listed in the university catalog, illustrated the resulting amalgam: students could take surveys of English literature, Shakespeare, English drama, eighteenth- and nineteenth-century English literature, Tennyson and Browning, and American literature as well as Anglo-Saxon, Middle English, etymology, the French element in English, and German philology.

In this time of changing definitions of literature study, from 1880 to 1940, the enlarging array of courses was not generally taught by doctorally trained literary specialists. After the establishment of Johns Hopkins in 1876, postgraduate work took root at Harvard, Columbia, Yale, Cornell, California, Michigan, and Wisconsin. By 1900, about 150 institutions had initiated graduate study, though less than a third of these offered the doctorate (Berelson 14). Between 1900 and 1920 the number of earned doctorates increased by 250 percent and between 1920 and 1940 another 500 percent, but the degree's first holders staffed the few doctoral programs or entered other professions and didn't greatly alter the makeup of undergraduate faculties (Berelson 23–25). As was true in other fields, college English professors before World War II were generally master's degree holders. At the University of Iowa in 1915, for example, as the university catalog indicates, the chair of the English department and dean of the College of

Fine Arts, to which English belonged, was Clark Fisher Ansley, who held the B.A. from the University of Nebraska. Of the five assistant professors, all male, two had the Ph.D., two had the M.A., and one had the B.A. The instructors were six women and one man, with six of them having the M.A. from Iowa and one having the B.A. from there.

To fill the class hour in the increasing number of new literature courses, teachers who might lack thorough grounding in current methodologies of linguistic criticism relied on some mix of philology, literary and cultural history, thematic interpretations, and simple appreciation. According to literary theorist Rene Wellek, scholars often "taught graduate students bibliography and sources . . . and meanwhile they read poetry to undergraduates in a trembling or unctuous voice." While various emphases could shape a class hour, they did not always indicate what students should do as writing assignments. Colleges generally had poor libraries, unfriendly places for students to continue historical or philological study on their own. In this period long before New Criticism, teachers did not generally assign the close readings so common after World War II. Instead, they frequently made assignments that required or allowed students to experiment with the genres being studied: poetry, drama, fiction, and the personal essay.

For several reasons, teachers at women's colleges were especially open to this approach. The percentage of teachers who had studied at German universities was lower, and their students generally did not plan to pursue graduate training in linguistics. These teachers were less bothered than their counterparts at men's schools that they might be creating unemployable poets or aesthetes. By the end of the 1920s, many women's colleges were withdrawing extended arts instruction as they tried to match the curriculum of men's colleges and assert their seriousness. Goucher and Salem, for example, offered history and criticism of art in 1926 but no courses in painting and ceramics. But literature courses with creative writing assignments provided a more acceptable arts opportunity, combining academic study and arts practice. Many stalwarts of the MLA, however, viewed this use of creative assignments as another form of "geisha girl" drivel. Beginning with the premise that "all teaching should start from a purely scientific basis," German scholar and Johns Hopkins Ph.D. candidate H. C. G. Brandt argued in an 1883 MLA paper against any teaching approach other than masculine, scientific philology and typified all creative alternatives as "final touches to be put on (to) young ladies in their seminaries . . . justly charged with affording no mental discipline" (32).

Even though many scholars disapproved, literature classes at women's colleges commonly provided students with the opportunity to pursue creative projects. At Barnard College in 1919, for example, Professor Minor W. Latham required students in Development of the English Drama to write miracle plays like those of the fourteenth century. Students created period costumes and sets and performed their plays on a temporary stage placed in the middle of Barnard's Brinckerhoff Theatre, "with the crowded audience pressing shoulder to shoulder around the actors as in a medieval market place." In the 1920s, Dr. Caroline Spurgeon, an expert on Chaucer and Shakespeare who was the first woman professor at the University of London, taught English poetry at Barnard as a visiting professor, providing students with a new terminology of "organic rhythms, symmetry, symbolism, cadences, patterns" (Miller and Myers 127–28). For their class assignments, students could write poetry, trying out techniques from various periods on their own subject choices. In an early 1920s course on Irish Epic and Romance at Barnard, Ethel Sturtevant asked students to dramatize an episode from one of the stories studied in class (Scobie 21). These assignments assumed that the practice of writing would help students not to become playwrights but to better understand and appreciate the literature.

These opportunities to practice creative genres, however, didn't occur solely at women's colleges. At the University of California in 1921, for example, Professor William Whittingham Lyman, a visiting professor from the Los Angeles Junior College who had done his graduate work at Harvard, offered an advanced course entitled Writing Based on Nineteenth Century Masterpieces, in which students read Darwin, Arnold, Carlyle, Wordsworth, and Hardy, and then wrote their own fiction and poetry imitative of either the writers' styles or themes. At Vanderbilt soon after he began teaching there in 1914, John Crowe Ransom began allowing students to turn in poetry instead of themes in his literature and advanced composition courses (Cowan 78; Young 127).

Opportunities to write poetry and work with language also occurred within classes in Latin and Greek, still a central part of the curriculum at liberal arts colleges. At Cornell where he began teaching in 1902, English professor and well-respected Aristotle translator Lane Cooper urged prospective writers to study the language and forms of classical poetry. In his course Translations of the Greek Classics, meeting once a week as a seminar for eight or nine students, Cooper assigned a few pages of a text, such as Aristotle's *De Poetica*, asking students to study the content, sentence styles, and word choices, and he repeated the assignment until they could argue cogently about each of the writer's choices. He intended this painstaking task, which students viewed as an easy assignment only for the first night, to teach them how language worked from the inside, a prerequisite for translating poetry and writing original verse, subsequent assignments in the class. Cooper believed that well-trained classics students could write with better grammar, vocabulary, clarity, and paragraph organization and with truer sentiments than those who just studied English composition (35–37). Instead of encouraging students to truly examine style and form, he argued in an MLA speech in 1909, English departments just imitated each other in "forcing the jaded wits of partly-trained instructors of English, sometimes known as 'English slaves,' to correct numberless themes, essays, and orations," focusing all their attention on error instead of rhetorical accomplishments (75). Classics professors at other schools offered similar assignments. At Vassar, for example, Latin poetry teacher Elizabeth Haight, who began teaching there in 1910, encouraged students to study poetic language and imitate classical poetic forms.

Experimenting with an Array of Genres in Advanced Composition Courses

As part of the evolving English major at the end of the nineteenth century, students could take not only literature courses with creative assignments but also advanced composition courses. These offerings began at men's schools to provide a haven for new generations of writers. In 1884–1885, Harvard's Barrett Wendell introduced English 12, an advanced composition course that became one of the most popular of Harvard's advanced electives, frequently enrolling 150 students split into several sections (Morison 75). In this course, Wendell drew from his own experiences as a novelist and journalist, attracting many talented students who wanted to explore a variety of genres and submit their work to a demanding critic/teacher. Robert Herrick wrote that Wendell "has had a greater influence upon the craftsmanship of the writer than any other American man of letters" ("Barrett Wendell" 7). Rollo Brown revered both Wendell and his colleague LeBaron Briggs for creating the supportive environment that he believed women students would undermine:

> But when some one sits down to explain why in the early years of the twentieth century the younger readers and writers of America began to concern themselves with something less hollow, less conventionally formed than much of the literature conventionally styled "New England," he cannot leave Briggs and Wendell out of consideration. They trained men to look at the world with their own eyes, and to write directly and honestly about what they saw, without regard for the traditional ways of looking at things. (*Dean Briggs* 59)

Although Harvard never created courses specifically labeled as poetry or fiction writing, these advanced composition courses allowed young men to write creatively, with an eye toward professional publication, first in campus journals such as the *Monthly* and the *Advocate* and then at presses like Scribner's where Harvard teachers published their own work and had influence with editors.

At Radcliffe during the 1880s and 1890s, Wendell brought this rigorous training to women by offering English 12 there regularly, meeting the much smaller classes, generally fewer than a dozen students, two hours a week instead of the three at Harvard (Simmons 268). At both schools, Wendell required that a page of descriptive prose be turned in each day before 10 A.M. Students chose their own topics for these "daily themes," but Wendell recommended that they write on current occurrences. Students frequently commented in campus publications on the assignment's artificiality and dullness, as in this recipe appearing in the *Radcliffe Magazine* signed with the initials M.V.A.:

> *How to make a Daily Theme.*
>
> Take one empty head, and fill with a stuffing composed of indescribably tempting sunsets, five different aspects of Harvard Bridge, and a firm conviction that the writing of daily themes is destined to be the cause of your premature death. Stir this mixture rapidly for about ten minutes with a fountain pen. One of these ingredients, in most cases your opinion on the subject of themes, will rise to the surface. Take this out, flavor to taste with commas, and serve on a sheet of white paper. This receipt may be varied occasionally by substituting for the sunsets, electric cars, and for the view from the bridge, small girls with conventional golden curls. (31–32)

Although students might argue about this argument's efficacy, Wendell intended these themes to improve their descriptive and investigative powers, as he described in his teaching notebook in 1887: "What I bid them chiefly try for is that each record shall tell something that makes the day on which it is made different from the day before" with the result that "each new bundle of these daily notes that I take up proves a fresh whiff of real human life" (Notes of Lectures in English 12). Throughout the term, he read daily themes aloud to provide examples of strengths and weaknesses. In addition to these dailies, students submitted longer fortnightly themes—often newspaper articles, poems, or stories. According to his lecture notes in 1885–1886, assignments included a short article or story on a current topic, a piece of fiction or nonfiction based on ideas from the works of Macaulay, and a description of something the students had actually seen, written in a newspaper format (Adams, *A History of* 40–52).

Like Wendell, many other teachers at eastern women's colleges taught creative writing and journalism within general advanced composition classes.

In her advanced classes at Vassar, Gertrude Buck asked students to write daily, to take on longer projects for various audiences—and to consider a future as writers. Her text *A Course in Narrative Writing* clearly leads students toward a goal not of more college themes but of publishable fiction. The chapters cover invention, story structure, point of view, scenes and transitions, character development, and settings, with the assigned readings including *Robinson Crusoe*, *The Vicar of Wakefield*, *Pride and Prejudice*, and anthologies of contemporary short stories. In 1914 at Barnard, according to the catalog, Professor Charles Sears Baldwin offered Composition: "Two consecutive hours, to be arranged, and a third appointment for criticism. This special course for a limited number of juniors and seniors is devoted mainly to story-writing and play-writing, with collateral reading." At Bryn Mawr in 1915, in Regina Katharine Crandall's Narrative Writing, an elective, students experimented with "the style and methods of the best modern writers of short stories, both English and French." Only students who had achieved a grade of merit in the freshman course could enroll. At Wellesley, Sophie Chantal Hart instituted similar advanced courses to allow students to probe their own experience: "to help an individual to possess, really to possess the content of her mind, to correlate ideas, to discover her reaction to ideas and connections between things which have just begun to dawn, enchantingly, on the horizon of the mind" and thus to create a "fusion of mind, sensibility, personal flavor" (373). Only by critically evaluating their own experiences and values, Hart believed, could women succeed as professional writers. From 1880 to 1890, only seven eastern colleges had this type of elective, but by 1920, twenty-nine of thirty-seven eastern colleges offered these courses that might cover several genres and involve lectures, class critique sessions, and regular conferences with teachers (Wozniak 129–32).

As these courses' alumni moved into teaching jobs, advanced composition electives spread to state and private universities across the country. In 1893, at the University of Chicago, for example, Barrett Wendell's student Robert Herrick offered a year-long general writing class, English 5: Advanced English Composition, which enrolled many women students, a trend that thirty-three years later in *Chimes* he would judge as having made the outnumbered men "ashamed of exposing their cruder mentality." Herrick felt the need for new ideals for writers, for both himself and his students, "in a country whose imaginative writing is so sloppily sentimental and romantic as is the case with ours" (Nevius 41): he wanted his advanced writing classes to move students to a greater realism and to a stronger connection with readers of all economic classes, goals reflected in his own novels, such as *The Common Lot* (1904), *The Memoirs of an American Citizen* (1905), and *A Life for a Life* (1910). "America is ready—or nearly ready—," he wrote in 1922, "for a reappraisement and a restatement of herself." Only through the more realistic "new novel," he claimed, would this reassessment occur ("The New Novel" 99). In his English 5, as in Wendell's English 12, students wrote daily themes and longer pieces. In the first term, they heard lectures on style and discussed their written work in class; in the second, they studied a variety of genres including fiction, history, exposition, argumentation, and criticism. As Wendell had also done, Herrick suggested that students write their six assignments on one subject, creating the parts that could coalesce into a novel or an essay collection. Herrick also taught English 6, a quarter-long course involving daily themes and longer projects, lectures on the development of English prose, and work on style.

Advanced writing courses, such as those taught by Wendell, Buck, Baldwin, Crandall, and Herrick, offered students a chance to review basic skills but also to break away from set forms and school-based tasks. Within these classes, students could experiment with new genres and meet regularly with their teachers in conferences, preparing work for publication. At both private and state schools, students in advanced writing classes began entering groups that included teachers and publishers, in which they were encouraged to consider their own work as existing within the sphere of the professional.

CONCENTRATING ON ONE GENRE OF CREATIVE WRITING

By the end of the nineteenth century, most colleges and universities had a few advanced composition courses in which students experimented with a variety of genres, but this method would soon be superseded by models of training experts evolving during the Progressive era. Change in writing instruction stemmed from the reaction against industrialization at the beginning of the new century. Progressive leaders, such as Bob La Follette and Teddy Roosevelt, argued that businesses should be allowed to continue their quest for profit, but more powerful would be an honest American government, strong enough to regulate industry and initiate social programs for the good of all. This view necessitated a well-educated, clear thinking populace, who would elect independent leaders instead of being cowed by local machines that offered protection. Progressive educators such as John Dewey at the University of Chicago and Sterling Leonard at the University of Michigan planned to change the lower-school curriculum of drill and memorization so that students could become active learners, able to associate their school work with their own experiences and with the values of their families and communities. Creative writing and the writing workshop, both Dewey and Leonard maintained, could provide a powerful means of developing citizens. "The setting for a class in creative writing should provide an atmosphere in which the student can believe that his own thoughts and his own experiences and his own feelings are intensely real and are as important as anything he might read out of a book," wrote Deweyan Lawrence H. Conrad of the New Jersey State Teachers College at Montclair for the Commission on the Secondary School Curriculum in 1937 (23). At the influential Lincoln School in New York City, students examined work in progress as a group of classroom citizens:

> When a good poem arrived, endless small matters of technique were the topic of general discussion. The poem is passed around and fought over, but the teacher is only one of many voices, each striving to be heard. In that hurried give-and-take, bombast, posing, unclear or insincere thinking, are laid bare in language more instructive than any adult could contrive. (Mearns 18)

Students' class work was regularly published in *Lincoln Lore*, a well-known monthly.

At the high school level, workshop experiences could help students prepare to work in citizen groups and explore their own ideas (Myers 104–107; Berlin, *Rhetoric and Reality* 78–81). Similarly, college courses in creative writing, as William Carruth, a Stanford professor who had studied with Barrett Wendell, argued in the preface to his 1917 text *Verse Writing*, could promote in students, as readers as well as writers, the development of "esthetic taste, of intellectual judgment, and of spiritual sensitiveness" (2–4). But at the university level the workshop and the writing major had another function. Under the leadership of Progressive politicians, university presidents, and faculty, the state university had begun to emphasize specializations of the modern expert. Included among the trained specialists would be writers who could educate and sway the populace. As Edward Bernays, a public relations specialist, commented in 1928, a large Progressive democracy mandated the ascension of such communicators:

> The conscious and intelligent manipulation of the organized habits and opinions of the masses is an important element in democratic society. Those who manipulate this unseen mechanism of society constitute an invisible government which is the true ruling power of our country. . . . We are governed, our minds are molded, our tastes formed, our ideas suggested, largely by men we have never heard of. (9)

By 1910, through writing workshops, Progressive universities were providing these mind molders, taste formers, and idea suggesters. Their new offerings reflected the practical structures of other new college majors as well as the development of American communication occurring, as Bernays commented, through "letters, the stage, the motion picture, the radio, the lecture platform, the magazine, the daily newspaper" (39). Thus, universities began to train not just sensitive readers and community participants but the creative writers who could influence and improve the populace through stories that described America's myths, moral imperatives, and visions for the future (Adams, *Progressive Politics* 37–38).

In college creative writing courses, instruction generally proceeded by a workshop method intended to involve students immediately in the daily routines of professionals. Percival Hunt, a fiction teacher at the University of Iowa, argued that to create powerful messages writers must move between their private and these public worlds:

> Our judgment of our writing usually is unsure, and often is wrong. Yet, while we write no one can be our intimate companion. Later, when part is done— or the whole—we may turn to someone as critic, and talk with him, and trust him. We may give him our gratitude in the extreme, and come home from him refreshed and sure of the justice of his judgment. (62–63)

By setting up their classes to emulate groups of friends, writing salons, and publishing firms, teachers attempted to supply both colleagues and editors, a professional world like the new agricultural stations, chemistry labs, and home economics kitchens then becoming a regular part of the university environment.

To form the mind molders that Bernays associated with modern democracy, many state schools made substantial commitments to creative writing courses combining lecture with the new workshop "lab" method. Verse-Making Class, operating as a large lecture, began at the University of Iowa in 1897. By 1914, Edwin Ford Piper's workshop version of the course was called Poetics, and Percival Hunt taught The Short Story. In 1915 at Stanford University, students could take workshops entitled Short Story Writing, Play Construction, Prosody and Verse Writing, and Versification. For creative writers at the University of Michigan, Fred Newton Scott instituted in his separate department of rhetoric a course in short story writing and an advanced seminar: "a limited number of advanced students who write with facility and are in the habit of writing," the university catalog indicated, would submit their manuscripts for correction by the class and study principles of criticism and revision. At the University of California at Berkeley, a combination of year-long and summer session programs enabled the school to train younger and older writers and help them market their work. In 1919–1920, the English department offered two courses, Play Construction and Modern Theatre, which involved lectures on production and stage decoration, practice in play writing, and discussion of plays in class. Other advanced offerings included English Verse Composition and Short Story Writing, which required a portfolio for admission as well as plans for projects that would meet the 12,000 word minimum. In the summer school, Berkeley teachers and colleagues from other schools, including well-known teachers and textbook writers such as Karl Young from the University of Wisconsin, offered classes for commuting students from around the state. From June 21 to July 31, 1920, for example, Advanced Narrative enrolled twenty-five students selected on the basis of manuscripts or published stories submitted with their application; those selected wrote at least two stories of over six thousand words during the course. Using Walter Pitkin's *The Art and the Business of Story Writing* as the text, teachers covered the various means of marketing fiction as well as writing and revising.

Along with short story, poetry, and playwriting courses, the Progressive emphasis led to another popular genre of creative writing, the pageant, through which students could enter professional writing careers and make a strong impact on modern thought. After playwright Percy MacKaye staged *Masque of the Golden Bowl* in Cornish, New Hampshire, in 1905, emulating an English performance, American towns became engulfed in a twenty-year enthusiasm for pageants. With participation from clubs and schools, many towns created outdoor spectacles, on historical themes or for national holidays, that involved large casts and elaborate costumes, often with interludes of dance and parading (Blair, *The Torchbearers* 118–42). As Thomas Dickinson of the University of Wisconsin and the Wisconsin Dramatic Society commented in 1915, pageants were a "potent instrument in the social programme," through which professionally trained dramatists along with local volunteers could awaken "social spirit and community cooperation." Community drama was for him the essential "democratic art": "It is laid upon drama by the conditions of its substance that it shall promote that social solidarity of which it is itself the outgrowth and the completest expression in art" (70, 147).

By 1910, towns across the country were hiring trained pageant directors and writers, many of whom had taken courses in pageantry and play production. The Carnegie Institute of Technology had a comprehensive course in drama, festival, and stage setting as did other separate drama schools, such as the American Academy of Dramatic Arts in New York; universities such as Cornell and North Dakota also taught rural community drama. At Kansas State in 1915, for example, Community English concentrated on activities and recreations of community life, with special study of the pageant and the rural community. The course's required text, *Pageants and Pageantry*, was written by Esther Willard Bates, who graduated from Boston University in 1906 and then wrote many historical and religious pageants for towns and clubs as well as full-length plays. In 1915, the University of Montana's English department offered a three-course sequence in Story Telling, Dramatic Presentation, and Pageantry. At Montana and elsewhere, such classes primarily enrolled women preparing to write and produce the often elaborate spectacles sponsored by women's clubs, little theatres, civic organizations, and civic governments.

Like coeducational schools, women's colleges also offered an array of creative writing courses by 1915. In fact, both coeducational state universities and private women's colleges developed creative writing programs while the more traditional liberal arts colleges for men retained only general advanced composition offerings. Newcomb College in New Orleans, for example, began offering a short story writing course in 1908 with emphasis on literary appreciation, historical development of the genre, and practical writing techniques; Tulane, the affiliated men's school, did not offer creative writing until 1939. Creative writing classes first entered women's schools through the aegis of art instruction for women, with poetry seeming especially suited to expressing their delicate thoughts to a private audience. But these classes soon reached beyond the realm of an appropriate pastime as structured sequences led to a professional level of achievement. At Smith College, Lee Wilson Dodd taught Constructive Study of the Drama, in two terms, which surveyed dramatic criticism and offered practice in dramatic writing. Only juniors and seniors with permission of the instructor could enroll. In 1925, Barnard had Story-writing, Playwrighting, and Writing and Criticism. At Mt. Holyoke, in 1925, creative writing courses included Structure of the Drama, Structure of the Novel, Verse Forms, Verse Composition, Prose Style, Literary Criticism, and A Course in Dramatic Action and Characterization.

At most schools, it was only in creative writing classes that students could study contemporary writers as well as canonical texts. By examining this prose critically—assessing its good and bad qualities instead of simply praising its glories as generally occurred with the approved canon of older texts—students began to enter a community of working writers. In Newcomb College's The Short Story, introduced in 1908 when the few literature classes taught there concerned English literature before 1900, students read Poe, Hawthorne, Bret Harte, George Cable, Lafcadio Hearn, and Edith Wharton. In the University of Chicago's two courses on short story writing, students read George Washington Cable, Joel Chandler Harris, Bret Harte, William Dean Howells, Brander Matthews, Arthur Conan Doyle, Octave Thanet, and Mary E. Wilkins. At Reed College, a creative writing course gave poetry student Mary Barnard her only opportunity to read what she considered "the real moderns," not Masters,

Sandburg, and the Benéts, but Eliot, Pound, H.D., Edith Sitwell, and Hart
Crane, writers castigated by her literature teacher, Barry Cerf, who argued that
the modern era had produced good criticism but no good literature (Barnard
35). Of Belhaven College in Mississippi, where sophomore literature surveys
offered during the 1930s ended with Thomas Hardy, Elizabeth Spencer wrote
in her autobiography, "[N]ewer writers were suspect and were hardly mentioned much less taught" (162). When Joseph Moody McDill came there in
1939 from Vanderbilt where he had studied with Donald Davidson, he set up
writing groups and introduced students to *The Waste Land*, as Spencer recorded:
"I felt I had turned the corner and found the modern era. I had been living in
it all the time, but no one had told me so" (166).

Although students could find themselves entering the larger community
of current writers, the most powerful group involvement in workshop-style
courses occurred with other students, small group of peers who were seeking
a definition as Writer. In *Verse Writing*, William Carruth recommended an informal class structure for the workshop:

> If possible a verse-writing course should meet out-of-doors, or at least in
> a private study and around a table. Stiffness and conventionality must be
> dispelled. So far as may be, the class should be like a club of friends gath-
> ered for common enjoyment and helpful suggestion and criticism. In such
> surroundings it is easier to draw out the real thought and the serious con-
> sideration of even the shy members. (54)

University classes across the country initiated such a structure, allowing students
to share their work as readers and critics, with the ultimate goal of publication.
At the University of Iowa during the 1920s, in classes taught by John Frederick, Edwin Ford Piper, Frank Luther Mott, and Wilbur Schramm, variations
occurred on Carruth's basic scheme: students either read their work aloud to
the group or they all read silently from dittoed copies; they reacted orally or in
writing to each other's drafts; teachers lectured on technique or let the work
itself guide the instruction (Wilbers 38). Mott often lectured for one period
and used parts of students' papers as illustrations during the next. With
advanced students, Piper conducted each session as a workshop in which the
teacher and participants gave their responses to work in progress, as his student
John Frederick described:

> Attendance is optional, but there are few of us who fail to find our way
> in the late afternoon to Mr. Piper's basement office, where we sit in
> nooks between bookcases or even share a table with heaps of papers and
> magazines, and read the stories and poems and essays we have written for

the comments of one another and of our leader. In that group, as rarely elsewhere in my experience, there was practiced by Mr. Piper the principle of criticism which I believe to be the only right one for dealing with student work: "Something to praise, something to blame." ("A Maker of Songs" 83)

Wilbur Schramm held classes in his home where his wife and child joined the group, with meetings called when class members had material ready for examination. He tried to enable participants to bring each other to their own best efforts, as student Barbara Clough Spargo commented:

> The students read aloud and "tore apart" each other's writings. . . . I believe [Schramm] felt a serious commitment to help each student develop according to each one's abilities. There was never merely one method or style that was right or best. He stressed that each person's writing should reflect something unique in that individual and represent a certain integrity of purpose, style, and content. (Dinger 12)

Of all the different genre workshops, those in playwrighting perhaps led to the most involvement among students. Jeannette Marks's Mechanics of Playwrighting, like similar courses led by George Pierce Baker at Radcliffe and Harvard, Hallie Flanagan at Grinnell and then at Vassar, and Charles Sears Baldwin at Barnard, stressed class cooperation through all stages of a dramatic project. Marks, who had studied at Wellesley with Katharine Lee Bates and had won the Welsh National Theatre prize, carefully chose a small group, never more than six juniors and seniors, with selection being "a mark of prestige among the undergraduate literati in the college" (Wells 162). She gave no lectures but instead allowed students to determine their own dramatic principles as they wrote one-act plays. At the beginning of the year, she read without comment a list of key words for playwrighting: characters, preparation, development, framing-in, economy, struggle, progress, suspense, surprise, tension, retardation, crisis, climax, audience. Then in class sessions, student began bringing in drafts of plays and critiquing each other's work, as a student commented:

> You begin by setting forth three or four floating ideas to the class. They are usually pretty nebulous—an interesting character, a clash of wills, something you picked up in the newspaper. Then you sit down on the steps and answer questions and ask them, while the class pulls your ideas apart and puts them together again to see what they are worth. These discussions are real discussions, not expressions of opinion. Nobody says, "I don't like that," We say, "I don't like that because"—and everything is open to question. ("Playshop Laboratory" xvii)

Throughout this process, Marks shared her opinions but worked hard to remain a member of the group. When a new playshopper asked whether she could develop her idea in a certain way, Marks responded, "You can if you can," because she wanted the student "to wrestle with her material and find out for herself" (xvii).

When a play was ready for production, the class first chose a director, assistant director, and stage manager, and then Marks's introductory classes submitted designs for the flats, which they constructed. After the casting occurred, primarily from the playwrighting class, each student was expected to work out her own part as others crafted the sets, costumes, and lighting. Students also handled the ticket distribution and ushering, as a final step of a complete group experience in theatre, as college historian Arthur C. Cole noted:

> A small group of Play-shop students had . . . wrestled their way through the many problems of stage and scenic design and of costume selection and construction; they had submitted their histrionic talents to the scrutiny of their associates and of their teacher; now under her watchful eye their results were submitted to public inspection. (310)

Although students were learning about production, their major emphasis remained on the writing, on working to bring forth the best possible version of the writer's intentions and then on enabling her to improve her play. To qualify for production, the play would first be revised in response to the in-class sessions. Further revision occurred during the rehearsal phase. At the three productions, members of the invited audiences left their comments for the author. At a postproduction meeting, she heard additional responses from the actors, directors, designers, and stage managers and initiated further revision plans. At the end of the year, after all the playwrights had gone through this process, Marks again read without comment her list of key words for writing and students discussed their own increased understanding gained through writing, revising, acting, directing, and stage managing.

BECOMING JOURNALISTS

Because the genre itself involved public performance, playwriting workshops encouraged students to understand their writing as public, professional work. Instruction in other genres also took on this professional emphasis—to enact the Progressive goal of having an active citizenry informed by well-trained writers. At the end of the nineteenth century, many universities, and especially state schools funded by the Morrill Act, began providing training in journalism and advertising as well as fiction and drama to form the influential rhetors nec-

essary for a modern Progressive democracy. In an address to University of Wisconsin students in 1904, Governor Bob La Follette argued that higher education's purpose was to create graduates who could serve and improve the state:

> The state welcomes the ever increasing tendency to make the university
> minister in a direct and practical way to the material interests of the
> state . . . the state has prepared you for this work and you are honor-bound
> to strike the blow or say the word which will make the state stronger, pro-
> mote a better public policy, insure a better government. ("Address")

The service of "saying the word" led, at the University of Wisconsin and many
other schools, to a commitment to journalism education because the newspaper, rightly guided, could be the most efficient means to "promote a better
public policy."

Since their goal was to train influential critics of American culture, journalism departments began with mostly male students and created various seg-
regating options as the numbers of women grew. During the 1900–1901 school
year, Wisconsin's School of Economic History, Geography, and Commerce
began offering a three-year tract in journalism, one chosen that year only by
men. This major included appropriate background courses for a Progressive
journalist: in economics, history, law, education, government, literature, ethics,
and sociology. To add training in specific writing techniques, English professor
Willard Bleyer began offering Newspaper Writing in 1905, a course in which
twenty-six men and only four women enrolled that year. This class was later
labeled by his colleague Grant Milnor Hyde as "the first course of journalistic
instruction which has continued without a break . . . 'the journalistic year one'"
("Taking Stock" 8). By 1915, when the program enrolled 116 majors of whom
over one-fourth were women, their presence had led to separate courses in
women's feature stories and in teaching high school journalism. In 1929, as
course offerings and student numbers continued to increase, the journalism
school established four separate tracks for its majors—advertising, general
newspaper, community journalism, and the teaching of journalism—with most
of the women students enrolled in the last two.

As the numbers of women students grew, Willard Bleyer evidenced con-
tradictory attitudes toward their presence in his program. He was popular with
men and women students because of his supportive advice and kindness, and
they often called him "Daddy," but his help was more forthcoming when
women students followed his advice that they seek employment as society
reporters or high school teachers. When they graduated, he would help them
find jobs, but not in hard news. Bleyer believed that the few women professors

should teach only courses for women students. Concerning Helen Patterson, who was hired for the women's feature course but soon lobbied to teach all requirements, he was said to tell colleagues at meetings: "Don't hire a woman; she might by like Patty" (Emery and McKerns 18). Bleyer was willing to write a textbook with an instructor, Margaret Ashmun, but when she insisted that her name be placed first on the cover because she had done most of the work, he withdrew from the project. His 1910 letter to Reading Publishers declared that he had expected his name to appear first because of "masculine superiority." Women should be glad for the limited opportunities that a journalism school might properly afford them, Bleyer believed, and should not push farther into the territory of male writer or professor.

Bleyer's attitudes were certainly not unique; many teachers at both coeducational and women's colleges insisted on offering only a few career choices in journalism to women. When Margaret Ball took journalism at Mt. Holyoke in 1898 (she would later become an English professor there), a woman reporter from the *Springfield Republican* spoke to the students about their place in the field, as Ball recorded in her class notes: "As a reporter on the daily [the woman] has no proper place. Almost impossible except for one extraordinarily constituted. . . . Book reviewing often done by women. This often mushy, using personal style" (Wagner 194). This speaker's opinion was that women should study journalism to understand more about the daily newspaper, but that few had the ability or temperament—or would encounter the opportunity—to enter the journalism profession.

This restrictive attitude was frequently reiterated in journalism textbooks, which often offered a psychological or physiological analysis to support their limited view of women's abilities and choices. In the 1903 text *Practical Journalism*, Edwin L. Shuman argued that "the newspaper is distinctively a masculine institution, offering women, with few exceptions, only the frills and fringes." In *The Reporter and the News* (1935), Philip Porter and Norval Luxon judged reporting as too physically demanding for women; its fast tempo "is such as to bar many women because of nervous temperament" (8). Most women, Porter and Luxon asserted, were incapable of covering the male worlds of police and court news; event reporting, at the fire or riot, involved too many harrowing scenes from which women would shrink because of their natural delicacy; they should also be excluded from the analytical work of editing because their thinking was naturally illogical. In the 1927 text *Writing and Editing for Women*, a book for courses on the women's page, Ethel M. Colson Brazelton, a lecturer at Northwestern University, argued that women could not succeed at editorial positions on large metropolitan papers. She did think, however, they could handle such positions in small towns because of their natural friendliness: "The qualities that render women good citizens, friends, and neighbors are just those that, backed by the necessary newspaper knowledge and training, make of them good community editors" (159). She defended a role for women on society pages by praising their "natural" ability to provide the "heart interest." Although all these texts recognized the increasing numbers of women taking journalism courses, they delineated a very limited job option—part-time work doing society reporting—as the farthest goal to reach for.

Not all journalism schools, however, insisted upon these separate courses and career paths for women. The University of Missouri journalism school, which admitted women from its opening in 1908, had required courses in reporting and copy reading with electives in management, illustration, advertising, and rural journalism, a summer course during which a professor took men and women students on a trip for several weeks, enabling them to act as correspondents for small daily newspapers. The school offered Feature Writing and the Special Article for students of both sexes and no separate courses on the women's page. From 1911 to 1918, women graduated in numbers of thirty-six to 128, or 22 percent (Williams 148–50). At the University of Michigan in 1909, Fred Newton Scott's rhetoric department began offering a program of study in journalism, with no separate curriculum for women.

Women's schools varied in their appraisal of journalism's purpose in the curriculum. As liberal arts colleges, most did not offer majors in any type of career training. The first journalism courses, offered by English departments, were intended to develop informed readers instead of writers. In 1937, Sophie Chantal Hart provided such a rationale for journalism at Wellesley:

> We give a journalism course not at all to make newspaper reporters, but, because everyone reads newspapers. The world needs intelligent appraisers and *consumers* of news, consumers who have standards and will bring the mite of their influence for better standards. Our students read their home town paper and the great metropolitan dailies, and then the best of dailies in England and discuss differences. (374)

As English departments began to offer more than one journalism course, however, the focus generally switched from informed reading to professional writing. Mt. Holyoke and Bessie Tift College added newspaper writing classes between 1900 and 1910 and then magazine writing. Barnard College offered Journalistic Writing by 1915, requiring it as a prerequisite for those students who wanted to enter the School of Journalism at Columbia for a one-year's

Masters of Science degree. In 1925, Baylor College for Women's new journalism department had its first four graduates.

At coeducational and women's colleges, whether or not their professors thought they should be preparing for jobs as reporters, women participated in workshop education, receiving feedback on work-in-progress, as in creative writing workshops. Here the analogy was not to informal groups of writers or salons, but to a newspaper's city room. At the University of Missouri in 1908, *The University Missourian* served as a laboratory for students who covered news and wrote features, edited copy, secured advertising, and circulated the paper on campus and in town. Many universities also developed relationships with local or regional publications. In 1894, Edwin M. Hopkins, head of the University of Kansas' English department, offered what he called a "highly experimental" course on newspaper writing to three students, to investigate social forces and the power of the press in shaping modern thought (O'Dell 35–36, 49). When he introduced his second news writing course, students wrote articles for a city publication to secure more practical training:

> In the fall of 1904 a volunteer section of freshman rhetoric was organized into a group of reporters, and the newspaper class proper into a corps of editors; beats were assigned, and edited. Matter was sent to the local papers including the *University Daily Kansan*. (O'Dell 49)

In Baton Rouge, students at Louisiana State University had their own news room at the local paper. There they worked on regular story assignments with the city editor, a member of the journalism faculty:

> All the work of students in this class is done under actual newspaper conditions and surroundings. They write stories, read copy, and build headlines with the sound of the linotype machines, telegraph instruments, and telephone bells in their ears. They learn how to work under pressure and to observe the "deadline." After the advanced students have a few months of such experience they are put in full charge for a day of the editorial department of the "State-Times." The classes have done some of their best work on these occasions, and these "journalism editions" have received editorial commendation from some of the leading dailies of the State. ("Notes of the Schools" 34)

By simulating the working environment of professional journalists, these courses prepared men and women students to succeed at their first jobs, proving to newspaper editors that trained college graduates could complete assignments without supervision and could cover the news well.

The feature writing classes often intended for women, such as those taught by Helen Patterson at the University of Wisconsin, also followed a workshop format. The preface to the textbook that Patterson wrote for her class, *Writing and Selling Special Feature Articles* (1939), claimed that sales for the ninety students she taught each year averaged $3,800, a large figure during the Depression (ix). This book records the process by which students wrote for various types of readers and magazines. After being encouraged to take investigative walks through town, one student remarked in class on a window display at a florist's shop, which seemed to attract customers. She decided to talk to the owner about how much business the window was generating and take pictures. For her article published in a trade magazine for florists, she received twenty-five dollars. Noticing a sculpture in front of the library when she went there to find a topic for a feature, another student talked to a librarian who knew the sculptor, secured an interview, and wrote articles for newspapers in cities where the sculptor had pieces. After talking with sociology and art professors, she also wrote an article for the *Christian Science Monitor* on an experimental sculpture class offered at a state penitentiary. In this class Patterson insisted on this learning by doing: on students' pursuing their own projects and discussing drafts in class while also studying other students' essays that were printed in the text along with notes on their research paths. This training enabled many of her students to continue their writing after college. Marvel Ings, who graduated in 1938, for example, worked as an assistant editor for *Everybody's Money* and as a contributing writer of *The Credit Union Magazine* and wrote a children's book, *Our Own Wisconsin,* and a prize-winning play, *Blackhawk.*

By 1940, journalism teachers were beginning to conclude that the workshop curriculum was too practical in its orientation, with too much daily practice and not enough history and theory. Randomly covering whatever happened on campus or in town for a term might not introduce students to the requirements and principles of real city journalism, as Curtis B. MacDougall of Northwestern University argued in *Journalism Quarterly* in 1938:

> These so-called "laboratory" methods, however, fall short because the student usually goes through the year handling nothing but speeches, meetings and interviews. Although it is valuable to have reporters proficient in covering Parent-Teacher meetings, there are many other types of assignments which the cub will receive early in his post-graduate career for which such training does not prepare him adequately. Fires, kidnappings, important accidents and similar events cannot be depended upon to occur conveniently as the proper chapters are being read by reporting students,

and, if they should, cooperating city editors are not going to allow amateurs to handle the stories even though the student's program of class
hours permits him the freedom to do so. (284)

Teachers in the 1940s responded to such critiques by adding courses on ethics,
public opinion, newspaper history, and the reporter's role in society while also
altering the existing reporting classes to include more theory and less practice.
But while the more practical curriculum existed, both in feature courses where
women students were welcome and in reporting courses where they were less
so, it gave these students an unprecedented opportunity to work together as
colleagues and to enter the writing profession.

Regardless of the genre—whether journalism, playwriting, fiction,
poetry, or pageants—women students of the early twentieth century had the
opportunity that Hannah Adams, Margaret Fuller, Elizabeth Cady Stanton,
Martha Louise Rayne, and Helen Grey Cone had fought for: they could seek
professional writing training. While they struggled with many types of segregation and prejudice, they increased their skills in literature courses, general
advanced composition courses, and workshops in both creative writing and
journalism. Although the path was certainly not a smooth one, these students
successfully prepared for writing careers—by becoming members of groups
that evaluated ancient and modern writers, struggled with language and meaning, gave and accepted criticism, developed products together, and made contacts beyond campus. Their own stories reveal the tremendous impact of this
new experience, first on individual writers' definitions of themselves and ultimately on the American definition of Writer.

CHAPTER THREE

TEACHERS AND STUDENTS

My small piece of America is singing in me.

—Gladys Hasty Carroll

In the years after 1880, coeducational and women's colleges initiated the literature and writing courses that would enable women to develop their skills and join groups of fellow writers. Literature and advanced composition classes offered a chance to experiment with different genres and evaluate respected texts; creative writing and journalism classes provided more small group experiences and publication opportunities. These classes brought women into the writing worlds of revered authors of the past, of contemporary authors, of college teachers, and of fellow students. These college experiences, though they involved many obstacles and complications, changed the expectations, skills, and futures of young women who wanted to write. Throughout their lives, in journals, novels, letters, and autobiographies, they recognized the tremendous impact of this instruction on their careers and on the larger issue of how women become writers.

IN WRITING WORKSHOPS:
THE TERRORS OF SELF-EXPOSURE

Although these college students had entered a world of exciting new possibilities, it was one fraught with difficulties—of working with male teachers and students, of revealing the self to a sometimes unsupportive group, of stating opinions openly where no pseudonym was possible. Certainly, they encountered teachers whose strong personalities and preferences could intimidate students

and inhibit personal response. Radcliffe student Annie Ware Winsor Allen, taking English 12 with Barrett Wendell in 1886–1887, recognized that asserting
themselves with overbearing male professors was especially difficult for women:

> I think women, besides really lacking independence, add to their apparent
> servility by their timid silence. Women students often disagree radically and
> emphatically with their instructors' statements and opinions, often have
> independent and sensible notions of their own; but they do not dare to
> express their dissent, or, feeling themselves ignorant, they do not feel justi-
> fied in propounding original theories to men who have spent years in study.
> They are not the mere receptacles which they seem to be. (Simmons 277)

In workshop settings, a student such as Annie Ware Winsor Allen might fear that
her writing as well as her judgment of other students' work would be harshly
denounced by a domineering teacher.

And what Allen feared did frequently occur: many women found that
entering workshops meant coping not just with their teachers' strong opinions
but with intimidation or ridicule. A student in the Harvard Annex's first class
in 1879, Abby Parsons MacDuffie, found Professor Adams Sherman Hill quite
daunting, especially when he read the students' themes aloud, inserting his
own "dry and sarcastic" comments: "He began reading and only a few words
proved the work to be mine! My horror may be imagined. Slash, bang, went
his caustic criticism, while slow, infinitesimal tears wet my cheeks" (11). Of
another session, she wrote home to her family: "There are six now in the class.
One, Miss ——— is very airy. She read aloud her first composition yesterday.
Mr. Hill would turn around and say, 'Young ladies, do you know what all this
means?' Poor thing, I've been all through it myself." On another day, she wrote,
"Mr. Hill said the other day that I was the most cheerful person he knew. I
hope he doesn't think I am an idiot and therefore cheerful" (24). When Elizabeth Spencer began studying with Donald Davidson at Vanderbilt in 1942,
she found him similarly terrifying, especially when she went to his office to
discuss her work. She recognized, however, that his strong presence could also
frighten the men:

> There was something about Donald Davidson that scared students to
> death. I used to actually shake when I had to go into his office, stand in
> his presence, and stumble through whatever I had to say. I have heard
> strong men relate how as students they felt exactly the same. (174)

Many students believed that Robert Herrick at the University of Chicago
wanted to devote his efforts only to the best students and that he could be a

harsh evaluator of the many he deemed unworthy: he had "little patience with the dull or mediocre ones and even less with the pretentious ones." A student who attended the university from 1908 to 1912 recalled that Herrick

> had a terrible reputation on the University of Chicago campus . . . as a vicious fiend who . . . lurked near unwary English majors and destroyed their chances for future success. The campus was full of tales of his sadism, and any of us who contemplated English 5 and 6 shook with sickening terror from the time we were freshmen. (Nevius 289)

While sadists filling a campus with terror was an extreme depiction, teachers did have a new power when they commented in class daily on student efforts instead of delivering lectures and grading papers. Whether these teachers intended to be cruel or not, many students interpreted their negative verdicts as an artistic death penalty.

Certainly, having to weather harsh critique could be debilitating, but perhaps even more damaging was the teachers' tendency to turn students into carbon copies of themselves. Dorothy Thompson felt that Dr. Edwin Herbert Lewis of the Lewis Institute and the University of Chicago insisted on too strict an adherence to his version of grammatical correctness: "Dr. Lewis seemed to think that the preservation of the English language in all its purity, had been exclusively entrusted to his care . . . that, for instance, to split an infinitive was some form of juvenile delinquency." In his classes, each paragraph had to have a set structure and each story had to begin and end with a clearly stated theme (Kurth 29–30; Sanders 14). Ruth V. Bortin, who wrote a book of verse for her master's thesis at the University of Iowa, found herself overwhelmed in workshops with Edwin Ford Piper because every poem and story had to emphasize Midwestern details. An avid collector of ballads about the Midwest and West and author of collections of poetry about the region entitled *The Land of the Aiouwas* (1922), *Barbed Wire and Wayfarers* (1924), and *Paintrock Road* (1927), Piper was known as the "singing professor," according to Bortin: "Reading 'Zebra Dun,' he was a cowboy talking to his horse. When he said 'whoa,' it was not as a professor reading to class members for their souls' edification, but as a top-hand who cajoled his pinto or mustang" (Wallace 1). By insisting that students emulate regional authors, he hindered Bortin's plans to develop a more personal inquiry:

> Piper himself was always very tactful and supportive, but he had strong ideas of what he liked. I was writing a long poem about my Grandmother, which I saw as a psychological study (not that I knew any psychology then) but he wanted me to make a tale of pioneer life in Iowa. (Wilbers 11)

Bortin felt that she had to acquiesce or leave the class; this writing workshop, like many others, supported only a narrow range of appropriate products.

Of course, not only male teachers could enforce their vision of appropriate styles of writing. Anna Mary Wells, who became a mystery writer and historian, found that in Jeannette Marks's playwrighting course at Mt. Holyoke professorial critique occurred "at every stage from idea through finished performance"; even though Marks wanted students to develop their own themes, by the end of the process many plays "had taken on a strong coloring of her personality and taste" (Wells 189). When student Frances Tatnall was writing a play that Marks thought could be made into a satire on the board of trustees' president, this student rebelled but then could not achieve her own goals for the project, as Wells recorded the incident:

> Frances was the most deeply rooted individualist among us, a Philadelphia Quaker on whom all my ideas of that breed have been formed. She could not or would not remodel her play to suit Miss Marks' ideas (the difference is not really important) and the result was that she never finished it. (189)

Especially at small schools, such negative judgments could reach beyond individual classrooms or offices. When Marianne Moore was a sophomore at Bryn Mawr in 1906, her teachers decided that she lacked the skills to become an English major. To her mother she wrote that they viewed her as one of the poorer writers: her essays were not sufficiently logical; she had a habit of moving from part to part by associative logic instead of by a college essay structure. When English professor Lucy Martin Donnelly told her that "I *might* fail and she would 'hate awfully to have me fail,'" Moore switched her major from English to history and politics (*The Selected Letters* 26). Then, in the spring term of 1908, as Moore wrote to her friend Marcet Haldeman, M. Carey Thomas, the college president, indicated at a chapel meeting of the entire faculty and student body that Moore's "Philip the Sober," which had appeared in a college literary magazine, was the kind of story, with its archaic language and medieval setting, that "made the college ridiculous to outsiders—phrases such as 'chop-chopping along in the half-dried mud,' 'Promethean-trained sensibilities'—that it seemed too bad that a girl who showed ability should be guilty of affectation" (*The Selected Letters* 48). After this second denunciation, Moore was hurt and angry, but she still planned to press on with her writing.

While the writing classes women entered could involve harsh public judgments by teachers, they also entailed the difficulties of a new class structure, the critique group. For Annie Ware Winsor Allen, whose 1886–1887 English 12 section enrolled an intimate but at times uncomfortable total of four women, group sessions entailed the terror of public revelation of self:

> At first a system of public criticism is certainly trying. It is always hard for people to get out of themselves and look at themselves with impartial eyes. This is what we are expected to do when our themes are criticized aloud in open class. It makes the shivers creep over one's cheeks, and the shakes go all over one's body at first. We are not used to sharing our peculiar difficulties with the general public. The process of getting used to it is not a pleasant one. (Simmons 275)

At the University of Iowa, Ruth Bortin also found the public critique by fellow students not always easy to accept, as in this incident involving her denunciation by a fellow student:

> The atmosphere sometimes became quite heated. I remember being completely squelched on my first reading by Bob Thackaberry's remark that he considered my poems "mere twaddle." When I got several years perspective on what I was then writing I could feel amused over that, but not at the time. (Wilbers 11)

Although Bortin had the drive to continue, other students who felt thus "squelched" in workshops may have given up on this process or on writing.

Blunt and cruel responses could be wounding and unconstructive, but at the other extreme class commentary could be too kind and uncritical, and thus offer the writer no real instruction or guidance. Mary McCarthy did not like the workshops at Vassar and never endorsed their methodology, even fifty years later: "It was so boring. We all wrote the same thing and then had to read what each other wrote. I think we hadn't enough experience to write a story—our experience was too fragmentary" (Gelderman 59). Many students, she complained, made only bland responses, thus adding to the generally insipid atmosphere of the class. As a student, however, McCarthy herself did not succumb to the trend toward unevaluative praise. Her own intense involvement in critique sessions, in fact, prompted a Vassar cartoon, published in a campus literary magazine while McCarthy was there, in which a very unhappy student is asked, "Miss Abbott, would you care to reply to Miss McCarthy's criticism of your story?"

INTERACTING WITH TEACHERS

Although writing classes could become cruel or cloying, and they certainly discouraged both male and female students, they also made writing seem possible for many determined women able to profit from the instruction and the collaboration, women who in earlier decades would have had to make their way alone. Through these classes, women were ultimately able to abandon their definition as Non-Writers: even if colleges and teachers did not intend to alter cultural definitions, the environment itself, which placed dedicated teachers in daily contact with apprentice writers, enabled these women to do so.

While their personalities could be strong and their criticisms wounding, many gifted teachers helped students to launch writing careers. Their intense enthusiasm for the process could make the students' own professional goals seem appropriate and any other career choice the unnatural or inferior one. At Lewis Institute, Fanny Butcher was excused from the freshman course in composition and instead took newspaper writing with Edwin Herbert Lewis, whose obstinacies Dorothy Thompson enumerated. For Butcher, Lewis came to symbolize the greatness of the venture because his obsession with writing validated her own:

> God or fate or whatever divinity that shapes our ends must have seen to it that I landed in a class in English taught by Edwin Herbert Lewis. He looked incredibly like William Shakespeare, was a purist in the use of words, and loved and respected them the way an artist loves his colors or a sculptor his clay. Dr. Lewis was also that rarest of the aristocrats of education, a born teacher. He wrote books (not unforgettable, alas), and he was able to communicate the sheer life-giving joy of writing, a bliss that to some authors I have known is what dope addicts seem to get out of their "trips." (20)

Even though like Thompson she recognized the frequent harshness of Lewis's tone, Butcher believed that this man introduced her to a professional career: "[H]e was more responsible than any other teacher in my life for my trying to be a writer" (205). Dorothy Thompson also knew that this teacher's enthusiasm for a literary life left a deep impression on students. He encouraged her to join the debating society, as its only woman student, where she learned to speak confidently and compete aggressively with words. According to the yearbook's report of one event, "[A]ll of the debaters, including Miss Thompson, acquitted themselves like men" (Kurth 29). And Lewis, who extended his influence through textbooks such as *A First Book in Writing English* (1897), *A First Manual of Composition* (1899), and *Business English* (1911), viewed his students' entrance into professional careers as his special joy, as Butcher testified: "[H]e used to tell me he was proud of having a finger in our newspaper pies" (21).

While many students prospered from this connection with teachers, they also established themselves as writers through the opportunity to analyze and critique established authors. Mary McCarthy found such freedom at Vassar. In English 105 taught by Anna Kitchel, author of *George Lewes and George Eliot* (1933), students studied literature and literary theory, beginning with Tolstoy's "What Is Art?" and Max Eastman on poetry (Gelderman 49). Kitchel's influence was sometimes trivial (her corrections caused McCarthy to stop putting circles over her *i*'s), but this teacher also reformed McCarthy's judgment of literary style, altering her assessment of Millay, Cabell, and other contemporary writers:

> "From too much love of living,/ From hope and fear set free . . ." I don't remember when those dearly loved words turned to derision in my ears. I guess I just dumped Swinburne without a backward thought. And Edna Millay? "You might as well be calling yours/ What never will be his,/ And one of us be happy,/ There's few enough as is." Did Anna Kitchel "kill" her for me with a jovial dart of satire? And James Branch Cabell? When did he go? (McCarthy 209)

Each week students were expected to try out—and perhaps improve upon—the techniques they encountered in the fiction and poetry. (And Kitchel would say as she picked the papers up, "Girls, hand me your effusions.") The best results, such as Mary McCarthy's description of a church's real emptiness, appeared in the class publication, *The Sampler.*

> Inside there is gloom and unreality; inside, there is a priest. Around a shadowy altar, a few feeble tapers burn. Grey wisps of incense salute a god, old beyond human understanding. A book is moved back and forth on the altar by small, puzzled boys. Their robes are like those of the priest, dark red, the red of old blood and time-worn sacrifices. A few Latin words drift down through the worshippers, dead ritual, in a dead language to a dead God. (Gelderman 49)

Through assignments involving careful reading, analysis, and imitation, Kitchel invited McCarthy and her classmates to enter a community of writers and not simply to revere published models from afar.

While helping students to critique published work, many teachers also stressed the students' ability to analyze current social situations and propose social change, instead of suggesting "true woman" accommodations like those found in women's morality novels of the nineteenth century. University of Chicago professor Robert Morss Lovett, a Harvard graduate who had served on the board of the *Harvard Monthly*, viewed all literature, including the Bible, Greek tragedy, Dante, and Milton, as a form of propaganda. The function of art, he maintained, was "the organization of experience toward the improvement of man's lot on earth" ("Literature and Animal Faith" 12). Thus, he wanted to make his students "aware of what experience they controlled" and the new vision of society they might produce. To have an impact on society, they had to seek publication, a professional focus that he and Robert Herrick thought had distinguished the Chicago program from Harvard's:

> We had in common our job—to develop writing at the university. In Herrick's view this implied writing ourselves and stimulating our young colleagues and students to write for professional publication. This was in marked contrast to the tendency at Harvard, where the *Monthly* and the *Advocate* were the goals. (Lovett, *All Our Years* 96)

Part of the "marked contrast" came from the inclusion of women in this professional arena of social reform and thus in the possible re-formations of American life.

One student whom Lovett helped to establish a professional career and an evaluative voice was Elizabeth Madox Roberts. A native of Kentucky, she taught after high school graduation in private schools and then went to Colorado to seek a cure for her tuberculosis. In 1915, her sentimental nature poems accompanied pictures of mountain flowers in *In the Great Steep's Garden*. James T. Cotton Noe, a childhood friend who was a professor of education at the University of Kentucky, wrote to Lovett about her and encouraged Roberts to enroll at the University of Chicago, which she did as a freshman in 1917, at age thirty-six (McDowell 25). With Lovett's help, she planned a fictional exposé of Southern rural poverty told through the perspective of a fifteen-year-old girl, a book published as *The Time of Man* in 1926. Roberts's career exemplifies what college courses could offer: as she studied creative writing in workshops, she moved from pretty verses about flowers to more complex poetry and to novels that evaluated the economic realities of her region and country. When she left the university, she continued to express her social views in fiction, in *My Heart and My Flesh* (1927), *Jingling in the Wind* (1928), *The Sacrifice of the Maidens* (1930), and other works.

Many of Lovett's other women students also established professional careers, continuing his emphasis on modern inequities but with their attention often focused on the struggles of women. Dorothy Scarborough, who wrote about Texas' plantation economy and its effects on family in *In the Land of Cotton* (1923) and *The Wind* (1925), reflected Lovett's goals in her cultural critique. His alumna Margaret Wilson wrote magazine pieces on women's plight in India, a topic she developed further for *Daughters of India*, and then, as Lovett wrote, she attempted a big novel of three generations about her ancestors in Iowa, which I tried to whip into shape with the conviction that here was the great American novel, but the canvas was too vast. Cut down to a single episode, it won the Pulitzer prize as *The Able McLaughlins*. Later, as wife of the governor of prisoners in England, she wrote *The Crime of Punishment* and *One Came Out*, which made me an active supporter of the League to Abolish Capital Punishment. (*All Our Years* 125)

His student Helen Hull taught three years at Wellesley and one at Barnard, before going to Columbia in 1916 as an extension professor and then as a professor of creative writing. She wrote a brief biography of Madame Chiang Kai-Shek, who had been her student at Wellesley. Her novels, such as *Labyrinth* (1923), *Islanders* (1927), *Hardy Perennial* (1933), *A Circle in the Water* (1943), and *Hawk's Flight* (1946), and a collection of short stories, *Octave* (1947), depicted the hazards and loneliness of marriage, child rearing, and careers for women. Katharine Susan Anthony came to Chicago after spending two years at the Peabody College for Teachers. After writing sociological analyses in *Mothers Who Must Earn* (1914) and *Feminism in Germany and Scandinavia* (1915), she turned to biography, creating psychological portraits of Margaret Fuller, Catherine the Great, Queen Elizabeth, Louisa May Alcott, Marie Antoinette, Dolly Madison, and Susan B. Anthony.

Many of Lovett's students were also successful in bringing social critique to journalism. After college, Anna Louise Strong wrote for the *Seattle Union Record*, a labor newspaper; her editorials and feature articles helped build the climate for the Seattle General Strike of 1919. When she traveled to Russia, she wrote a defense of Bolshevik economic policy, *The First Time in History* (1924). Her books and film scripts, such as *Song of Russia* for which she served as technical advisor, publicized Russian heroism during World War II. After the war, she traveled to China and began writing about Mao Tse-tung and the Chinese Communist party.

Like Kitchel and Lovett, many other teachers encouraged students to probe their own experience and judgments, and especially to reconcile in writing their new perspectives with the values inherited from home. Willa Cather entered the University of Nebraska in 1890 after spending a year in the school's preparatory department. As she wrote in *My Antonia*, "There was an atmosphere of endeavour, of expectancy and bright hopefulness about the college that had lifted its head from the prairie only a few years before" (168). Her English instructor, Herbert Bates, a young poet and fiction writer who had studied with Barrett Wendell, was greatly impressed by her story, "Peter," a tale of an immigrant who commits suicide on a bleak Nebraska farm. Bates sent this story, an early version of Mr. Shimerda's death in *My Antonia*, to a Boston magazine, *The Mahogany Tree*, which published it in May 1892.

In *My Antonia*, Cather wrote about this experience with Bates in her portrait of a teacher, Gaston Cleric, who sees Jim Burden's talent and helps him to initiate combinations of the old and new:

> I shall always look back on that time of mental awakening as one of the happiest in my life. Gaston Cleric introduced me to the world of ideas; when one first enters that world everything else fades for a time, and all that went before is as if it had not been. Yet I found curious survivals; some of the figures of my old life seemed to be waiting for me in the new. (167)

As he learns from his teacher, Burden senses the power that his "old life" can have in his work:

> Mental excitement was apt to send me with a rush back to my own naked land and the figures scattered upon it. While I was in the very act of yearning toward the new forms that Cleric brought up before me, my mind plunged away from me, and I suddenly found myself thinking of the places and people of my own infinitesimal past. They stood out strengthened and simplified now, like the image of the plough against the sun. (170)

Burden especially remembers a key day in class that helps him define his own subject matter. Cleric had quoted from the *Georgics*, "*Primus ego in patriam mecum . . . decucam Musas*—for I shall be the first, if I live, to bring the Muse into my country"—and explained to the class that *patria* did not mean nation or homeland or the capital, but Virgil's own little "country," his father's fields: when Virgil realized that he would not be able to complete the *Aeneid*, he was still thankful for being the first to bring the Muse into this small country of his own. Burden then thought that perhaps a "particular rocky strip of New England coast" was Cleric's own *patria* (172). Later that day, reviewing this class meeting in which "we had been brushed by the wing of a great feeling" (172), Burden realized—as did Cather herself—that rural Nebraska would be the *patria* that his own widened perspective would enable him to describe, critique, and transform.

For many African American students, writing classes presented a means of critiquing their own *patria* and thus developing a literature of protest. In the University of Michigan's English 149, a class in dramatic writing, Kenneth Rowe encouraged Doris Price to write stories that would not be acceptable to the commercial theatre. In *The Bright Medallion*, which Rowe included along with her *The Eyes of the Old* in a published collection of plays in 1932, she uses dialect to portray a suburban town in Texas in 1919 and the plight of a poor black man who steals a war medal and attempts dangerous deeds to convince townspeople of his worth. Rowe arranged for her play *Sokta* to be produced in the University Laboratory Theatre with a black cast by the Detroit chapter of Delta Sigma Theta, which also produced her *The Bright Medallion* and *The Eyes of the Old*.

For North Carolinian Pauli Murray, Hunter College and New York City offered the chance to interact with poets such as Dorothy West, Countee Cullen, and Langston Hughes. In 1933, her final year of college, she was profoundly influenced by Stephen Vincent Benét's "John Brown's Body," assigned in a poetry class. She began, in fact, to create new poetry in response to his call to black writers to express their own reactions to American history, to reassess the past in a "blackskinned epic . . . a match for any song sung by old, populous nations in the past." Murray's year-long American history course had contained no mention of any black citizen, but she vowed to change that established record through her own poetry and stories. In her class notebook, in response to Benét's call, she started a poem called "Dark Anger"; after she met him in 1939 and began sharing her work with him, she revised this work and retitled it "Dark Testament," changing it from a short statement of frustration into a long poem on the history of slavery in Africa and America, the entrapments of religion, and the hypocrisies of American ideals (85, 131–32).

Besides encouraging a more complex rendition of personal and political themes, writing teachers gave a level of attention to language that most students had never encountered before. When Laura Z. Hobson, who later wrote *Gentleman's Agreement* and other novels, entered Cornell in 1919, Lane Cooper told her, as he had told many other students, "[I]f you wish to write, study Greek. Study the Greek classics. Educate yourself. If the writing is there, it will flow" (Hobson, *Laura Z* 63). Hobson later recognized that his class' careful examination of original texts and translations fostered her lifetime habits of revising:

> How many times in my working life, when I have gone back at some balky paragraph again and again, gone back at some unsatisfying scene over and over, rewriting and rewriting, shifting emphasis here, subtracting verbage here, clarifying, striking out what I always called "pear-shaped prose" in so-called beautiful writing by various contemporary authors— how often have I acknowledged my debt to those impossible Lane Cooper assignments that trained me to reject surfaces and dig below, to keep at it and at it and at it. (*Laura Z* 64)

At Bryn Mawr, Marianne Moore was introduced to close analysis of style by Georgiana King, who was then working on a play in rhymed verse, *The Way of*

Perfect Love. As a senior, Moore took King's Imitative Prose, a class that included detailed analysis of prose stylists such as Sir Thomas Browne, Francis Bacon, and Samuel Johnson. To her friends and mother, Moore proclaimed King the best teacher with whom she had studied, and she was often to cite Bacon and Browne as major influences on her style. Like Hobson and others, Moore found that careful study of stylistics led to better control over each word and sentence.

Many teachers also recognized that class sessions on precise language could be reinforced by careful theme marking. At Boston University, Dallas Lore Sharp taught advanced composition courses beginning in 1902. Trained at Brown and Boston University, he was known for his descriptive essays on nature, published in collections such as *Wild Life Near Home* (1901), *A Watcher in the Woods* (1901), and *Roof and Meadow* (1904). Esther Willard Bates valued Sharp's focus on language in a sophomore course, Rhetoric and English Composition:

> These were hours when time took wing, when the young instructor, rosy and brisk, fetching corrected theses, bearing away new ones, told us once and for all how to write and write well. Clear-eyed and direct, he had swiftness and resilence of mind and the instructor's thorough paced interest to teach his class what they should know and no bones about it either. He was not in a hurry, but he wasted no time. He taught fundamentals,— freshness of diction, freedom from cliches, orderly thinking, clarity of phrase. (Ault 42–43)

Bates recognized that Sharp ensured each student's participation in this instruction by carefully marking each paper, attending not so much to error but to missed possibilities. He especially liked to suggest changes in the phrasing, locations where a writer might consider "a new phrase concocted of old words or an old phrase illuminated by a new word" to engage readers more fully in the content (Ault 43). Sometimes Sharp would bring scissors to class and snip off bad sentences, especially in introductory paragraphs, and let them fall onto the floor. He asked students to revise their own work with equal ruthlessness.

Many students found their determination and confidence growing as they interacted with their teachers. When Era Bell Thompson arrived at the University of North Dakota in 1924, she found out, in a conversation with her new landlady, that she was the only African American student at this school:

> "Aren't there any colored students at the university?"
> "Lord, no! I think there was one boy a long time ago. He was studying to be a doctor or lawyer or something. I don't remember which, it's been so long." (170)

Her freshman rhetoric teacher, Professor Lewis, "was young and good-looking and human—so human he stopped right in the middle of class one day to see if he could hear a pin drop" (173). After he praised her autobiographical theme in class, she began to meet with him regularly: "I followed the theme into Mr. Lewis' office." There, "he was magnificent. His phrasing, his tonal quality, his word shading, and his gestures were beautiful, dramatic." And he treated her as an author, providing praise and firm suggestions: "You write well, I guess you know; you spell abominably, I guess you know that, too. . . . It's about time, Miss Thompson, that you remember to forget that you're clever and get down to the brass tacks of learning to put your cleverness into civilized art" (177). This censorious but encouraging friend, who always took her work seriously, led her to the magazine *Student*, to the *Grand Forks Herald*, and to a new confidence on campus: "I didn't walk down the back road so much anymore" (180). To satirize his stinging remarks, she gave him a garter snake bedecked in pink ribbons as an end-of-the-year present, a token named Little Thunder that he thanked her for profusely before turning to the window to throw it out of its fruit-jar cage.

Training in idea development and style, obtained in class and in office visits, led students to labor over their own texts thoughtfully, and even to assert intentions that conflicted with those of their professors. At Bryn Mawr, for a class with Henry Neville Sanders, Marianne Moore wrote "Ennui," a poem that stemmed from her fascination with the transformation of Caliban in *The Tempest*, which had recently been performed on campus:

> He often expressed
> A curious wish,
> To be interchangeably
> Man and fish;
> To nibble the bait
> Off the hook,
> Said he,
> And then slip away
> Like a ghost
> In the sea.

In class, Sanders told her the poem was "dithyramb glyconic," and he suggested this rewriting of the last four lines to make them metrically smooth:

> He'd nibble the bait
> like any man

And then take a weed
and be fish again—

At this point, Moore argued with him about content as well as style. She claimed that in his smoother version no change occurs; the fish "nibbles" at the idea of changing forms but is finally content to eat weeds and remain fish. She had instead tried, through a jarring rhythm, to portray a divided state and a desire to learn from, but not be constrained by, the different realms (Molesworth 59–60). Her poem "The Plumet Basilick," written twenty years later, contains her lines about man and fish and an image of metamorphosis: "the basilick portrays / mythology's wish / to be interchangeably man and fish" (79–81).

During her senior year, Moore frequently asserted her views with other teachers, approaching them as collaborative colleagues. By that time, in fact, Lucy Martin Donnelly, the teacher who had suggested that she not become an English major, had become her friend. Moore and Donnelly enjoyed debating the symbolism of women's fashions, a subject that Donnelly was then studying and that Moore later wrote about also. In their frequent conversations, they worked through their opinions on other social issues, and especially on women's freedoms and restrictions, while also discussing their works in progress.

Like Marianne Moore, many other students had the disturbing but wonderful experience of recognizing the weaknesses in the artistic advice given by teachers that they respected. In a creative writing seminar with Lloyd Reynolds during her junior year at Reed College in 1931, Mary Barnard eventually discovered the shortcomings of the teacher who had led her to a new poetic voice and to a supportive class group: "It was only in Lloyd's creative writing class where discussion revealed what the other students were not perceiving that I discovered what I knew" (37). As the term proceeded, she began to see his limitations: he was better able to motivate writers, teach general techniques, and judge completed poetry than to give specific advice for revision:

> Lloyd sometimes said, "I think your poem is wonderful!" which made me feel good, especially as he bent a sparkling gaze upon me as he said it, but it told me nothing. Once he said of two poems I had put in his box, "It was a mistake to have written those two." When I handed in the final draft of the collection I had put together, he handed it back without comment, and said to type it for submission. (41)

Barnard recognized that each teacher and group of students had special strengths and that ultimately she would have to carefully consider their enthusiasms and their criticisms to create her own best possible products.

For many African American students, recognizing the professors' limitations might involve a confrontation with their perspectives on race and activism. Marita Odette Bonner, a regular contributor to her high school's literary magazine, was told by a counselor that she should go to Radcliffe to study writing with the well-known Charles Townsend Copeland. Bonner recalled, "At the time I was in high school, Copy's class was limited to twenty students each year and admission was on a competitive basis. Students came from all over the world to take his course" (Roses and Randolph 18). Bonner appreciated his encouragement and his careful critique of her works-in-progress. But she found his advice limited when he warned her not to appear "bitter" in her stories. This was "a cliché to colored people who write," an attempt, she believed, to keep her from pronouncing harsh judgments on white America. Her determination to express her own vision of institutionalized hatred only grew in his class, as evidenced in the stories she published in *Opportunity* and *The Crisis* soon after her graduation in 1922.

As students entered more equal relationships with teachers, critiquing their values and advice, they often established friendships stretching beyond an individual course to years of collaboration. Milicent Washburn Shinn, who entered the University of California in 1874, took a leave of absence in 1877 to teach school, and returned to graduate in 1880, was greatly influenced by the poet and literature professor Edward Rowland Sill, who taught at Berkeley and had also been her high school teacher. She felt that he had challenged his high school students to love learning:

> He was fond of bringing any great idea, all his own chief topics of spiritual meditation, to the schoolroom. The object of human existence, the *summum bonum*, the chief end of man, the Good, the True, and the Beautiful, the service of humanity, the ideals of medieval chivalry, of Hale's Ten times One, were everyday subjects to us. (Parker 135)

In his high school and college classes, Sill encouraged students "to talk freely, to argue back and criticise, and would take more of that than any teacher I ever knew" (Parker 136). When Shinn left college and returned to her high school as a teacher, Sill wrote to her from Berkeley to encourage her to keep writing and to avoid becoming too critical of her own work, especially during the drafting process:

> You should be writing a good deal, in odd moments. Send me anything that's good—after it gets cold:—so that you needn't feel that it's *going* to be sent while writing; for what we all need is to keep clear of restraining

influences—these obscure, subtle ones, that throw us out of *rapport* with ourselves, and make us think of the writing instead of the thing to be written. I believe we could all of us write something worth while if we could get free from everything but the looking clearly at the inner thing we are trying (or should be) to transcribe. (Parker 157–58)

After Shinn returned to college, Sill helped her to secure an editorial staff position at the *San Francisco Commercial Herald*. Then in 1880, she became a regular contributor of poetry and prose to the literary magazine, *Californian*. After it reopened with its older name, the *Overland Monthly*, Sill encouraged her to take the position as editor, which she held from 1883 to 1894, and he acted as her consultant and as an anonymous contributor until his death in 1887.

Sill encouraged other students to pursue poetry writing seriously, causing an *Overland Monthly* reviewer to comment in 1883 of his career at the University of California: "That this should result in an era of poetry-writing is no more wonderful that that Agassiz' sojourn at Harvard produced a crop of naturalists" (Ferguson 160). Sill believed that all educated women, such as Milicent Shinn, needed opportunities other than just the one choice of teaching, as he wrote to President Daniel Coit Gilman at Johns Hopkins in 1878:

> Here we graduate every year a number of intelligent and virtuous and industrious young women—but what are they to do? Teaching, of course, is open, but sometimes they don't like that, and are not suited for it, or haven't the nerves to stand the public school drudgery. . . .
>
> They drive me to my wits' end every year, with the impossibility of seeing anything for them but teaching or getting married.
>
> Do you know of any one in the East who would act as an intelligence officer for educated girls? . . . By the way, when are you going to open Johns Hopkins to girls? (Parker 176)

To help many students become writers, Sill served as their colleague and advisor long after they graduated and worked with them on a variety of creative projects.

LEARNING AND GROWING IN A GROUP

Many writers vividly remembered their positive interactions with writing teachers; they also frequently recorded the transforming impact of working within a group in class. At its best, as Paulo Freire indicates, a workshop could resolve "the teacher-student contradiction": "to exchange the role of depositor, prescriber, domesticator, for the role of student among students would be to undermine the power of oppression and serve the power of liberation." His preferred modes of education thus consist of "communication and of the common experience of a reality perceived in the complexity of its constant 'becoming'" (62, 99). This type of communication and becoming could be especially complex for women, conditioned to silence and to nonprofessional education, but the first generations of female college students found in this complex environment a bridge to professional life.

Many writers noted that after their initial fears subsided and a group relationship developed, they began to feel comfortable with the regular oral commentary. Taking The Mechanics of Playwrighting at Mt. Holyoke with Jeannette Marks, many women at first found the workshop situation daunting, but their total involvement in the process soon eased the pressure:

> Having always been one of the "young and secret," who retire beyond locked doors when engaging in creative attempts . . . my first reaction to the role of auditor was that of extreme embarrassment. Had I been asked to criticize my neighbor's newborn babe, I could scarcely have felt more rude. However, I soon became so engrossed in the general discussion of the plays that I forgot to worry about the personal element involved. ("Playshop Laboratory" xvii)

After noting her initial terror of studying in a group of four with Barrett Wendell, an opportunity not available at Harvard where class sizes were much larger, Radcliffe student Annie Ware Winsor Allen recognized the growth that these class sessions had engendered. Using imagery of health and illumination, she wrote about her growing comfort with critique sessions:

> It is a good thing to learn that our faults are not precious possessions like our life-blood. We can part with our faults without injury; it is not a vital pain when they are touched. And our good qualities—we do well to understand that they are not sacred invaluable possessions which are profaned by being looked upon. If somehow we can get to see that a mental fault is not a virtue we have gone far toward a healthy state of mind. We are learning to live to see ourselves and other people in the natural light of day. The nearer we get to this state of mind the easier it will be for us to learn and for our instructors to teach. (Simmons 275–76)

Although Annie Allen could not receive additional credit, she enrolled in Wendell's class several times, choosing her own readings and writing assignments to vary the work. As she continued to participate in this workshop situation, Allen did not remain a silenced or unconfident woman. In fact, after college, she became a teacher at Brearley School in New York City, director of the Roger Ascham School in Scarsdale, and then manager of the State Training School for

Girls in Hudson. And she became a writer, publishing books on education such as *Home, School and Vacation: A Book of Suggestions* and prose and verse in *Without and Within*.

In their first novels, written soon after college ended, many women writers described the intensity and commitment of workshop sessions, writing clubs, and of groups of writers living together in dorms. This college-novel genre gave them a means of analyzing their own experience and of showing younger women what college and writing workshops could offer. Julia Schwartz's book of vignettes, *Vassar Studies*, published in 1899, three years after she graduated, portrays several students, like the author herself, for whom writing is the focus of the college years. Alice describes herself to her roommate as nervous and uncertain, "prickly all over," when reviewing her work with an older student who serves as a teacher's assistant:

> "The criticism was all right, but the critic was telling how she is mistaken for a freshman every year, and she said, 'It seems very strange, considering my gray hair.' I popped out, 'Why, I should think so!' and then I remembered and exclaimed, 'Oh, no! I mean I shouldn't think so.'" (14)

Although their working relationship begins awkwardly, Alice soon finds herself working profitably on drafts and revisions with this assistant, as with the class group, thus forging a profitable literary routine that Schwartz recommends to her readers.

Another sketch, on "The Genius," a student described by her roommate as a nervous literary type, concerns the competition among workshop students for their teachers' approbation as well as their genuine desire to see each other succeed at this chosen craft:

> Her first essay was returned, marked in red ink, "Rewrite." She put me in a fidget by lying on her bed, face downward, all the afternoon. I am so sensitive that such demonstrations wear me out through the drain on my sympathies. About twilight, getting up, she said that she had decided to go home, because it was only a waste of time and money for her to remain. Instantly I began to ponder which of my congenial friends I should invite to room with me. Of course, I was sorry for her, but sometimes we just have to bow our heads to fate. Well, while she was starting to pack, I happened to pick up the essay, and discovered on the last page another note which she had not seen. It said that, although in mechanical execution the work was faulty, in power of conception and treatment it was far above the average. That girl acted half crazy—danced around the room, flung her arms about me, and kept exclaiming that she was too happy to live. Wasn't it ridiculous for her to depend so entirely upon another person's opinion?

Now, as for me, I knew my essays were good although generally the critic did not like to commit herself.

So the Genius stayed in college, and after a while she began to get "Excellent" on her essays, and have her stories and poems printed in the college magazine. I never could understand how she accomplished anything with her peculiar methods. The truth is that she had no method. After wandering around alone in the Pines, she used to steal away to the attic to write behind big ghostly tin pipes, or, in the spring, to the orchard or the fields. Nearly every Saturday—that was our day for writing themes—I was obliged to spend a long time in looking for her to tell her that luncheon was over. Now, when I wrote, I had system. . . . I always worked at a definite time and then stopped. . . . One thing I never permitted myself to do—the Genius was perfectly conscienceless regarding it—and that was to skip a meal.

As a result my thoughts were clearer and more simple than those of the Genius. My handwriting was better too. . . . Once I offered to copy something for her, because it seemed a pity to have that poem scrawled—it was her competitive poem for Founder's Day, and it was pretty good, and I was anxious that she should win the prize;—she snatched the paper away as if my touch might spoil it. The Genius cared considerably for that poem, and she was wild to have it chosen as the best from the whole college. That friend in Maine would then see that she had not been mistaken in believing in her. It would be, too—well, a sort of advertisement of ability. The reason why I wanted her to win was, first, of course, for her own sake, and then so that I might be able to point her out to my guests as my celebrated room-mate. You know, all the boys from the other colleges come here on Founder's Day. Think of the glory of having your own poem read before that great audience! At one time I intended to try for the prize myself, but I happened to be too busy with extra work the second semester. (68–71)

As in this excerpt, Schwartz attempts to portray these students' complete dedication to writing, as demonstrated in their classwork and their involvement in campus magazines and competitions. The narrator certainly envies her roommate's "genius" and wonders why her own hard work doesn't yield better results—an eternal quandary of writers. But even though, or perhaps because, they feel competitive, these women spur each other on to better work.

In her novel *Elinor's College Career* (1906), Julia Schwartz uses the experiences of four Vassar roommates, all from Ohio, to move from vignettes on teachers and classmates to a fully developed picture of a dedicated writing group, working within the larger community of college writers. In fact, one dorm resident declares, "Sometimes I believe I'm the only girl in the United States who doesn't believe she can write" (149). These four roommates and their friends enjoy sparring in lines from Shakespeare, conducting their own poetry contests, and viewing themselves as future "Literary Celebrities." They consider Derrick, a member of the Poetry Club, a regular contributor to the literary magazine, and a poetry prize winner, to be "the Literary Figure of the College" (135). Ruth, a student with considerable literary talent, forces herself to get over a crush on a roommate so that she can focus her energy on writing. She writes frantically as a sophomore and skips classes to get her literary magazine articles turned in on time and earn a place on the magazine's editorial board. Her friends joke with her about what her mother would say: "It must be that Ruth is working too hard over the magazine this fall. She surely looks miserable, and she never has time for anything outside of classes and that editorial business" (224). Myra prepares a story for the senior prize, but decides against submitting it because it denigrates her friend Elinor, to whom she explains the situation:

> Elinor, do you know that the story is about you? I wrote it at a time when I was angry—but it is a picture that will be recognized. Miss Ewers recognized it when she read the manuscript. She says that the story will be likely to win one of the prizes or at least be bought for publication. And she also said that I would not submit it if I cared for you. (260–61)

But Elinor insists that Myra submit it; she will weather the results for the sake of her friend's aspirations. Although their own writing occupies their attention, class readings often do not, as another roommate declares:

> There's the bell, and I haven't looked at my literature yet. Elinor tells me that it takes two hours to read a play of Shakespeare's. Just watch me scamper through one in the next forty minutes. People make me tired by being afraid of superficiality. I think it is like consistency, which Emerson says is the "hobgoblin of little minds," you remember. (156)

In these situations, Schwartz shows that women can use their mutual esteem to help each other achieve their goals, to enable them to put the work first: they have come to college not just to get a liberal education but together to seek the label of Writer.

MOVING FROM CLASSES TO CLUBS AND PUBLICATIONS

In these novels, the close groups often move beyond classes and dorm rooms to taking advantage of every club and publication that could help them move into the professional world. In *To Remember Forever*, Gladys Hasty Carroll used her own college journals, which she kept from 1922 to 1923, to present a picture of a young woman who discovered in college the possibility of a personal sort of authorship existing outside of the traditional enclaves of male privilege and tradition:

> In the twentieth century in America one does not have to be Sophocles, or Shakespeare, or Browning, or even Melville or Hawthorne or Walt Whitman to be read by his fellow citizens. He has only to be swept by an urge to create, to *re*-create the America—even the small piece of America—he knows, and to discover how to do it. . . . Oh, glory hallelujah! Because my small piece of America is singing in me, waiting to burst through, and I want nothing so much as to see it spilling out; my whole ambition is to be a local laureate. (7)

For Carroll's heroine Gladys, the key moment of college is being chosen to join the Spofford Club, a literary group for which only fifteen members are chosen. When she is asked to join, her sarcastic thoughts indicate the moment's importance: "Would I like to be presented to the Queen? Would I like to be in the Hall of Fame? Would I like to travel the seven seas on a tramp steamer with Shakespeare, the Brownings, Hawthorne, Melville, Ibsen, Conrad, Willa Cather, and Sarah Orne Jewett?" (125). After attending her first club events, she believes that her life is taking a new course: "[T]hey are almost a promise that I can be a writer if I try hard enough" (131). This group actually does enable her to travel with influential writers of all eras and to see herself as a professional writer going along with them. Like Gladys Hasty Carroll, many other women wrote about the professional settings on campus where they could deal with deadlines and finances, the requirements of real readers, and the egos of fellow writers. Coeducational schools did not always encourage women's participation in "the men's" newspapers and clubs; and the extracurricular activities at women's schools did not always stress connections to professional arenas. But, in both coeducational and women's colleges, women found ways to form new groups and to enter and transform existing extracurricular writing groups.

In nineteenth-century colleges for men, debating societies and literary clubs provided a major locus of college life. These clubs, which often had private libraries larger than the college collection, held forensic contests involving students from other clubs and other schools (Gere, *Writing Groups* 11). To create the complete campus environment, new women's schools quickly initiated such debating societies and teams: Mount Holyoke and Wellesley, for example, had active groups soon after their opening. At men's schools that were becoming coeducational, official opinions varied on whether women should be able to participate in such active, combative groups. When the College of California became a state school in 1869, women could enroll in this new University of California, but the debating societies remained all male (Gordon, "Co-education" 173–78). At Grinnell College, administrators maintained separate social societies for women through the mid-1920s and barred them from entering or forming debating clubs.

As attempts to bar women from campus groups at coeducational schools began to fail, their presence transformed the clubs themselves. Many societies began to downplay oral argumentation and instead stressed oral performance of literature, a less controversial activity for young ladies. Some of these clubs also offered members a chance to critique assigned readings, which might include the fictional or scholarly efforts of members. Thus altered, these clubs "attracted students who harbored secret ambitions to be writers, poets, actresses, or journalists" (Solomon 105). Most coeducational schools first inaugurated separate literary societies or clubs for women, but by the beginning of the twentieth century many also sponsored coeducational groups where men and women read fiction and poetry together and critiqued their own work.

Writing professors frequently sponsored such literary groups because they viewed these informal gatherings as an additional site for group work among dedicated students. Writers' clubs formed in Iowa City around 1890, out of older debating societies, to provide a place where students and faculty could read their own work and seek response. George Cram ("Jig") Cook took part in the founding of one club while he was still a student at Iowa. Then after studying at Harvard with Barrett Wendell, he returned to Iowa to begin teaching poetry courses and holding informal writing club meetings at his room, which he shared with another teacher: "You sat by an open fire, and were given rum in your tea when you came to see them. There were Chinese hangings. Iowa City was not quite sure." Cook especially wanted the club to serve as a catalyst for those few who thought creatively, who could see beyond Iowa: he "talked to the dozen who knew what he was talking about, and let the others make what they could of it" (Glaspell, *The Road to the Temple* 82–86).

Besides such informal groupings, the University of Iowa sponsored more formal writing clubs. Clarke Fisher Ansley, chair of the English department from 1899 to 1917, became an advisor to four such groups. In 1921, professors John Frederick and Frank Luther Mott organized the Saturday Luncheon Club, to extend the education of young writers by bringing in outside speakers. With very little money, they secured Robert Frost, Carl Sandburg, Sherwood Anderson, and Clarence Darrow as guests. Mott's Times Club and SPCS (Society for Prevention of Cruelty to Speakers) also brought in prominent writers, but their most anxiously awaited speaker was one who never arrived, Gertrude Stein, whose plane was grounded in Waukesha, Wisconsin, during a snowstorm.

At the University of Chicago in 1917, Robert Morss Lovett decided that his course on versification didn't give dedicated students adequate time to craft their work, and thus he started the Poetry Club along with student Harold Van Kirk. The club began at a meeting of five students with *Poetry* editor Harriet Monroe at Lovett's home: "After dinner the poets read their verses, which Miss Monroe pronounced deplorable" (Lovett, *All Our Years* 122). The club later sponsored other more congenial visits from Monroe, who published student work in *Poetry*, as well as visits from Edgar Lee Masters, Robert Frost, and Carl Sandburg. More commonly, however, meetings involved Lovett and the group members reading their own verses and seeking response; as Van Kirk remembered, "[W]e called each other's verse to task with a fine fervor and freedom" (Lovett, Preface n. pag.). The group had begun with only men and in 1918, in fact, they were asked to leave their meeting room in Ida Noyes Hall, a women's dorm, since "we were a merely masculine assembly." In the next few weeks, the club began admitting women (perhaps to keep the meeting room), among them Gladys Campbell, Janet Lewis, and Elizabeth Roberts, who served as the club president in 1920. In his 1923 anthology of poems by club members, Lovett included work by nineteen women and thirteen men. In the preface, he spoke enthusiastically of the individual voices and the spirit of experimentation that this club had nurtured:

> It is fortunate that this association of young poets came about at a time when the technique of poetry is undergoing rapid changes, when the subordination of formal considerations to self-expression is in the air, and the impulse to experiment is strong. I like to think of these poems as part of the experience of the writers of them, a part of life, not merely a decoration of it or the pursuit of a separate interest in it. One use of art is to strengthen our impression of reality. (n. pag.)

For all these writers, the club's anthology provided a first means of publication; Lovett's contacts with Monroe and with Boston publishers led them from the collegiate to the professional.

At many other schools, women's entrance into clubs that began with men caused deeper consternation, even when the emphasis was no longer on oral debate. When they began entering small groups of male friends, their intrusions seemed even less tolerable than in required courses. Many men regretted losing their private enclaves and found the women's dedication and skill to be intimidating. In the late nineteenth century, the University of Nebraska had several literary societies, including two that were coeducational, the Palladian and the Union. According to Willa Cather's friend and fellow student Alvin Johnson, the coeducational group revealed the high quality of women students, which the men had to find excuses to explain:

> Perhaps our literary performance was mediocre, but the association through years with eager young people of both sexes was worth while.... The Palladian girls were an admirable group, not, however, set apart from the girls of the general student body, who were in the vast majority earnest students, better disciplined intellectually than the boy students and gaining top rank in their classes so frequently that the male students, in self-defense, had to fall back on the antique dogma that the female mind is acquisitive, not original, and that the girls won honors by reflecting faithfully the professors' wisdom and foibles. (92)

The successful movement of women from classes into literary groups such as the Palladian was often the occasion for rationalizations, and for alarm.

Although their presence often caused dismay, many women found a circle of colleagues in these coeducational groups. When Mary Barnard came to Reed College in 1928, her professor Victor Chittick was sponsoring the Gawd-Awful Society, which almost always met at his home, as she described it:

> This group was composed of would-be poets for the most part, and girls for the most part, though the membership fluctuated greatly from year to year.... In this group I encountered for the first time in my life other people who wrote poetry. We would meet on Saturday nights about once a month to read our Gawd-Awful poetry and our Gawd-Awful prose. Gawd-Awful was one of Victor Chittick's favorite adjectives, hence the name. I was invited to join almost immediately upon my arrival at Reed, a high compliment, I believe, because most members were juniors or seniors. (35–36)

At club meetings, when Barnard read poems that she had written in high school, she enjoyed the enthusiastic response. She also began learning about new poetic styles: "It seemed that I was the only rhyming poet on campus. Everyone else wrote free verse" (36). As an avid collector of western stories and scholar of contemporary literature, Chittick encouraged group members to experiment with their own subject matter and the prosody appropriate to it.

To further encourage their most dedicated writers, many schools sponsored not only several literary clubs but also elite groups for the best writers. The honorary society Blackstick at Mt. Holyoke, for example, admitted to membership only the most skilled writers. Katharine Lee Bates, who later wrote six volumes of poetry and published studies of English and American literary history while teaching at Wellesley, was allowed to join the chosen few soon after she entered college in 1876 (Campbell 25, 31). As an undergraduate, she published "Sleep" in the *Atlantic Monthly*, and when the Blackstick Club visited Longfellow, the poet spoke approvingly of that piece. Beginning in 1915, distinguished American poets began to speak at a series of monthly Poetry Shop Talks arranged by Professor Marks for the Blacksticks and for other interested writers (Cole 305). Speakers included Robert Frost, Grace Conkling, and Amy Lowell. In 1926, this series was enlarged to Play and Poetry Shop Talks, with George Pierce Baker as one of the invited speakers. At Bryn Mawr, students also sought entrance into select groups. During the 1913–1914 senior year, Katherine Sargeant White, who became a long-time *New Yorker* editor and writer, belonged to several clubs, including the six-member Inner Shrine and the nine-member English Club, which required senior class status and at least one A and two Bs in English. Their purpose was to provide serious critique of the students' coursework and of pieces intended for publication (L. Davis 37).

While these clubs extended interest in writing, they also provided specific goals for members through their annual writing prizes. At Mt. Holyoke, members competed for the annual Sigma Theta Chi Alumnae Poetry Prize. The Kathryn Irene Glascock Poetry Prize, named in memory of a literary prodigy of the Mt. Holyoke class of 1922, involved writers from many eastern schools, with winners coming from Mt. Holyoke, Barnard, Smith, and Vassar as well as Yale, Brown, Wesleyan, and Dartmouth. A panel of distinguished writers awarded the prize and then conducted readings along with student writers.

At schools around the country, this regular contact and serious work, involving clubs as well as classes, made a future of creative writing seem possible to a large student population, a new situation for American women. Harriette Arnow, for example, studied in Berea College's normal school program from 1924 to 1926 and then became a teacher in Pulaski County, Kentucky. She later recognized that if her education had ceased there, as it would have in earlier generations, she would have never become a writer. In 1928, however, she enrolled in the University of Louisville where she took writing courses and belonged to Chi Delta Phi, a small literary group that met once a week at lunch to listen to the members' latest efforts and choose pieces for club pamphlets. There, as a member of a group, a biographer concluded, "she became more or less firmly wedded to the idea of writing" (Eckley 36). Her first novel *Mountain Path* came out in 1936. Like Arnow, many other women writers found in the extracurricular club an extension of the writing class' group emphasis and a connection to professional life.

Like literary clubs for creative writers, university press clubs gave journalists a chance to hone their skills and make valuable contacts as they worked together in groups. Whereas at state schools literary clubs tended to quickly become coeducational, separate press clubs were common for women there, perhaps because they needed an especially supportive environment within male-dominated journalism schools and because they were not generally welcomed into the virile pursuits of newspapermen. Theta Sigma Phi journalism sorority was established at the University of Washington in 1909, with support from Merle Thorpe, originator of the journalism program there and later editor of *The Nation's Business*. By 1915, eight universities had chapters. In 1929, thirty-two active chapters shared the purpose of uniting women college students, conferring honors on distinguished writers, and improving conditions for women journalists. High grades were a membership requirement. The organization published the *Matrix* and maintained the Women's National Journalistic Register, an employment bureau for women headquartered in Chicago and with branch offices in Kansas City, New York, and Seattle. After leaving the University of Wisconsin in 1923, Ruby Black edited the organization's bimonthly magazine, with news of alumnae chapters as well as inspirational pieces, practical guidance, and book reviews.

Besides these sorority chapters, most schools had press clubs that recruited student writers to serve as stringers for local papers. At Barnard, Emma Bugbee joined the campus press club, whose members wrote about college events for various New York City newspapers. She decided to apply for a college stringer position at the *Tribune*, wrote to the editor, and was accepted immediately with a note asking, "Where were you yesterday? We wanted you to cover the basketball game" (Belford 180). After graduation, Bugbee began teaching Greek at a high school, but a year later a Barnard classmate and fellow press club member, Eva vom Baur, a reporter at the *Tribune*, asked her to serve as her summer substitute while she visited relatives in Germany. When vom Baur decided to stay abroad, Bugbee was given a permanent job. In women's schools that might have just one or two journalism courses intended for enrichment, such activities and the contacts they generated provided an essential connection to the profession.

Like Gladys Hasty Carroll, Bugbee wrote fiction for young women that stressed the importance of participating in writing clubs. Her character Peggy, featured in her series of novels about a journalism career, joins a press club in the first book, *Peggy Covers the News* (1936), and uses this association to get a college stringer job. She writes her first story about a swim race that the lead swimmer, the granddaughter of a Senator, forfeited to save a drowning dog. Although the editor instructively repeats for her the old anecdote of the rookie who misses the news value of a called-off society wedding, the well-educated Peggy already knows that the kindly forfeit will provide her lead. When a boat sinks in the New York harbor, she suddenly goes from reporting college events to interviewing passengers brought out of the sea. As a press club stringer, she gets regular advice from a mentor, successful reporter Kate Morrison, a woman whose skills and panache she greatly admires:

> Usually Kate was out on an assignment of her own when the girl arrived, but before the college story had been finished—she still toiled over each paragraph, seeking clarity of style and perfection in the detail of names and addresses—the older woman bustled in, flung open her typewriter, and plunged into her work without taking off her hat. She always had time, however, for a brisk smile at Peggy, and a quick:
> "Hello, how are you getting on?"
> And Peggy would linger at some pretended task, perhaps to write a letter or copy off some college lecture notes, just for the pleasure of watch-ing Kate Morrison at work.
> Would she herself, she wondered, ever acquire so much assurance, so unerring a sense of how to tell her story, how to select the most inter-esting items from the mass of detail that to her inexperienced mind still befogged the narrative? (67–68)

Peggy cannot be sure of a positive answer to her questions, but it is her college training and press club experience that enable her to ask them.

Besides helping women to gain professional experience, press clubs spon-sored talks and other activities for women students that could further involve them in the career. At the University of Wisconsin, for example, the Women's Press Club, involving university and Madison women, held biweekly meetings with talks by professionals. At the University of Missouri, Journalism Week brought professional speakers to campus each year. Along with women faculty and the Missouri Writers' Guild, the Theta Sigma Phi chapter sponsored talks throughout the week, with the emphasis during the first years on feature writ-ing jobs, but with more varied topics as the years passed. In 1910, at the first Journalism Week, Winifred Black, who had written for Hearst's *San Francisco Examiner* and *New York Journal* as Annie Laurie and was then working for the *Kansas City Post*, spoke on "The News as the Newspaper Woman Sees It." In 1913, speeches included "City Journalism for Women"; the Missouri Women's Press Club met; and women students and professionals met together for a tea and for dinner. In 1914, Elizabeth Gilmer (Dorothy Dix) spoke on "How the

Press Views the Feminist Movement"; other talks included "A Woman Journalist in the Far North." In 1916, women spoke on "Experiences in Writing Motion Pictures," "Writing a Story from a Child's Viewpoint," and "The Problems and Struggles of a Beginner" (Williams 164–80).

At women's colleges and coeducational universities, literary and press club involvement frequently went along with work on campus literary magazines and newspapers. These publication outlets, like writing clubs, did not always welcome women, but they did provide further training for professional careers. With their regular meetings in designated rooms on campus, these publications in fact provided the first professional offices that women students entered and made their own.

If a magazine did not serve as a component of class work, it might be sponsored extracurricularly by a writing teacher. At the University of Iowa, John Frederick involved students in editing *Midland*, a regional literary journal. Frank Luther Mott, who came there in 1921, acted as advisor to the *Iowa Literary Magazine*, which published student work. Although teachers offered guidance, students were generally allowed to assume editorial control of campus magazines. On the *Barnard Quarterly* in 1931, students formed committees to choose among the submissions. As one student commented, "[I]ts poetry is very deep, with a vague and lovely other-worldliness. Its stories are long and serious and almost invariably tragic" (Miller and Myers 132).

Involvement in these publications allowed many women to define themselves as writers. Zona Gale had written constantly before she went to college, starting in elementary school: "My school mates were bound to believe that I was going to be a writer—because I had told them all so! I wrote when I should have been studying, I wrote through recess, and took home my tablets and wrote" (Derleth 30). In high school, she began sending her pieces out to magazines, but to no avail: "The heavy manuscripts fell with an unmistakable sound; and often, even when I was upstairs, I could count them as they dropped, and know just how many of my stories had come back" (Derleth 31). When she entered the University of Wisconsin in 1891, she felt lost in the large student body and intimidated by the sorority system. In 1918, twenty-three years after her graduation, she wrote a letter to the editor of the student paper, the *Daily Cardinal*, about her isolation:

> I hope that no one will mind too much my questionable taste in admitting that the sorority situation clouded my own university life to such a degree that, much as I love the campus, I never go back there without experiencing again, through memory, something of the unhappiness of those days which ought to have been happy. (Simonson 23)

Although college social life seemed daunting, Gale soon found her own place by joining the staff of *The Aegis*, a literary magazine. In November 1891 when the magazine offered prizes for the best poems written by students, she entered several pieces and her poem "A Rose" won second place. She then began working on the editorial committee, became the magazine's editor, made friends with fellow writers such as Anne Scribner, and met the university president Charles Kendall Adams, who frequently invited her to his home. While at the university, she won two additional literary prizes, for an essay and a poem. To extend these opportunities to others, when her *Miss Lulu Betts* was awarded the Pulitzer Prize for drama in 1921, she established scholarships for students whose talents lay in the creative arts, particularly in writing. Gale's first beneficiary was Margery Latimer, a fellow resident of Portage, Wisconsin. After one of Latimer's short stories appeared in a local newspaper, Gale called her and encouraged her to attend the university and participate in the literary life available beyond the classroom there.

At other schools and for students farther from familiar surroundings, college literary magazines also provided a home base. When Pearl Buck came from China to Randolph-Macon Woman's College in Lynchburg, Virginia, in 1910, she felt lost on campus, surprised that so few students wanted to hear about her experiences as a daughter of missionaries in China and that so many were wrapped up in campus social events. But during her freshman year she began to feel more confident about the university and her place in it as she wrote stories for the college literary monthly, *The Tatler*, and other campus publications while also acting in and writing class plays. For her efforts, she won two campus literary prizes in her senior year, for the best short story and best poem, and was voted member of the modern literature club, a select group of eight. When she submitted a translation of a Chinese poem to the club's magazine, one of the editors helped her with poetic style:

> There was one odd thing about the verses. Pearl had rhyme but the meter just wasn't there. I asked why she hadn't written them in meter, and she said she had never had meter called to her attention. She asked for a lesson and we sat right down and patched up the lines and scanned several other examples. The result was an overnight miracle. (C. Spencer 122)

As a senior, she wrote a play about a freshman with no money, dressed in absurd clothes, who is rebuffed in her efforts to enter any of the school's social cliques, but her classmates wouldn't accept this piece for production because it made them look like cruel snobs. Buck directed the senior class follies even though her classmates were unwilling to confront the behavior that had made her so glad to find *The Tatler*.

Along with offering a place to find a supportive on-campus group and to seek publication, literary magazine involvement could lead to notice by professional magazines and writers. Mildred Gilman, the first woman editor of the *Wisconsin Literary Magazine*, felt emboldened by the authority of that post and began corresponding with H. L. Mencken and Sherwood Anderson by first sending them fan letters: "I had a wonderful correspondence with Sherwood Anderson about writing techniques. It was like having him as a teacher" (Belford 249). While at college, she also began selling magazine articles and finished her first novel, *Fig Leaves*, about her adolescent years in Grand Rapids. She began working as a journalist after college, a career path she described in her novel, *Sob Sister*.

When Zora Neale Hurston started college at Howard University, Stylus, the campus literary club, admitted her to its group of writers and editors because of her superior performance in English classes and in May 1921 published her first short story, "John Redding Goes to Sea," in its literary magazine. She wrote in her autobiography, "My joining The Stylus influenced my later moves" (*Dust Tracks* 167). This piece was her "calling card on the professional literary world," causing Charles Spurgeon Johnson of *Opportunity Magazine*, who was introducing new African American writers, to ask her for more publishable material (Howard 18). After she sent him the stories "Drenched in Light" and "Spunk" and a play *Color Struck*, Johnson suggested that she come to New York, where he and his wife befriended her. At the first *Opportunity* award dinner, she won second prize for "Spunk" and met Annie Nathan Meyer, a founder of Barnard who arranged for her to have a scholarship there.

Besides providing a means of securing that first professional notice, literary magazines also offered women the chance to gain editorial and management experience, to learn how publication worked. In December of her freshman year, Willa Cather, a member of the Union Literary Society, became associate editor of a new campus magazine, *The Lasso*, and in the beginning of her sophomore year joined the staff of the oldest campus literary publication, the *Hesperian*, a semimonthly magazine of sixteen pages published jointly by several literary societies. As a member of an editorial board for all campus publications, she even encouraged a high school student, Dorothy Canfield, daughter of the college president, to co-write a story for the 1894 university yearbook, *The Sombrero*. Canfield recorded the occurrence:

> At a football game where we happened to be on the same grandstand, I gave her the idea of a football story—of all things! A fancy that had just occurred to me. She wrote the story, and very generously, I thought, put my name with hers as if I had helped write the story although I would

have been perfectly incapable of that at that age. The story got a prize, $10.00—all of that! She gave me half of it. I thought it was generosity itself and still do. (21)

By editing a paper and helping other writers, Cather established a professional ethos that gave her the confidence and knowledge needed for establishing her own career.

For some older students, these college classes and publications provided the opportunity to extend or restart careers instead of to begin them. This pattern may have been especially common for students, many of them African Americans, who could not afford to enter college directly after high school. Mary Burrill, for example, studied at Emerson College after she graduated from high school in 1901, but she returned to earn a bachelor's of literary interpretation in 1930. She had published two plays in 1919, *Aftermath* and *They Sit in Darkness.* Her writing continued when she returned to school where her *Unto the Third and Fourth Generations: A One Act Play of Negro Life* appeared in the college yearbook and was awarded Best Junior Play of the Year. Shirley Graham DuBois had studied music and written two plays before entering Oberlin College in 1931 at age thirty-five. At Oberlin, she wrote her first musical, *Tom-Tom*, drawing on traditional African themes and rhythms to dramatize the harsh realities of the Middle Passage from Africa to America. When it was produced by the Cleveland Summer Opera Company in 1935, *Tom-Tom* was the first professionally produced all-black opera. When DuBois left Oberlin, she secured a teaching job at Tennessee State and then directed the Negro Unit of the Chicago Federal Theatre.

Other students further extended their professional training by initiating their own publications, thus asserting their ability to assess drafts, guide revisions, and determine policy, skills stressed in their writing classes. Elizabeth Bishop, who went to Vassar College in 1930, joined the editorial staff of the campus *Vassar Miscellany News* to which she contributed a humor column, "Campus Chat," a parody of the campus scene with bits of verse, parodies, and jokes (Fountain and Brazeau 47). During her junior year, along with Mary McCarthy, Frani Blough, Margaret Miller, Muriel Rukeyser, Eunice Clark, and Eleanor Clark, she helped found a new literary magazine to compete with the conservative *Vassar Review.* The friends met at a restaurant off campus, chose a more open editorial policy, and settled on anonymous publication to protect contributors, mostly themselves, from censure. They then wrote and revised their own pieces, advertised for manuscripts, and put up their own money to publish this *Con Spirito*, a name picked by Bishop to represent both their spirit and conspiracy. (Mary McCarthy had suggested *The Battleaxe.*) They picked the best works in group sessions:

> We of *Con Spirito* would meet in a room in Students (later in the Pough-
> keepsie red-wine-and-white-coffee-cups speak-easy owned by Signor
> Bruno); manuscripts for submission were put, unsigned, on a wooden
> chair, to be read and argued over. (McCarthy, *How I Grew* 257–58)

When T. S. Eliot visited Vassar in May 1933, Bishop interviewed him for the campus newspaper; she was pleased when he complimented both the contents and
design of their independent magazine. The summer after her junior year, she
began sending her writing out to magazines: although *Hound and Horn* and the
New Yorker returned her submissions, she had a story and poem published by *The
Magazine*, whose editors had read *Con Spirito*. Mary McCarthy also used her literary magazine experiences at Vassar to move from classwork to her first publication. When she went to *The New Republic* offices to see the book editor, Malcolm
Cowley, bringing a *Con Spirito* issue containing her book reviews, he allowed her
to write a review for the magazine, for which he paid her five dollars.

At women's colleges and coeducational schools, women students found
a place in campus literary magazines. Such involvement seemed to their teachers and to male students to be a natural extension of their creative natures and
their presence in English departments. But finding their way on campus newspapers proved more difficult: as we have seen, even schools of journalism that
encouraged women's enrollment in classes judged daily journalism as a career
closed to them. At coeducational universities, men controlled the major newspaper publications although women did receive some professional experience
there. At women's schools, which generally did not have journalism departments or schools, teachers gave more support to literary publications than to
daily newspapers.

Even though the charter of the University of Chicago pointed to the
importance of coeducation, at the beginning of the century its university
papers, like so many others, did not welcome women's participation. The *Daily
Maroon* reflected a man's perspective in its coverage of fraternity activities and
sports although it did have a separate women's page at the back, which ensured
the limited participation of some women writers. Women also wrote for the
University Weekly, but held no editorial positions. A female staff published *The
Women's Weekly* once a year to dramatize their minimal role on the regular
papers. Grinnell College also offered only limited participation on campus
publications, as evidenced by special annual women's editions, beginning in
1905, of the student newspaper, *Scarlet and Black* (Zimmerman 165).

At the University of California, the *Daily Californian*, published by the
fraternities, not only refused to involve women writers but frequently included
editorials against women's presence on campus. Since removing women from

the university seemed unlikely, the newspaper urged that education for women occur only in separate classes. Elsie McCormick, women's page editor of another campus publication, *Brass Tacks*, complained in a 1916 article "An Etiquette for Coeds" of the *Daily Californian*'s essays on the differences between the sexes. She made fun of their specific advice to women students: "Do not study anything useful. Co-eds should specialize in English, and a diluted form of art history." Like *Brass Tacks*, other newspapers such as *Student Opinion*, the *Pelican*, the *Dill Pickle*, and the *Raspberry Press* gave women some opportunity to express their opinions and publish fiction, but not to control editorial policy or report news.

Even when newspapers served as part of the classwork and not as an extracurricular activity, women students were often kept from leadership roles and wrote only for a women's page. At *The University Missourian*, sponsored by Sara Lockwood as part of class work, women wrote a regular column called "Marylou Goes Shopping." Women also regularly worked on the newspaper's extracurricular activities, such as the "Yellow Extra," a newspaper designed to be a "horrible example of what a newspaper should not be," and the "Scoop Dance" where a "Scoop Extra" was sold. But from 1911 to 1918 when eighty-four students held editorial positions at *The University Missourian*, twelve each year, women comprised 3.5 percent of this membership whereas, as we have seen, they graduated in numbers of thirty-six to 128, or 22 percent (Williams 148–50). Although they might organize a dance or work on a humor issue, they were not chosen for regular editorial or reporting positions.

At women's colleges, the school newspaper offered a less combative place to develop journalistic skills although often an uncertain one because of these schools' weaker commitment to journalism instruction and to career experiences generally. The newspaper *Mount Holyoke*, for example, had trouble getting sufficient funding, and so in 1908 it was reorganized into a literary magazine to gain a larger clientele and more faculty support.

Although their tenure might be short, newspapers at women's colleges did offer the opportunity for editorial experience and political training. In 1935, Katharine Meyer Graham, who had originally gone to college to study German, went to Albany with the local chapter of the American Student Union to protest a proposed law requiring a loyalty oath for public school students. This political involvement led to her becoming an apprentice editor of the *Vassar Miscellany News* and then to her joining its regular editorial staff as a social critic. Among other subjects, she wrote on conservative control of American film:

The censorship of Sinclair Lewis' novel *It Can't Happen Here* proves that Hollywood means to dedicate its technological advance to the cause of reaction. Under the control of dictators such as Williams, Hays, and Hearst, the vast potential mastery of the movies promises to play an actively anti-social role. . . . Any progressive leaning, any fundamental truth will be eliminated in order not to diminish a picture's box office appeal, annoy a foreign or Fascist government, or encourage disagreement with the status quo which is after all the faithful watch dog of the movie interests. (D. Davis 59)

By 1936 she was one of several progressives in charge of the paper, she was a member of the national board of the American Student Union (ASU), and she went to Washington to support the American Youth Act, a New Deal social program. When she transferred to the more radical University of Chicago after her sophomore year and a summer of work at her father's *Washington Post*, she founded a weekly ASU bulletin, her first work as a publisher (D. Davis 71–72). Then she went from college to a position at the *San Francisco Daily News*.

As an extension of classroom activities, clubs, contests, newspapers, and magazines created a path of literary distinction in college, an apprenticeship leading from the classroom to the profession. And many women took advantage of all of these possibilities, combining them to create an immersion in writing that would lead to successful careers. Edna St. Vincent Millay went to Vassar in 1913 because her goal was to become a writer. She had already sent poems to the Poetry Society of America and told Arthur Davison Ficke, a poet whose work had appeared along with hers as winners of a contest at *The Lyric Year*, "It is quite true that I have yet to learn the ABC's of my art. I am hoping that college will help me;—but if I should come back a suffragette instead of a poet wouldn't it be dreadful?" (Brittin 27). When she took writing courses at Barnard in 1913 to prepare for college admission, she studied with William Tenney Brewster, a Harvard graduate and close friend of Robert Morss Lovett who was a Dryden and Carlyle scholar and author of a freshman composition text. When she first read her poetry aloud in his class, she feared for the results, as she wrote to her family:

If he takes a dislike to anything he delivers it accordingly & I was scared to death for fear he would read it & I should be obliged to go up and take it away from him.

So this morning, after reading two rather indifferent short poems on *Spring*, he picked up my *Interim*, and I felt a pang. "Gosh," I said to the girl at my right, "I wish he wouldn't read that. He reads verse so *wretchedly.*" "Yes, doesn't he?" she agreed, and he began.

"Here," he said, "is a very interesting piece of verse that I want to read to you, that is well worth reading."—I noticed that there wasn't even the twitch of a twinkle in his eye, and you may be sure I was watching for it. "It is called *Interim*," he said, and he didn't even smile at the odd title, "and I'll tell you a little about it, tho it's easy enough to understand. It's supposed to be the thoughts of a man about the woman he loved who has died very unexpectedly & very recently. The attitude is naturally rather tense. It is written in blank verse.—Well,—it is called *Interim* then," and he began.

He read it beautifully. I was never so astonished in my life. He had really got hold at last of something he liked, and he was a changed man. He seemed to understand every bit of it. Nothing struck him funny. Even the *Santa Claus* figure at the end and which some people have thought ridiculous, you know, he read with understanding, and when he stumbled over one line (it was a sixth or seventh carbon, & very faint) he went back and did the whole paragraph over.

When he had finished he asked, as usual, "Any comment on this theme?" (The girls, by the way, are crazy about it, of which more anon)— and when somebody suggested, "Well. it certainly isn't very amateurish," he said "It isn't amateurish at all." Then he went on, "No, it is a very remarkable production for a girl in college. The verse is very smooth, and there are a great many striking figures. For instance, this,—" and he read over the part about the planets spinning "like tops across a table." (Macdougall 42)

Brewster also read aloud her story "Barbara on the Beach," which the other students had critiqued in draft form during the previous class session. He helped her to revise this story further and to consider possible places for its publication; she published it in *Smart Set* in November 1914 (Brittin 5). When she entered Vassar, Millay continued to write poetry and participated in plays performed each week and in musical performances. She was also among the first to enroll in Vassar's Workshop Theatre, a playwriting course set up by Gertrude Buck to resemble George Pierce Baker's course at Radcliffe and Harvard. She wrote three plays during the course, and she starred in the workshop's production of *The Princess Marries the Page* in May 1917. By the time she graduated, the new combination of courses, clubs, college magazines, and college theatre groups had prepared her for a writing career.

In different circumstances, as an older student at a state college, Josephine Herbst profited from the same array of involvements, treading like Millay a path that only college could provide. Herbst started at Morningside College in her hometown of Sioux City in 1910, taught in Stratford, Iowa, and then went to Berkeley to finish her education in 1916. As an older student, she found it difficult to adjust to the University of California's social life, as she wrote to her sister:

> I guess I have seen too much of reality to swallow the stick candy side of college life. I can't stand around on one foot and pull off sweet nothings. . . . The student body is smug and comfortable. They are very proud of their contented state and contribute it to student government. Why student government should shrivel up their capacity for thinking, I can't see, but they don't put it that way, of course. (Langer 48)

There she took an English composition class with Harold Bruce, a 1915 Yale Ph.D. who had written a thesis on the structural characteristics of comedy and was then working on a study of Voltaire and the English stage. Recognizing her superior skills, Bruce read her stories aloud and invited her to lecture to his other classes about modern writing. During 1917–1918, with his encouragement, she published several poems in the campus literary magazine, the *Occident*. Bruce introduced her to the writers' community in San Francisco and Oakland, led by Max Stern and Carl Hoffman, editors of the *San Francisco Bulletin*. Her fellow student, Genevieve Taggard, also came to these sessions.

Taggard, too, had found in college classes and groups a life-changing experience. The daughter of missionaries, she grew up in Hawaii under a stern mother's edicts. When she left the islands for Berkeley in 1914, she studied with poet Witter Bryner, took Leonard Bacon's writing course English 106, became editor of the *Occident*, and met with her teachers' socialist friends. Of these new influences, she wrote to a friend: "Am I the Christian gentlewoman my mother slaved to make me? No indeed. I am a poet, wine-bibber, a radical; a nonchurchgoer who will no longer sing in the church choir or lead prayer meeting with a testimonial" (James III 422). Of all these new literary connections, she wrote to her mother, "I always knew that somewhere in the world were people who could talk about the things I wanted to talk about and do the things I wanted to do and in some measure at least I have found them" (Langer 44). After graduation and several odd jobs, Taggard joined Herbst in New York and became a reader for *Smart Set*, lived in Germany, Italy, and Paris in a socialist group, and then returned to Greenwich Village in 1926 to interact with other writers and work for *Scribner's*, *New Masses*, *American Mercury*, the *New York Post*, and the *Nation*.

Like Millay and Herbst, Taggard made new connections and entered new networks as her career developed, but the beginning occurred in the groups that college made accessible. For many other students these experiences offered real involvement in writing and entrance into the professional world, which students could approach as Writers, crafting messages and exploring genres without having to disguise themselves as financially strapped mothers or temporary crusaders—as Non-Writers. Certainly not every student who entered these classes and extracurricular activities desired a professional career, and some who did left discouraged, but through this process of education, many women writers found their own voices and began to find their own futures.

Willa Cather, as editor of her college paper, University of Nebraska, 1892. Courtesy of the Dorothy C. Fisher Papers, Special Collections, University of Vermont Library.

Willa Cather and the *Hesperian* staff, University of Nebraska. Courtesy of Willa Cather Pioneer Memorial Collection, Nebraska State Historical Society.

Marianne Moore at her Bryn Mawr graduation, 1909. Courtesy of the Special Collections Department, Bryn Mawr College Library.

Edna St. Vincent Millay seated under the porte-cochere of Main Building, Vassar College. Photograph by Madeline Benedict Foster, 1917. Courtesy of Special Collections, Vassar College Libraries.

Clarissa Scott Delany's senior picture in the Wellesley College annual, 1923. Courtesy of Wellesley College Archives.

Editorial and business boards of *The Vassarion*, 1934, with editor-in-chief Elizabeth Bishop in the center of the bottom row. Courtesy of Special Collections, Vassar College Libraries.

The Higher Types

"The Higher Types" in the *Vassar Review*. Clockwise from upper left: Mary E. St. John, editor, the *Vassar Miscellany News*; Mary M. Crapo, president of the students' association; Virginia Wylie, chief justice; and Elizabeth Bishop. Drawn by Anne Cleveland, 1937. Courtesy of Special Collections, Vassar College Libraries.

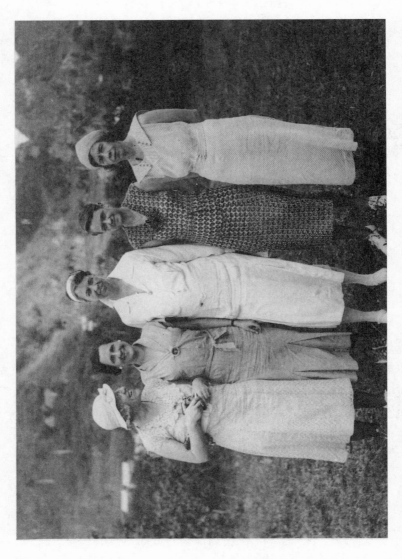

Eleanor Roosevelt and members of her press group in Puerto Rico, March 1934. Left to right: Emma Bugbee, Dorothy Ducas, Eleanor Roosevelt, Ruby Black, Bess Furman. Courtesy of Franklin D. Roosevelt Library.

Gladys Hasty Carroll at the Bread Loaf Writers' Conference, Summer 1935. Reprinted with the permission of Abernethy Library, Middlebury College.

Zora Neale Hurston, at the Federal Writers' Project exhibit, *New York Times* Book Fair, 1937. Courtesy of Photographs and Prints, Schomburg Center for Research in Black Culture, The New York Public Library, Astor, Lenox and Tilden Foundations.

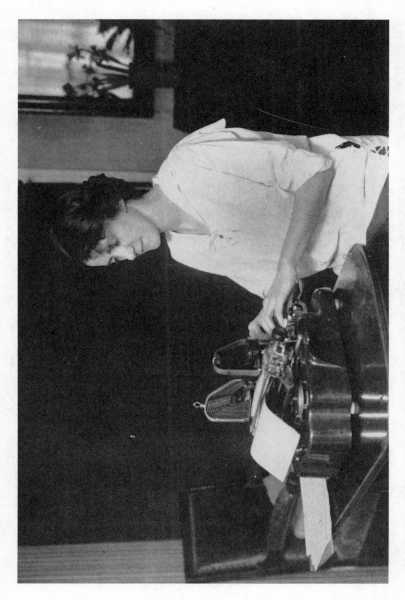

Susan Glaspell working on fiction at home. Courtesy Berg Collection of English and American Literature, The New York Public Library, Astor, Lenox and Tilden Foundations.

CHAPTER FOUR

A WRITING CAREER
AS SUBJECT

Art of every kind is an exacting master, more so even
than Jehovah. He says only, "Thou shalt have no other
gods before me." Art, science, and letters cry, "Thou
shalt have no other gods at all." They accept only
human sacrifices.

—Willa Cather

As we have seen, an array of college writing experiences helped women prepare for newly defined careers in writing. Classes, clubs, magazines, newspapers,
and contests enabled them to work together, gain experience, and begin viewing themselves as writers (Ault 75–76). During and after college, these women
wrote about their days spent in dorms, classes, and clubs, processing new experiences and making them real for readers. But while writing about college life,
they also turned their attention to the realities facing them as they attempted
to begin writing careers after graduation: the expectations of family and friends
that they would marry and forget college dreams, the isolation of the working
writer, the pressures caused by editors and readers. On this subject, young
women created a large body of work, their realistic discussion of the hardships
ahead replacing the etiquette manual or cookbook of earlier generations as a
common first book project. These texts, written at a time when the writers
were still considering the path ahead and the first hard choices they had made,
create a realistic, and even pessimistic, literature but one that emphasizes the

true value of the goal. In the nineteenth century, women defended themeselves as writers by declaring their own normalcy, their place in the secure home and community. Harriet Beecher Stowe and Fanny Fern described the writer as the loving homemaker and model mother; Eliza Leslie contended that "the best writers will be humble in front of men and fully dedicated to the home" (*The Behaviour Book* 259). But this literature from twentieth-century writers clearly posits an opposite: that the claims of family and of convention provide no protection for the writer and ultimately can only stifle creativity and end careers. Here there is no romanticizing of the naturally elevated place an author might occupy in society as a moral authority; there is no belief that a writer can thrive if she just pretends to be a humble do-gooder or inoffensive neighbor. This literature breaks through excuses and rationales to look realistically at the costs and benefits of the way ahead.

At the end of the nineteenth century, when women began crafting these texts, writing about a literary life was also a common choice of male writers, especially those involved in the aesthetics movement. Marianne Moore's biographer Charles Molesworth discussed her college writing, in fact, as reviewing "the problem as it was posed by the aestheticism of the late 1890's: one must choose perfection of the life or the work" (70). He thus placed her writing in the tradition of *fin de siècle* authors whose texts, such as Oscar Wilde's *The Picture of Dorian Gray*, Anton Chekhov's *The Seagull*, and Thomas Mann's *A Death in Venice*, focused on the superiority of the artistic temperament and on the necessary isolation of the artist, a man with heightened perceptions and unconventional habits. Among American writers of the period, Henry James may have best portrayed these themes in *Roderick Hudson*. In this novel, the main character, an artist, feels misplaced in small-town America and doomed by his family's expectations that he will marry his cousin and forget his dreamy goals. A patron's invitation to Rome, however, suddenly allows him to adopt new garb and manners—the heightened life of a genius—but he dies consumed by passion for an adventurous beauty whom he cannot obtain because she chooses wealth over love. In this novel, as in other texts from this period, the male artist is portrayed as a sensitive loner who reaches for fullness of experience and thus clashes with puritanical authorities and petty socialites, obstacles to a beautiful life and to its rendition in art.

Charles Molesworth rightly notes that several recurring themes of this literature—and especially the concentration on an artist's isolation—appear in Moore's work. But when he states that in defying conventions ultimately "one must choose perfection of the life or the work," he may not be fully recognizing that Moore is not the usual "one," but a woman for whom dedication to art was certainly more complicated than for a man. This women's literature on art and the artist's choices focuses less on the romantic plight of the author, although this theme does surface, and more on the difficult day-to-day decisions ahead, on responsibilities to parents, husbands, children, and friends that cannot easily be denied or combined with this new goal. These works provide realistic warnings, especially of the harsh difficulties of proceeding without the group life that made writing seem so possible in college. Writing, as we have seen, was not a particularly lonely choice for college women who took classes, joined clubs, and lived in dorms with others who shared their enthusiasm. In poetry and especially fiction, written in college and after, these women wrestled with the intense isolation from family and community that a writing career would entail once they left this environment if they were forced, like women of earlier generations, to proceed alone.

THIS CHOICE OF LIFE

In these texts, many women wrote about the moment of choosing an artistic life, of making family and peers understand that writing was not just a college notion. Some writers treated these conflicts lightly and ironically, recognizing that few among the large groups of college workshoppers actually had the courage to fight accepted mores and achieve their dreams. In "After Vassar—What?," a poem in the 1917 college annual, the *Vassarion*, the writer presents five students labeled from A to E whose dreams of suffrage work, social work, and war opposition fade into school teaching, cooking, and social life. But F, the author of the poem herself, still holds on tenuously to her goal of writing:

> For F, you see, was I
>   The little Shakespeare-still-to-be
> Throughout the coming century—
>   Unless *my* bubble bursts on me.

This poem portrays a writer, the last student in a long list, whose radical plans could be as vulnerable as soap bubbles floating on air. She realistically knows that her bubble could burst around her, that she may not be able to turn away from all traditional expectations to continue with writing.

Similarly, in her novel *Herbs and Apples* (1925), Helen Hooven Santmyer used Wellesley College roommates to focus attention on marriage as the much likelier choice than art. These four women swear a solemn oath at commencement: "'Down with Matrimony, up with Art, Fame before Forty or bust!' They decide together on a bet: 'Let's wager on our futures—bet on the first one to publish, and make it worth while: a new hat to be contributed by the losers to the winner on our fifth reunion'" (167). Like the Vassar poet and her characters A to F, these women realize that their career aspirations will probably devolve into marriage and school teaching, but they don't want to abandon the possibility of reaching what to them seems a completely separate but much more rewarding goal. By the time that she finished this first novel in 1923, when she was twenty-eight and still single, Santmyer was deciding to wager on her own future: she left an instructorship at Wellesley to go to Oxford as a Rhodes scholar and working novelist.

Other writers went beyond a general listing of the choices to further portray the specific expectations that would greet a graduate as soon as she returned home, where college would automatically be judged as an isolated interlude not an entré into professional life. For a skit written for an Alumnae Vaudeville Show in 1914, Newcomb College alumna Elizabeth McFetridge, who became a medical writer and served as associate editor for a multivolume history of surgical practices during World War II, created a character who had flourished within a group of college writers, who wanted a writing career, but who returned home as a dutiful daughter with only vague plans for an escape into art. As the character writes to a friend,

> Yes, I'm going to stay home next year. I did want to go up north—I know I could *easily* get a position on the *Atlantic* or *The Century* or one of those magazines; Miss Stone and Mr. Butler always gave me A on my essays— but mother and father won't hear of it.—Yes, after all, a woman's sphere is the home. No, I won't do the actual housekeeping. Mother will do that, but I'll attend to the rest.—And, Jane, we *must* keep up our French and German and read together for a couple of hours a day. And then our settlement work—I intend to devote *all* my time to that. And I expect I can write something, even here. (42)

As Newcomb students watched an actress speak these lines, McFetridge intended for them to carefully consider their own decisions about the future.

The family's complex combinations of love and guilt—the strong tentacles it fastened onto the female child—also interested Ruth Suckow. In *The Odyssey of a Nice Girl* (1925), she sends her character Marjorie from an Iowa farm to the school in Boston that Suckow had left the local Grinnell College to attend, the School of Expression, which offered Practice of Dramatic Art, Vocal Expression, and Study of Poetry. Marjorie finds there an underfunded and unorganized school that cannot live up to its catalog descriptions:

> The class in English Composition and Literary Study, that had sounded so
> wonderful in the catalogue, is taught (when held at all) by Miss Caroline
> Lee, the assistant in the wine-coloured suit, who says that the compositions
> were lovely, and tries fearfully to ward off questions about punctuation and
> spelling. (189)

But, even with this limited teacher, Marjorie exults in the closer connection
to literature that she achieves: "A shiver of delight went through Marjorie
when she wrote down words all steeped in a distant, glamorous beauty. The
lyrics of Herrick and Shakespeare, and the new things, in *Poetry*, that had
about them a marvelous freshness like a painting not yet dry" (242). At
school, she dreams new dreams, of leaving home, perhaps as a teacher but
preferably as a performer or writer. When she writes home about her desire
to find a job at a New York publishing house, her parents reply that "no doubt
New York would be very interesting to be in" but that she should come home
before making any further decisions (247). Ruth Suckow left Boston to pursue graduate training in writing at the University of Denver, but Marjorie
goes home, for what she plans as a short visit, where she finds that her parents have arranged a teaching job for her and fixed up her room: "If only they
hadn't done over the room! It meant that they expected her to stay" (262).
When she seeks a teaching job away from home, she feels the full force of
family needs and guilt:

> All the arguments came down to one thing. This school was so far away
> from home. She had been away from them for two years. They would be
> alone next year if she left them. How could they let her go again? . . .
> Mamma's thin shoulders, her little face, were drooping and pitiful as she
> went silently about the house, cooking the things that Marjorie liked and
> laying her clothes, all mended, upon the bed. (269)

Her final means of leaving home and establishing her own life is through marriage to a local man, not through writing or teaching in some distant city.

Certainly the claims and wiles of parents were not the only obstacle that
occupied these writers' attention. They knew that young women had to also
consider love and marriage: could they combine a career with family life or
would they have to completely turn away from the choice of a husband and
children to continue to write? In *A White Bird Flying* (1931), Bess Streeter
Aldrich considers various living situations in which women might continue
their writing. The story concerns Laura Deal who goes from her hometown in
Cedartown to the University of Nebraska in Lincoln, where she takes Narration, English Composition, Magazine Article, and Novel Study and publishes a

short story and a poem in *The Prairie Schooner*, the campus literary magazine: she "always had poetry at her tongue's end" (101). Her grandmother had told her, "Laura, you'll have a fine education and you'll do some of the things I never did" (110). Having married instead of pursuing a musical career, she hopes for her granddaughter to do "some genuinely creative thing" (110). And Laura pays careful attention to the contrast between them:

> She could hardly break away from any thought but doing the thing she did. But here I am . . . different . . . in a modern setting . . . a University education . . . free . . . a sort of "heir of the ages," all that stuff you know,— and I can choose deliberately. But I've got to be free, as free as the wind blows, with no entanglements of any kind. (114)

After graduation, Laura plans to go alone to a big city and become a writer, but then she is given two other choices: her elderly uncle and aunt offer to support her if she vows not to marry and to attend to their needs; her boyfriend Allen offers her married life on a struggling farm. Even though Allen argues that she could marry him and continue to write and she does try to pursue some free-lancing after their marriage, she decides that her choice of an isolated life on the plains is not compatible with a writing career.

The choices Aldrich presents to her character are more limited than those she made, but she well understood the difficulties of combining marriage and writing. Aldrich went to Iowa State Teachers College, taught school, and then married and moved with her husband Charles Aldrich to Elmwood, Nebraska. She wrote fourteen novels, including *The Rim of the Prairie* and *A Lantern in Her Hand*, before her husband died, after which she devoted herself entirely to her writing and her children. Her novel *Miss Bishop*, about a schoolteacher, was made into a movie, *Cheers for Miss Bishop*, in 1933. Although Aldrich wrote throughout her life, she did so by balancing the claims of this career with marriage and child raising, a difficult choice that her Laura rejects.

Other writers presented characters not controlled by family ties but still buffeted by cultural expectations and the difficulties of establishing a new way of life. For the novella *A Part of the Institution*, which appeared in *Smart Set* in 1923, Ruth Suckow created Hester Harris who had grown up in Adamsville, the location of Adams College, a stand-in for Suckow's Grinnell College. Her family owns a boarding house where many young women from the college, including members of its literary Elizabeth Barrett Browning Society (E.B.B.), live. From this site, the young Hester avidly observes the college careers of her older sister and brother as well as the many boarders:

> She knew Alma's and Russell's old Annuals—the "Pioneer"—by heart. The
> names of all the prominent students who had ever gone to Adams. She was
> sick if some popular Freshman girl turned down E.B.B. for Ionian [a social
> club]. She went to every one of the Commencement events, and tried not
> to weep when one of her favorites crossed the platform of the Congrega-
> tional church to receive her diploma with a dipping bow. (60–61)

When Hester happily becomes an Adams student, she excels in her writing
classes, joins E.B.B., and works on the annual literary magazine, the *Pioneer*, a
central part of campus life, as she conveys in this scene of publication day:

> They got an old covered wagon, and the boys scoured the county for
> oxen, renting them finally from an old farmer near Sandy Creek; and
> they made a gratifying commotion driving upon the campus, the girls
> dressed in calico and old sunbonnets, the boys in broad-brimmed hats.
> They handed out the *Pioneers* from the back of the wagon. Big Bill wore
> a false beard and overalls, with an enormous plug of tobacco sticking out
> of his pocket, and he led the oxen. "The cleverest *Pioneer* stunt ever
> pulled off." (91)

After college ends, her parents die and she achieves financial independence
through the boarding house. But, even though Hester dreams of a writing job
in a big city and she lacks the family responsibilities that constrained many
women, she finds herself remaining in Adamsville and working at the college,
as everyone else had always assumed she would, easing into a routine that leaves
her unsatisfied. Written during a year in which Suckow was living in her
father's parsonage in Earlville, Iowa, but beginning to work with John Frederick at the University of Iowa, the novel recognizes the creative drive many
women felt—but also the conventions that made the choice difficult even for
those without parents, a husband, or children.

THE DAY-TO-DAY STRUGGLES OF WRITING

As these examples indicate, women created a large body of work about the
complexities of the initial post-college choice, describing the glory of the goal
as well as its agonies and posing no easy solutions. Since they frequently created characters who did not make the choice they themselves were making,
they were perhaps revealing their own ambivalences and regrets; the "odyssey
of a nice girl" might in fact be the better choice, and no one could easily walk
away from its attractions. In none of these texts does the writer imagine that a
traditional life could easily accommodate new goals. These complications of the

initial choice of life, however, are not the only subject of the many texts about writing. Women also constructed characters who had already made the commitment, as they themselves had, and were dealing with the continuing consequences of that choice.

Family was again a common topic, but with the emphasis now on the ongoing response to the decision. One writer who carefully considered family reaction was Marianne Moore. After entering Bryn Mawr in 1905, she used the literary magazine *Tipyn O'Bob* to analyze the requirements of her writing goals. Here she recognized that, after the writer began a career, rebellion against family would continue to war with desire for approval. In her story "Pym," although her main character wants to be respected as a serious author, he admits to himself that one of his motivations for beginning a career was "to prove to him [his uncle] that he was wrong and old-fashioned" in his disapproval of this choice (13). When Uncle Stanford keeps insisting that Pym study law and abandon his "literary trifling," Pym tries to explain the irresistable attractions of his craft:

> There are times when I should give anything on earth to have writing a matter of indifference to me. Then I add with a glance modestly askance, that it is undeniably convenient, in times of expressionary need, to be able to say things to the point. And, irrelevantly, that I like the thing for the element of personal adventure in it. (14)

When his uncle continues to argue that Pym cannot succeed and that his purposes are not sufficiently serious, Pym throws his work in the fire and decides to enter the family business for a time, with his future path not clear because he does not know if he has the determination to continue to defy his uncle and live without his approbation, a difficulty that Moore knew she might also face when she acquainted her mother and brother with her plans.

In another story for *Tipyn O'Bob*, "The Discouraged Poet," Moore again considered the possibility of defying a guardian—although here she also recognized the limitations of the guardian's world view and judgments. In this story, the poet states his artistic anxieties after a painful visit to a mentor who criticized his work: "The famous bard is quite right. I do not know enough ever to become famous. I shall not try to write" (8). He tells his guardian, "I have come to say that I am no longer a poet," greatly pleasing this man who has suggested more traditional careers. "'My lad,' said the guardian, with a frown, 'you are young. You do not know enough to write.'" But this response finally angers the boy: "'I don't know?' he queried, hesitatingly. 'The bard—may know, but you—my careful guardian, you don't know about verse—or me. To the winds with distemper. I'll roam the woods and then, if I wish, I'll write.'" This poet is spurred to continue because he knows that the guardian is unable to judge creativity, but he is still hampered by a lack of confidence that causes him to react strongly to each judgment rendered by authorities.

Only Moore's woman artist, in her "Wisdom and Virtue" for *Tipyn O'Bob*, seems confident and serene, prepared to cope with the vicissitudes of her choice. She is visited by her Uncle Duckworth, a publisher, who represents to her conservatism and stern judgment: "[P]ious women, clever men, and obedient children, were the order of things in his world" (27). He finds her rooms too cold and her work "rather a puddle." But when he leaves, she smiles and thinks to herself: "Gloomy, Janus-headed man. Wisdom palls upon him" (30). She does not seem hurt by his rebuffs, and she certainly does not abandon her career because of them; she can calmly assess his own need for dominance and the limitations of his judgment. In this story, Moore perhaps creates a model for herself. This writer has confidence in her abilities; she has achieved financial independence; she acts respectfully toward her family but does not depend on their approbation. This character's equilibrium—and quiet sense of joy—come from achieving the emotional and financial independence needed for her work.

Certainly the complex ties of family figure heavily in these stories, but women also realistically examined the daily routine that the choice would require. Moore recognized that the isolation of this work could take writers away from communal purposes and pleasures. In another *Tipyn O'Bob* story, "A Pilgrim," she explores the selfishness—and even futility—of the future she proposed. At first, a young boy seeks what is to him a perfect world of the intellect: "'It is a place,' he said, 'where people do as they please. The flowers gleam, and there are always poets about, and actors and artists and architects. Time is to be had for the asking, and the finding of an occupation is not short of a pleasure'" (10). A man he meets on his way offers him steady work pruning willows and digging a well: "'The work is not hard,' said the old man. 'Compared with making verses and roaming the high-roads it is play.'" The boy replies that, "It is not that I cannot do it, but that I hate it" and leaves the man's house (10). But after wandering aimlessly, he returns from the road to join this man and his companions, adopting what he now considers "the ideal life": participation in a community of useful workers instead of the undirected and fanciful pathway of art (12).

At the University of Nebraska, Willa Cather also used her college writing assignments to probe the difficulties of the path that lay ahead. In her class essay "Shakespeare and *Hamlet*," which her teacher Percival Hunt reprinted in two parts in the *Nebraska State Journal,* on November 1 and 8, 1891, she separates the true artist from the pretender and focuses on "the solitude and the loneliness" that authentic work requires:

> Modern authors admire the great creations of thought, oh yes, and they would like well enough to produce them, but they are unwilling, either for the sake of the idea itself or for the sake of the truth which inspired it, to undergo the pain, the suffering, the separation from other men, the solitude and the loneliness which thought learning involves. (434)

As the essay proceeds, Cather continues to probe the great loneliness of the committed, professional writer, the lifetime separation from love and sympathy:

> It is not an easy thing, this separation from the world. Authors are not made of marble or of ice, and human sympathy is a sweet thing. There is much to suffer, much to undergo: the awful loneliness, the longing for human fellowship and for human love. The terrible realization of the soul that no one knows it, no one sees it, no one understands it; that it is barred from the perception of other souls; that it is always alone. (435)

While Shakespeare is her announced subject here, Cather writes about the sacrifices required of all artists, and certainly of herself.

For an English literature course with Ebenezer Hunt, Cather wrote "Concerning Thomas Carlyle," a paper that she later thought had turned her into a writer (Woodress 71). It was published simultaneously by the college magazine *Hesperian* and by the *Nebraska State Journal.* Here she again carefully considers the isolation, sacrifice, and singleness of purpose involved in this most demanding of life choices. Looked at honestly, she concludes, writing required a stronger commitment than religion:

> Art of every kind is an exacting master, more so even than Jehovah. He says only, "Thou shalt have no other gods before me." Art, science, and letters cry, "Thou shalt have no other gods at all." They accept only human sacrifices. (423)

Cather felt that few women were able to trod this path; with their daily family burdens, they found it especially difficult to "love an abstract ideal" (423). In later years, she looked at these essays as having helped her decide to become a writer— she had planned to study medicine—and to face the real impact of her choice.

Willa Cather continued after college to write about the singleminded commitment required by art, most notably in *The Song of the Lark* (1915), a

novel based on the life of opera singer Olive Fremstad, whom Cather had interviewed for *McClure's Magazine* at a time when she was leaving the magazine
and making the commitment to full-time fiction writing. In this story, Cather
tells of her Thea's path from Moonstone, Colorado, to the Metropolitan Opera
and her repeated need to isolate herself from family claims, from social ties, and
from would-be artists who don't have the talent and dedication needed to succeed. When she travels to Arizona, a site of great inspiration for Cather herself,
Thea recognizes in decorated potsherds the eternal desire of women to create
art—to reach toward a larger purpose even as they toiled in traditional homes
and communities.

Many writers also recognized that the writing life involved other difficulties, beyond the family's needs and values. In her college essays, Willa Cather
acknowledged that economic necessities could hinder the artist's attempt to fulfill her potential. Edgar Allan Poe's ability to maintain his high level of artistic
accomplishment throughout his financial difficulties seems astounding to her:

> How in his wandering, laborious life, bound to the hack work of the press
> and crushed by the ever-growing burden of want and debt, did he ever
> come upon all this deep and mystical lore, the knowledge of all history, of
> all languages, of all art, this penetration into the hidden things of the East?
> ("Edgar Allan Poe" 158–59)

She argues that, in contrast, Thomas Carlyle's need to earn money for his sick
brother had done irreparable harm to his art, had cut away his very being:

> [F]or his brother's sake he wrote for money. It seemed to him like selling
> his own soul. He wrote article after article for reviews, and cut up his
> great thoughts to fit the pages of a magazine. No wonder he hated it; it
> was like hacking his own flesh, bit by bit, to feed those he loved. (*The
> Kingdom of Art* 424)

Cather examines not only the financial need, but also the possible burdens of editors and readers. True artists would have to somehow keep not just
family but also the preferences of readers at a distance, refusing to become business managers or slaves to current taste, as she notes about Carlyle:

> He never strove to please a pampered public. His genius was not the tool
> of his ambition, but his religion, his god. Nothing has so degraded mod-
> ern literature as the desperate efforts of modern writers to captivate the
> public, their watching the variation of public taste, as a speculator watches
> the markets. (*The Kingdom of Art* 424)

Marianne Moore also feared this duel between the editor's priorities and the author's vision. In "Pym," she expresses these conflicts in gendered terms. Cob, Pym's editor, accuses him of being overly sensitive—"effeminate"—when he insists on his own artistic vision. But to fight back successfully requires determined aggression, the male urge to "lay down his life" in battle for a noble cause:

> I can no more write according to Cob's requirements and at the same time approve what I write, myself, than I can make it rain. I've got to buck up. Now that I've begun I have to stick it out. Revolting beast that Cob. I can hardly stand him. Says I am supersensitive, effeminate and perverse, charged too heavily with "scruples," always full of excuses and explanations. I may have bad judgment and fall short of the mark a little too often, but conscience—! If I can scrape a pretext, in the shape of one provocation more, I shall throw up the sponge. A derelict life has in some ways attractions, it can't be denied. It is in all the copy-books that a man may lay down his life for his individualism. I begin to be convinced. (*The Complete Prose* 13)

Moore realized that this seemingly unnatural combination of sensitivity and fierce determination, of female and male, was crucial to the artist.

Women who wrote about a career in journalism also recorded the battles with editors that could rob the writer of artistic integrity. In Mildred Gilman's *Sob Sister* (1931), Jane Ray goes to New York to take the only job available to her: interviewing murderers and both victims' families to create piteous front-page exposés. When she attempts a more in-depth analysis of crime, her editor, Baker, says, "What's the matter with you, Jane? Slipping? There's no sex in this, no kick" (57). When "a wow of a story" appears—a former chorus girl adopts two children, all three disappear, and then human bones are found in the woods—Baker directs Jane: "Make every mother that reads the *Courier* feel as if those were the bones of her own baby lying out there, bleaching in the sun, being tossed about by the dogs. Lay it on thick and dig up a sex angle" (65). Jane regularly competes for front page headlines by exaggerating and even concocting details, techniques that other reporters apply to her case when she is kidnapped by two gangsters. After she becomes a story and takes her turn in the press' spotlight, she quits reporting. In this novel, Gilman warns her female readers about becoming caught up in the crass pursuit of scandal, abandoning the career's best principles and practices so that more papers will sell. This plot stemmed from her own two excursions into becoming a story, when her phone discussion of a case led police to accuse her of a murder and when she was sent out as part of a decoy couple to lure a serial killer, who later sent letters to newspapers about following "the tall, blonde

Miss Gilman." Like Jane, Gilman quit her newspaper job when she realized that the readers' enthusiasm for sex and violence had changed her from journalist into tabloid character.

When these writers were still in college, they wrote about the isolation that would greet them as soon as the four years ended. Then, after they graduated, they continued to write about the vicissitudes and joys of a professional career. These texts realistically tally the costs, of upsetting parents, leaving hometowns, forgoing love, facing self-doubt, earning a living, and struggling with the ethical conflicts inherent in being a hired pen. Unlike their male counterparts, these women rarely focus on the writer as a doomed and misunderstood romantic rebel. Instead they carefully consider the qualifications and liabilities of daily involvement in this work—and especially the social ties that a woman has to sever to go on. They also look realistically at the difficulty, even the impossibility, of proceeding alone, fully acknowledging the bleakness of a writing life without supportive groups. As these young writers created this literature of warning, envisioning the worst scenarios that past generations of women had endured and that could be their own futures, they began carefully working at crafting another sort of writer's life for themselves, involving an unprecedented extension of college forms of collaboration. Even as they wrote these texts, they were establishing in their own lives the very networks and connections that could have altered the fates of their heroines. It would ultimately be the group that would enable the woman writer to embrace the isolation and personal rebellion required for writing without being destroyed by the demands of her art.

CHAPTER FIVE

CONTINUING THE GROUPS

When I read Yeats's statement that by the time he was
in his mid-twenties he knew all the poets of his generation, I felt near to despair.

—Mary Barnard

In fiction written in college and after, women explored a writing career: its isolation; its incompatibility with the roles of daughter, wife, and mother; its heavy
requirements of talent, training, and discipline. These writers realized that one
of the worst exigencies would be to proceed alone, without colleagues like
those that had surrounded them in college dorms and classrooms, without the
critique and encouragement of a group. Seemingly in response to their own
bleak assessments, and unlike any generation before them, these writers began
to forge writing groups almost as soon as they began their careers, extending
the college model of collaboration. Certainly not every woman writer made
the way easier for her colleagues. Fighting to gain a place within patriarchal
structures, many women felt pressured to denounce their peers for seeking solidarity or for acting or writing like women. But, despite contrary pressures,
group support, both for an individual work in progress and for a career, flourished with the first generations of college-educated women, those who wrote
so frequently about the high price of proceeding alone. The groups that they
chose to form and enter might primarily have civic or political goals, they
could be male-dominated assemblages that admitted women only under duress,
they could involve competition as well as support, and they could narrowly
define appropriate genres or content—but they continued the atmosphere of
collaboration so hard to achieve after college ended and jobs and marriages

began. This unprecedented array of clubs and connections, networks that provided opportunities for growth and for success and that ultimately involved college graduates as well as many other women, would change the road taken by women writers and ultimately the definition of American writer and American writing.

SUPPORT NEEDED FOR THE ROAD AHEAD

However well trained they may have been, women found they needed networks of peers because, as their fiction documented, they faced serious obstacles from the moment they left school. Many journalists, for example, chronicled the difficulties, even with a college education, of landing any job. Rheta Childe Dorr in *A Woman of Fifty* (1924) wrote that only "a few women, even in 1898, were in the newspaper world, although I never knew with what burglar's tools they broke in" (74). William Allen White of Kansas, reform journalist and editor of the *Emporia Gazette*, declared, "In our office, which was free of the female taint, we gossip bitterly and salaciously about the foreman and the printer girls of the other shop. Perhaps all this was the instinctive fear of a tide of feminism" (264). Florence Finch Kelly recorded the usual stereotypes and excuses she heard as she looked for a reporter's job in Boston: the publisher and managing editor wouldn't approve, the men didn't want women around, no woman could withstand the daily physical grind of the work, women didn't have the mental capacity for analysis, and the all encompassing "we don't believe in women in journalism" (158). In Martha Gellhorn's *What Mad Pursuit* (1934), Charis Day comes up against these prejudices in the personage of an editor whose boss, Poole, had hired her without consulting him:

> Being unschooled, he felt that no reporter was so foolish and useless as one college-bred. He also upheld the outworn, chivalric tradition that young women cannot be exposed to the same rigors as men. Especially young, tender women—with pale freckles on their nose (or noses), who speak careful English and wear brogues. Mac was both disgusted and at a loss. What did Henry T. Poole expect him to do with this lady? For Charis was branded at once by the entire staff as a lady—a pretty nasty position to be in. (27)

Family values reinforced the rightness of the male city room. In fact, a woman who insisted on entering there might be branded as unnatural, as a bitter spinster or lesbian. Robert Lynd and Helen Lynd's 1929 ethnographical study of Middletown, a city of between 25,000 and 50,000 citizens intended

to be representative of Midwestern life, reported that when in 1899 a prominent citizen's daughter became the first woman court reporter in the city, an
old friend of her mother's protested that such work would "un-sex" her (25).
Edna Ferber in *Dawn O'Hara* spoke of the middle-class stereotype that
branded as an unattractive spinster any woman who chose a writing career:
"Mother had never approved. Dad had chuckled and said that it was a curse
descended upon me from the terrible old Kitty O'Hara, the only old maid in
the history of the O'Haras, and famed in her day for a caustic tongue and a
venomed pen" (29–30).

For women, choosing to write fiction instead of journalism might seem
easier: literature was genteel; it did not involve the downtown office and late-
night beats; it called forth those supposedly natural skills of observing detail and
focusing on family life. But this profession was in some ways a more difficult
choice because it was rarely taken seriously and it occurred farthest from
groups and networks. At the beginning of a foray into fiction, women might be
financially dependent on parents or husbands and have to work within family
domains. Although Edna Ferber had spent long hours at the office as a reporter,
she found no sacrosanct writer's place when she began writing a novel at home:

> I settled down as best I could to write a certain number of hours daily in
> a bedroom with the family life swirling about me. Here there was no con-
> venient spidery little lean-to off the dining room into which I could creep.
> I made no elaborate arrangements for my daily stint of writing because I
> didn't regard myself as a writer. I just wrote. I worked in a bedroom
> because I didn't dream of affording a separate workroom. Sometimes I
> thought vaguely that it would be marvelous to work without interruption,
> but that this actually could be achieved was beyond my imagination. . . .
> People don't understand. One's family mysteriously doesn't understand. It
> all seems so easy—a typewriter, or a pencil and a piece of paper. Nothing
> to be fussy about. For years my mother spoke of my work as "Edna's type-
> writing." The fact that creative writing is a good deal like having a baby
> every day for so many hours daily doesn't occur to the layman, and he
> wouldn't believe it if you told him. (*A Peculiar Treasure* 166)

Her character Dawn O'Hara expresses similar sentiments when she returns to
her family after becoming ill while working as a journalist in New York: "It's
hard trying to develop into a real Writer Lady in the bosom of one's family,
especially when the family refuses to take one seriously" (40). When Dawn is
asked to finish cooking dinner while her mother goes out, she comments about
the story she is writing, "What heroine could remain calm-eyed when her cre-
ator's mind is filled with roast beef?" (42). When Vera Caspary began writing

fiction after spending three years at an advertising agency, her mother completely disregarded her creative efforts:"Although she loved to read, she was not impressed that I was writing a novel. 'You kept me awake again last night,' she said on many mornings, as though I'd worked past midnight for the sole purpose of disturbing her" (74). When Gertrude Atherton, from San Francisco, began to write at home in 1883, her husband and his family were very critical of this wasteful use of her housekeeping time:

> For the first time in my life I was supremely happy. George was furious and made a nuisance of himself, stalking in and out of the room, pounding on the door if I locked it, and reviling the fates for inflicting him with a wife so different from the wives of other lucky fellows. Of course it was impossible to conceal from him that I was writing a book, but there was no need to ask him to keep my secret, for not only was he ashamed of the fact that I was demeaning myself, but was confident that it would never see the light. What was I but a child anyhow? Who would want to read any book of mine? I must have taken leave of what little sense I ever had. (*Adventures of a Novelist* 93)

When women such as Ferber, Caspary, and Atherton wrote at home, mothers and husbands expected the day-to-day needs of family to take precedence over a long-term project. Asserting one's professionalism in a kitchen or extra bedroom could be difficult indeed.

PROBLEMS IN ESTABLISHED MALE GROUPS

These women isolated in their writing spaces, as part-time freelancers at the newspaper or as novelists tending to the roast beef at home, found at first few established groups beckoning them to join. In the 1920s and 1930s, newspaper associations across the country, such as the all-male Gridiron Club in Washington, provided social and professional enclaves for men. The common term "newspaperman" revealed the accepted definition of who was welcome there.

For the creative writer of the early twentieth century, the existing groups and literary movements also seemed to say, "Women need not apply." Modernism was certainly not an easy alliance for women. Eliot and Pound used new stylistic techniques to express a longing for an older social order in which intellectual white men created literate culture. Pound, in fact, believed that male creativity was literally carried in the sperm and deposited in the female as a receptacle, to create the male poet. Eliot praised another influential group, the Southern Agrarians, for their opposition to industrialization in the South and the resultant loss of tradition and social order: "The old Southern society, with all its defects, vices and limitations, was still in its way a spiritual entity." John Crowe Ransom, in his essay "The Poet as Woman," discussed Edna St. Vincent Millay, a representative of all women poets, as "deficient of masculinity." He describes women as naive and earthly, unable to extricate themselves from their mire of feelings and make intellectual statements. Millay's poetry

> fascinates the reader but at the same time horrifies him a little too. He will probably swing between attachment and antipathy, which may be the very attitudes provoked in him by generic women in the flesh, as well as by Emily Dickinson, Elizabeth Barrett, Christina Rosetti, and doubtless, if we had enough of her, Sappho herself. (783–84)

Certainly individual artists, such as Mary Barnard and Marianne Moore, interacted profitably with these new Brahmins, but their primary goal was not to further the careers of young women.

Alain Locke's 1925 article helped create another movement for writers in which women found some encouragement along with marginalization. Locke's article discusses the advent of the "New Negro," involved in the Harlem Renaissance or New Negro Movement: "The mind of the Negro seems suddenly to have slipped from under the tyranny of social intimidation and to be shaking off the psychology of imitation and implied inferiority," with the most extreme and positive change occurring "in the life-attitudes and self-expression of the Young Negro, in his poetry, his art, his education and his new outlook" (4–5). In that same year, however, Marita Bonner published "On Being Young—A Woman—and Colored," arguing that the old stereotypes Locke had dismissed were continuing to constrict black women, creating silence, entrapment, paralysis—a double ghetto of race and sex not addressed in the new manifestos for progress. Although writers such as Claude McKay, James Weldon Johnson, and Langston Hughes attained national reputations, the Harlem Renaissance was not a male phenomenon; it also involved Jessie Fauset, Zora Neale Hurston, Effie Lee Newsome, Angelina Weld Grimké, Nella Larsen, Gwendolyn Bennett, and other women. But, like modernism and agrarianism, this movement often cast women in the role of inferior protégé or enthusiastic reader.

WOMEN SUPPORT EACH OTHER: ROLE MODELS AND GUIDES

With few established groups to draw upon, women began to offer support to each other. The older writer often served as a role model, if sometimes an intimidating one, while providing specific advice on writing and publishing. As women entered professional careers, they even began to create chains of influence and success, a pattern that previously had involved only men. After graduation from the University of Wisconsin, Zona Gale worked her way into reporting jobs by applying everywhere, accepting freelance work, and then finally securing a full-time position at the Milwaukee *Journal*. She then took a job at the New York *Evening World*, covering a regular downtown beat; her next step was to quit the *World* to write fiction: stories for *Outlook* and *Smart Set*, a series of tales about her hometown called *Friendship Village*, and then the novel *Miss Lulu Bett*, for which she won the Pulitzer Prize for a play adaptation in 1921. Her path from a small town to college to local and national success in both journalism and fiction provided a role model for other women. When Edna Ferber started out, she first worked for her home-town paper in Appleton, Wisconsin, the *Daily Crescent*, and then went to Milwaukee to work for the *Journal*, causing one of her father's friends to declare, "Wonder a girl like that wouldn't try to do something decent, like teaching school" (Ferber, *A Peculiar Treasure* 130). Although she had some success with writing fiction, she found the routines of daily journalism more stable and professional:

> Though I had sold all the short stories I had written I still was afraid that this golden gift would be snatched from me. It didn't seem possible that one could earn a living just by sitting home cozily in front of a typewriter and bringing people to life on paper. As soon as I could summon the courage I paid a visit to the Chicago Tribune office in search of a steady job. (*A Peculiar Treasure* 168)

At the paper, other journalists told her that writers could not move from journalism to a career in fiction writing; all she would find, they said, was discouragement:

> Some of the boys on the copy desks or in the local room used to talk about fiction writing, darkly. They must have had dog-eared manuscripts and rejection slips in their desk drawers and boarding-house bedrooms to account for the bitterness of their tone. Disty, on the copy desk, used to say, with terrible definiteness, "You can't earn a living writing short stories." (*A Peculiar Treasure* 145)

But then she heard of one *Journal* writer who had tread the path to fiction successfully: Zona Gale. Ferber, however, viewed her as a faraway presence, too successful to emulate. As Ferber remained at her job, in fact, she "grew to hate the sound" of this name; the two words even sounded "made-up and affected." But "then, one day," as she recorded in her autobiography, "there was a great to-do down the hall":

> One heard the voice of Campbell, usually harsh and grating, now dulcet as the dove. He appeared, hovering calf-eyed over a fragile and lovely creature whose skirts rustled silkenly as she moved.
>
> She had great dark tragic eyes in a little pointed face; the gentlest of voices; a hand so tiny that when one took it in one's grasp it felt like the crushing of a bird's wing. I was introduced and mumbled something inadequate. This was the first real writer I had ever met. I wasn't envious. I was impressed. . . .
>
> At the desk behind mine sat Jean Airlie, who conducted the People to the Journal column. She had known Zona Gale in her reporter days. They talked together now, the successful fiction writer and the weary-looking newspaper woman. Blandly I listened.
>
> "Tell me the name of a good writer's agent," Jean Airlie pleaded. (So she was trying to write, was she!)
>
> Zona Gale mentioned a name. It sounded highly floral and faintly improbable. "Send your stories to her," Miss Gale said. "She placed my very first things, years ago."
>
> Tidily I tucked the name away in my memory and closed the door on it. (*A Peculiar Treasure* 145–46)

After meeting Gale and considering her successes, Ferber began work on a novel, *Dawn O'Hara*, about a young woman's path through the newspaper world. When she finished, she sent the manuscript to the New York agent that Gale had recommended.

For would-be journalist Lorena Hickok, Edna Ferber served as the admired role model. When Hickok was in high school in Battle Creek, Michigan, Ferber's *Dawn O'Hara* introduced her to the aggressive woman journalist and to Ferber, still in her twenties, who was from nearby Kalamazoo. Hickok then went to Appleton, Wisconsin, to attend Lawrence College and work at the *Daily Crescent*, partially because Ferber had gotten her start in this town. When she left school, she worked as a cub reporter for the Battle Creek *Evening News* and then landed a reporting job in Milwaukee in 1915, determined to again follow her fictional and real role models, O'Hara and Ferber, as she recalled later in letters to her friend and fellow journalist Eleanor Roosevelt (Faber 341–42). Following a line of professional commitment from Zona Gale and Edna Ferber, Lorena Hickok worked all her career within influential groups of women. She was assigned to cover Eleanor Roosevelt during the 1932 presidential campaign, became her friend, and helped her arrange the more than

four hundred women's press conferences that provided employment and support for women journalists during the Depression and World War II.

   While Gale served as an inspiration for many younger writers, throughout her career she was also influenced by colleagues and mentors. One powerful influence was Edith Wharton, with whom she frequently exchanged letters about works in progress and completed texts. In September 1922, two
years after the publication of *Miss Lulu Bett*, Wharton wrote that this novel
had represented a crucial "turning point" in Gale's work, away from the
overly sentimental stories she had written earlier. But Wharton questioned
Gale's use of a simple and even barren prose to portray truths of domestic life:
"[Y]ou have needlessly limited your field of expression, and produced an
expression of monotony in your style as well as in the lives of the people you
depict." She warned against a style lacking "inflections, modulations, twists,
turns, surprises, heights and depths." In her reply, Gale characterized herself
as under the spell of this letter, and in another letter written two weeks later
she claimed that the criticism had come "at precisely the moment I needed
it, was restless because of the need of it. . . . Since my new book left my hand
I have been haunted by just this verbal insufficiency, unwise compression,
inflexibility, monotony." While Gale worked on *Faint Perfume* in 1923, they
corresponded about the use of a wise and sensitive woman character who
seemed very different, perhaps too different, from the rest of her family. In
one of these letters, Wharton described her new project, which would
become *Preface to a Life*, as "a certain brooding hope which leaves me quite
breathless" (Simonson 82–83).

   Writers such as Edith Wharton, Zona Gale, Edna Ferber, and Lorena
Hickok served as role models and inspirations, starting as mentors but growing into colleagues. Following the workshop pattern of college classes, many
other women entered circles of writers after college, relying on each other
for ongoing critique and encouragement. During college, Marianne Moore,
who so dramatically portrayed the solitary life of the writer in her college
stories, tried unsuccessfully to have her poetry accepted at *Literary Digest* and
The Atlantic Monthly and to secure employment at the *Ladies' Home Journal*.
Throughout these early failures, her Bryn Mawr friends, such as Peggy James
and Margaret Ayer Barnes, a *Tipyn 'O Bob* editor, kept her working toward
her writing goals. Her friend Margaret Morison read her stories and made
critical responses in the margins, trying out the literary vocabulary of their
classes and comparing Moore's works to the canon they had studied, with
comments like "typical villain" and "like Kipling but good" (Molesworth 48).
Moore continued throughout her career to depend on critical judgments and

encouragement from women friends, such as Laura Benét, Louise Crane, Alyse Gregory, Louise Bogan, and Hildegarde Watson. H.D. and Bryher frequently corresponded with Moore to critique her work, and they sponsored the publication of a book of her poetry. In 1937, Bryher read a chapter of Moore's novel-in-progress and praised it highly; in the early 1940s, Moore returned the favor by making several pages of suggestions about Bryher's novel *Beowulf* (Molesworth 325).

Elizabeth Bishop met Moore in 1934 and established a long relationship, which began with Moore serving as mentor and grew to a reliance on each other as fellow writers. That year Moore recommended Bishop to Ted Wilson of *Westminster* magazine and helped her publish the anthology *Trial Balances* by contacting Edward Atell at Houghton Mifflin and even typing her manuscript. This assistance and support helped Bishop decide to devote herself to poetry and abandon her plan for a medical career. As Bishop indicated in a letter to Moore in October 1936, she was able to value the advice without letting it overwhelm her own intentions:

> Thank you so much for all your, and your mother's, trouble with my story. It is very sad to be capable of such mistakes—even in grammar and spelling! I sent off a copy to *Life and Letters*. . . .
>
> You helped me so much with "The Baptism." I'm afraid that I was quite ungracious in that I accepted most of your suggestions but refused some—that seems almost worse than refusing all assistance. I have almost finished now a second story, which I feel is much, much better—although I suppose that is just a "phase." I am hoping that you will think it worth sending to *The Criterion*. (*One Art* 47)

The two poets frequently discussed issues of prosody, such as the impact of various rhyme schemes, and Moore asked Bishop to help her with many of the rhymes in *Fables*. Their friendship and frequent letters led to an interweaving of styles, especially noted by critics who reviewed Bishop's poetry collection, *North and South*. The authors themselves were well aware of this energizing form of collaboration, as Bishop noted in a letter from January 1937:

> This morning I have been working on "The Sea & Its Shore"—or rather, making use of your and your mother's work—and I am suddenly afraid that at the end I have stolen something from [Moore's] "The Frigate Pelican." I say: "Large flakes of blackened paper, still sparkling red at the edges, flew into the sky. While his eyes could follow them, he had never seen such clever, quivering maneuvers." It was not until I began seeing pelicans that my true source occurred to me. I know you speak of the flight like "charred paper," and use the word "maneuvers." (*One Art* 54)

Moore, in fact, had not used "manuevers" in her poem, but Bishop might have thought so since their discussions and letters led to many forms of overlapping.

In her position as editor of *The Dial*, from 1926 to 1929, Moore extended her vision of writers working collaboratively into a model of publication. Before her arrival, the journal had a policy of either accepting or rejecting work, without commentary. As she wrote in a memoir on her editorship, she soon substituted a policy of "non-exploiting helpfulness to art and the artist" (Molesworth 209). In February 1926, for example, in a letter to Yvor Winters about a poem describing an old man left like rubbish in the snow, she gave careful attention to each line:

> I like "The Barnyard," in which I don't feel the beard to be irrelevant. My objection was to the cadence of the line about the beard. I am tempted to wonder if you might care to reinstate the beard—to substitute it perhaps for the wall of hell, which is confusing to me. (*The Selected Letters* 223)

Like Moore with Henry Neville Sanders, her writing professor at Bryn Mawr, Winters took only some advice: he didn't reinstate his line about the beard, but he changed "wall of hell" to "this old man / wrinkled in / the fear of Hell" (18–19). With each year, Moore grew more confident with this method: in 1928, for example, she asked Ezra Pound if she could omit a few pages of his introduction to a translation of Guido Calvacante's "Donna Mi Prega"; she asked Mabel Luhan Dodge to consider wording changes in her story "Southwest" (Molesworth 220–21). She also tried to advise younger writers, such as Martha Gellhorn, then a Bryn Mawr student, on how to craft their work. Some writers had difficulty with this collaborative mode of working. Hart Crane, for example, accepted her substantial changes and new title for his poem, "The Wine Menagerie," but then complained to his friends of her abusive treatment and asked them to protest this indignity, which he had tolerated, he said, only because of his need for money. In a later interview, Moore noted the difference between Crane and herself concerning collaboration: "[His] gratitude was ardent and later his repudiation of it commensurate—he perhaps being in both instances under a disability with which I was not familiar" (Molesworth 220).

Although Moore generally had positive experiences with fellow writers such as Elizabeth Bishop, e. e. cummings, and Ezra Pound, others found the mentor role more problematic. At its extremes, it could lead to writers becoming too dependent on the approbation, too wounded by the critique. Zona Gale found the necessary mutual respect and distance difficult to achieve with Margery Latimer, who grew up in Portage, Wisconsin, where Gale was living. In 1917, when Gale was forty-two, she phoned Latimer, who was then in high school, to congratulate her when her story appeared in a local newspaper. Gale then helped Latimer to sell other stories to the *Woman's Home Companion* and provided her with a scholarship to the University of Wisconsin, making Latimer feel like a chosen person who could become a writer. Latimer wrote to Gale from the university of her intense feeling of gratitude and respect: "I thought I would like to serve you, serve you, belong to you. I feel as though now for the first time I am bound to beauty" (Loughridge 218). In her *We Are Incredible*, however, Latimer created a mentor who was an intimidating and controlling figure, who wanted adulation but lacked a proper concern for the younger person's ongoing struggles, and she told friends that she meant for the story to anger Gale and secure more of her attention. Latimer became very upset when Gale adopted a child and married without even telling her about these decisions, since she believed that they should both be devoted only to art and to other artists. Latimer then created another unfavorable portrait of Gale in her story "Guardian Angel." Their friend and fellow writer Meridel Le Sueur felt that although Latimer's combination of reverence and revolt filled the relationship with confusion and pain, even such a difficult connection was better than none at all: "Margery might not have written at all without her" (231).

THE REGULARLY MEETING GROUP

Besides relying on individual friends and role models after college ended, women also formed their own regularly meeting groups or clubs of writers, further extending habits acquired in college. These groups often consisted entirely of women, meeting in homes and libraries—like the college club and dorm settings where serious work occurred in a supportive and relaxed atmosphere. After college, back home in Vancouver, Mary Barnard wanted to form her own extension of Reed College's workshops and club meetings: in her autobiography, she recalled feeling that men, especially those from Eastern colleges, had a natural access to the world of letters that she lacked:

> Their biographies had not yet been written; but I had a vague sense that they seemed, usually, to have gone to Harvard and begun publishing in the *Harvard Advocate*. They left college, no doubt, with introductions to editors. When I read Yeats's statement that by the time he was in his mid-twenties he knew all the poets of his generation, I felt near to despair. (51)

By talking with librarians about possible members, Barnard formed a regular study club that discussed readings and critiqued their own writing. With the group's urging, she looked up Ezra Pound's address at the library and sent their

poems to him, beginning a correspondence that led to his urging her to experiment with ancient Greek verse forms, work that she pursued throughout her
career. His friendship later brought Barnard into a wider circle in New York,
including William Carlos Williams and Marianne Moore, and at the Yaddo
retreat for artists and writers. Her first published poem appeared in *Poetry* in
1926, she wrote in her autobiography, "after Marianne Moore had opened the
door for me" (30).

Many clubs became well established, enrolling generations of women
who wanted to collaborate on authoring, critiquing, and marketing their work.
At the turn of the century, the Virginia Writers Club had a membership of
forty-five, and many members contributed fiction and poetry to magazines. In
the Students' Writers Club that this group sponsored, all members were
required to send poetry or fiction to a magazine at least once each year. When
Alice Caldwell Hegan Rice joined the Authors' Club of Louisville, this group
had assigned itself an exercise to improve their skills: they would all write short
stories on the same subject and compare the results. As Rice recalled in her
autobiography, "The subject, absurdly enough, was 'A Young Girl Alone in a
Barber Shop at Midnight.' In a day when young girls did not visit barber shops,
either by day or by night, this was considered almost risqué!" (*The Inky Way* 51).
Their six stories on the improbable visit appeared in *Black Cat*, a popular magazine. Then, "demoralized by this dazzling success," they began a joint novel, *A
Comedy of Circumstance*, for which each member wrote a chapter from the point
of view of one of the characters. Although Rice commented that "it is doubtful if a poorer book ever got itself on paper," it was published in New York and
London in 1911 (*The Inky Way* 52). The "writer," whom they named Emma
Gavf by using the first initial of each of their names, answered requests for auto-
graphs and questions about the story. In this group, Alice Rice received encouragement to write her first novel, *Mrs. Wiggs of the Cabbage Patch* (1901), which
drew on her experience working in a Louisville settlement house. "In this fer-
tile field [of the writing club] my modest talent flourished," wrote Rice. "The
criticism and enthusiasm of my co-workers were alike inspiring, and when my
publishers asked: 'Are there any more stories in your Cabbage Patch?' I joyfully
answered 'Yes!' Life seemed all too short to chronicle the stories that swarmed
in my brain" (*The Inky Way* 53). The group encouraged the efforts of other
members, resulting in the publication of more than seventy volumes, among
them Annie Fellows Johnston's *The Little Colonel* (1895), the first book in what
became a popular series about this character; George Madden Martin's *Emmy
Lou: Her Book and Heart* (1902); Abby Meguire Roach's *Some Successful Marriages*
(1906); and Frances Little's *The Lady of the Decoration* (1906) and *Little Sister*

Snow (1909). The group also included Ellen Churchill Semple, a Vassar graduate whose sister began the club in 1890. With the members' encouragement,
Semple began publishing studies of American history and geography, which led
to a lectureship at Oxford.

African American writers, encountering great difficulties after college
as they continued to write and sought publication, met regularly in each others' homes to discuss texts and opportunities. At her house in Harlem, Regina
M. Anderson Andrews, who had attended Wilberforce University and the
University of Chicago, established a meeting place for members of a new
Writers' Guild and for amateur dramatic groups. On March 21, 1924, she
organized a Civic Club dinner to honor Jessie Fauset and other young black
writers such as Gwendolyn Bennett and Clarissa Scott Delany. In the 1920s,
when she served as literary editor of the NAACP's magazine *Crisis*, Fauset
published many works by younger writers and invited them to literary club
meetings in her home. Bennett's column in the magazine *Opportunity*, named
"The Ebony Flute" after a line in a William Rose Benet poem, "I want to
sing Harlem on an ebony flute," acquainted readers with club meeting dates
and cultural events.

Although Harlem writers saw their own city as the true site of a New
Negro Movement, Bennett recognized in one of her columns the arrogance
of that judgment: "[I]t is ever so refreshing to be brought sharply up against
the fact that here and there in other less motley cities are little knots of people writing, reading . . . perhaps hoping and certainly thinking" (Roses and
Randolph 13). While Clarissa M. Scott Delany was a student at Wellesley College, she began to attend Literary Guild meetings in Boston where young
writers met weekly to discuss their own works and hear speeches by published
authors such as Claude McKay. In Boston also, beginning in July 1925, the Saturday Evening Quill Club met regularly, with a membership of generally
about twenty-five, of whom half were women. In 1928, the group began planning a serial, the *Saturday Evening Quill*, which they published annually. Florence M. Harmon served as assistant editor of the magazine while also working at the *Boston Post* with the club's president Eugene Gordon. Poet Helene
Johnson met frequently with the *Quill* group before moving to New York
with her cousin Dorothy West and joining A'Lelia Walker's Dark Tower,
another literary club. Poet Grace Vera Postles began attending in 1925 when
she was working toward a bachelor of literary interpretation at the Emerson
College of Oratory.

In Philadelphia, writers such as Bessie Calhoun Bird, Mae Crowdery,
Nellie Bright, and Evelyn Crawford Reynolds took part in the New Negro

Movement by meeting together in groups such as the Piranean Club and the Beaux Art Club and publishing a literary anthology, *Black Opals*, in 1927 and 1928, which was edited by Nellie Bright and Arthur Huff Fauset. (Bright's poem "Longings," published in the first issue, gave the magazine its title: "I want to look deep in a pool at night, and see the/ stars / flash flame like fires in black opals" (Roses and Randolph 24)). Ottie Beatrice Graham, playwright and short story writer, came to this club environment after studying writing at Howard University and Columbia University. She had begun considering herself to be a writer after winning prizes at Howard and an Alpha Kappa Alpha sorority prize for her short story "To a Wild Rose." Group member Isabel Yeiser, a graduate of the University of Pennsylvania, published a travel essay in the Christmas 1927 *Black Opals;* she went on to publish poetry in the major African American journals, *Crisis* and *Opportunity*, and to produce two volumes of poetry. The group also encouraged writers in local high schools. In 1927, when she was a high school senior, Mae Virginia Cowdery published three of her poems in *Black Opals'* spring issue, the year she entered Pratt Institute in New York. When she returned to Philadelphia, she rejoined the Beaux Art Club to continue her writing and to encourage younger writers.

In Washington, D.C., poet Georgia Douglas Johnson, who had studied at Atlanta University and Howard University, opened her home to the Round Table literary group in the 1920s and 1930s, with members including Langston Hughes, Alain Locke, W. E. B. DuBois, and Countee Cullen but with primarily women as members: Marita Bonner, Mary Burrill, Clarissa Scott Delany, Alice Dunbar-Nelson, Jessie Fauset, Zora Neale Hurston, and Mary Effie Lee Newsome. Howard graduate May Miller, a playwright who fostered African American theatre through her involvement in several little theatres and her publications such as *Plays and Pageants from the Life of the Negro* (1930) and *Negro History in Thirteen Plays* (1935), came down from Baltimore regularly to attend the Saturday night meetings (Roses and Randolph 201–02, 235–37).

Another African American writers' group in the 1930s met in several Texas towns and published a literary magazine, *Heralding Dawn*, edited by J. Mason Brewer. This publication drew from the works of club members in Houston and Dallas, such as Maurine L. Jeffrey and Birdelle Wycoff, as well as works by other writers, such as Gwendolyn Bennett, who were born in Texas but by then were living elsewhere. Poet Lillian Tucker Lewis, a graduate of Prairie View College (now Prairie View Agricultural and Mechanical University), published in the journal while also meeting with the Priscilla Art Club, the Ladies Reading Circle, and the City Federation in Dallas.

CONTACTS THROUGH WOMEN'S CLUBS

Besides forming these authors' groups, women also involved themselves in professional writing through women's clubs. These groups began meeting across the United States between 1870 and 1900, drawing most of their membership from older women who through their club memberships conducted scholarly research on literature, became politically active, and extended their skills as speakers and organizers. By 1900, more than two million women participated in clubs affiliated with the General Federation of Women's Clubs, the National League of Women Workers, the National Council of Jewish Women, and the National Association of Colored Women (Gere, *Intimate Practices* 5, 8). Agnes Surbridge's novel *The Confessions of a Club Woman* (1904) testified to the importance that club activities, and especially the writing and speaking that they entailed, could have in a woman's life. As Surbridge tells us in the book's first paragraph, her heroine Johnnie chose marriage primarily because there were no other acceptable choices.

> I was raised in a town where marriage was esteemed the only career worth considering for women; where not to have achieved matrimony by the time one was twenty-five was evidence of some lack of charm, mental or, worse yet, physical; where to go on to middle life without prefixing a "Mrs." was to drop into the deadliest level of insignificance possible to women. So, when during the summer I reached my twenty-first birthday Joseph Henning came down from Chicago to our little town in Kansas to visit his aunt, our neighbor, and fell in love with me, I accepted the proposal the gods provided and married him without delay. (3)

Because marriage and child rearing did not completely fulfill her, Johnnie enriched her life through women's clubs. This lifelong involvement offered her a chance to write and speak about suffrage, to take on various leadership roles, to serve as a patron of local theatre, and to work with her mother and her daughters. In speeches, such as the following one given to her club, she was able to consider the limitations of the adult role she had initially assumed:

> "The club woman of the future, the ideal club woman," I began, "will have nothing to do with her house except to let herself out in the morning and into it again at night with her own latch-key"—I could feel my audience gasp and tighten and brace itself. "The idea that home is sacred because the dinner is cooked there should be exploded, and will be some day. Home is sacred only because love and congeniality and real companionship are there. The club woman's ideal home will be one where she is as free as the man who calls himself the head of it." (87)

Although women's clubs generally emphasized civic activism and intellectual development and not professional careers, they also provided a supportive environment for many writers. Women wrote papers shared with other clubs, published magazines such as *Club Woman* and *Club Worker*, and sponsored plays and pageants. The League of Women Workers' *Club Worker* regularly published poetry, such as Ela Wheeler Wilcox's "Which Are You?" and Mary Low Dickinson's "If We Had But a Day" (Gere, *Intimate Practices* 231). Clubs sponsored lending libraries that accumulated impressive collections of books by women writers, about which members wrote critical essays discussed in meetings and published in club journals. Clubs often invited writers to speak at meetings and asked them to provide poetry, short fiction, and pageants for celebration days. In May 1921, for example, the California Federation of Women's Clubs performed Gertrude Atherton's pageant, *California, The Land of Dreams*, outdoors at Yosemite, as part of their twentieth annual convention. Its six episodes focused on women's contributions to state history. Clubs also provided financial support for young writers and scholarships for students who wanted to study the arts (Blair, *The Clubwoman* 38).

THE DRAMA LEAGUE OF AMERICA

Another group opportunity for women writers, involving many of the same women who participated in women's clubs, occurred through the Drama League of America. Initiated by Alice C. D. Riley in Evanston, Illinois, in 1901, the first group read and discussed plays and then performed individual scenes for local YMCA meetings. As the idea of drama clubs spread, many groups produced bulletins to alert residents to the best local and traveling productions. Frequent conventions allowed members to discuss their bulletins and see productions. This organization had 100,000 members by 1915, by which time its emphasis had begun to shift from the bulletins to the formation of little theatres (Blair, *The Torchbearers* 39).

Although drama leagues didn't initially form to encourage women writers, they soon provided many women with an extension of their college theatre experience. League conventions created a regular showcase for college theatre groups. The Vassar Players came to a Chicago meeting in 1921, for example, to perform Edna St. Vincent Millay's one-act play *Aria da Capo* and attend a production of Percy MacKaye's religious pageant *The Pilgrim and the Book*. League theatres also sponsored productions and publication of plays by new women writers, such as Hallie Flanagan from Des Moines, who became a Vassar teacher and leader of the Federal Theatre Project sponsored by the New

Deal. Throughout the 1920s, the Pasadena Playhouse, one of the leading little theatres formed from a drama league, featured works by new women playwrights, including Zona Gale, Alice Caldwell Hegan Rice, Susan Glaspel, Alice C. D. Riley, Rachel Crothers, and Lula Vollmer (Blair, *The Torchbearers* 143–77). Additionally, Pasadena league members could take Playwrighting Class, meeting twice a month, with University of Southern California English professor Laurabelle S. Dietrich. Like women's clubs, these drama leagues and theatres provided ongoing group involvement and support, both for women who considered themselves amateurs and for those seeking professional status.

African American theatre groups also offered opportunities for women playwrights. W. E. B. DuBois helped to found Krigwa, the Crisis Guild of Writers and Artists, to support theatre about, by, and for African Americans. This group inspired Regina M. Anderson Andrews to become a playwright and helped her to rewrite her *Climbing Jacob's Ladder*. Andrews wrote for the Krigwa Theatre, the Harlem Suitcase Theatre, and the Harlem Experimental Theatre, housed in the basement of the library where she worked. In 1928, the Krigwa Players performed Mary Burrill's *Aftermath*, concerning a black veteran of World War I who returns to his home in South Carolina to find that his father has been lynched. Eulalie Spence's *Fools Errand*, about a young man pressured into marriage by hypocritical church members, was produced by the Krigwa Players at the Little Negro Theater of Harlem and then won second prize at the National Little Theatre Tournament in 1927, a success she followed with nine other plays.

ELEANOR ROOSEVELT AND THE WOMEN'S PRESS CLUB

As women writers left college, not only the creative writers sought group involvement; journalists also formed groups with other women to ease their passage into careers. In the 1930s, Eleanor Roosevelt and her colleagues provided a powerful enclave for professional women writers. During her husband's first term, Roosevelt gave commercially sponsored talks on the radio, wrote articles for women's magazines, and started "My Day," a syndicated column for United Features. Beginning in December 1935, the column appeared in sixty-two newspapers, reaching an audience of up to four million by 1936. Here she shared her opinions and analyses—on White House entertaining, household management, and child care as well as political and social issues that affected women, including safety conditions in sweatshops, the minimum wage, salaries for teachers, women's military service, relief efforts and work programs for women, immunization, old-age pension plans, and family nutrition. Like her

column, the press conferences, for women only, included commentary on politics as well as the home (Beasley, *Eleanor Roosevelt* 82–99; Chadakoff). About
seventy-five women attended the first press conference; regular attendance was
between thirty and forty. Roosevelt thought that by allowing only women at
the press conferences, she could discuss women's issues more openly as well as
provide jobs for women reporters. Her friend Ruby Black, a former University
of Wisconsin professor who ran her own Washington news bureau and maintained an employment bureau for the Theta Sigma Phi journalism sorority,
feared that her decision might lead to the barring of women at other official
press conferences, but in fact it led to more women at all meetings and to more
attention to women's issues in newspapers. Roosevelt also held joint conferences with women in the administration, such as representatives from the
Bureau of Home Economics, the Children's Bureau, and the Women's Bureau
(Black 163). The entire women's press group went out to tour settlement
houses, agricultural experimental stations, and other areas of interest. Reporters
also accompanied Roosevelt when she traveled to investigate the impact of the
Depression and New Deal: when she went to Puerto Rico in 1934 she was
accompanied by Lorena Hickok of the Associated Press, Emma Bugbee of the
New York Herald Tribune, Dorothy Ducas of International News, Bess Furman of
the Associated Press, and Ruby Black. Other reporters earning bylines and
writing lead stories because of their access to important news via Eleanor Roosevelt were Genevieve Forbes Herrick of the *Chicago Tribune*, Marjorie Driscoll
of the *Los Angeles Examiner*, Grace Robinson of the *New York Daily News*,
Eleonore Kellogg of the *New York World*, and Ruth Finney of the Scripps-
Howard chain (Ware 76–78). Through the press conferences, Emma Bugbee
became a close friend of Eleanor Roosevelt, whose activities she reported on
from 1928 to Mrs. Roosevelt's death in 1962. Lenora Hickok left her position
at the Associated Press in 1939 and moved to Washington to be nearer to Roosevelt; in the capital, Hickok worked as a writer for the WPA and then for the
women's division of the Democratic National Committee.

With Roosevelt's help, the Women's National Press Club greatly
expanded its functions as a supportive group for women journalists. It had
begun in 1919 to combat what its first president, Cora Rigby, chief of the
Washington Bureau of the *Christian Science Monitor*, called "the conspiracy of
men to keep women off the newspapers—or at least to reduce their number,
wages, and importance to a minimum." The suffrage campaign had helped
launch the club as women found new opportunities by reporting on suffrage
rallies and legislative negotiations. Women in public relations also joined to gain
clients and visibility. At weekly lunch meetings, members discussed their own

activities and heard talks by people in the news, thus discovering stories to report as well as making personal contact with newsmakers. Because of the group's concentration on hard news, many feature and society writers withdrew in 1932 to form their own Newspaper Women's Club, which allowed women featured in society columns to become members along with reporters and press agents (Beasley, *Eleanor Roosevelt* 43–54).

Members of the Women's National Press Club debated allowing Eleanor Roosevelt's entrance into their group because although her "My Day" ran in hundreds of newspapers, she did not earn her living as a journalist. She was proposed for nomination by Doris Fleeson, a political columnist of the *New York Daily News*, and seconded by Ruby Black, Bess Furman, and Frances Parkinson Keyes, then a magazine writer and later a best-selling novelist. The group ultimately asked Roosevelt to join and then found her support unflagging. On April 29, 1933, Roosevelt invited women officials and journalists, primarily members of the press club, to the White House on the same night that the president attended the all-male Gridiron Club dinner for the White House press corps, a tradition she continued each year, greatly increasing the group's public recognition. Beginning with twenty-eight members, this group had grown to one hundred by 1937. Among its presidents in the 1930s were many friends of Eleanor Roosevelt and participants in her news conferences, including Ruby Black, Genevieve Forbes Herrick, and Doris Fleeson.

Like many of her colleagues, Emma Bugbee realized that these press conferences were creating an unprecedented opportunity for women, one she wanted young journalists to know about and other public figures to extend. In her second "Peggy" novel, *Peggy Covers Washington* (1937), she focused on publicizing the conferences as a model for professional development. Her heroine, now a college graduate, works at *The New York Star* where she finds herself ostracized by the young men in the office who consider her just a "stunt girl" suited only for sensational feature writing. Then she goes to Washington to report on an international conference, called Women of Tomorrow, taking place with Eleanor Roosevelt's guidance. The book highlights Roosevelt's support for young reporters and the camaraderie they achieve as a result. After the conference, Peggy seeks work in the capital, where she gets a reporting job made available because of the new press conferences and special events. Bugbee herself began her fifty-six-year career at the *New York Herald Tribune* writing recipes such as "an eccentric Eastern salad consists of pineapple and celery, dressed with mayonnaise and served with lettuce," covered suffragist marches, and then got the opportunity to write on the New Deal and other social issues when her association with Eleanor Roosevelt revealed her strengths as a political reporter (Belford 180).

SUMMER WORKSHOPS

As women extended college models and gained confidence and knowledge through their own personal connections, clubs, theatres, and press organizations, they also took advantage of opportunities to join institutionally sponsored groups that involved both men and women. Although women may not have been asked to join men's private clubs and associations, they could not be so easily turned away from new classes and workshops through which colleges expanded on their successes with undergraduates. Whether they were welcome or not, their large numbers and fierce dedication enabled many continuing-education workshops to thrive. As women pursued careers, such new workshops offered a chance to return to college workshop classes, this time with a group of more experienced writers.

Bread Loaf, a summer workshop directed by men, involved women as faculty and students. The large number of women students, in fact, helped to keep the conference financially solvent. Joseph Battel donated his Bread Loaf Inn to Middlebury College in Middlebury, Vermont, at his death in 1915; in 1920 the college opened the Bread Loaf School of English, a six-week graduate program in literature and composition, providing an additional two-weeks' summer income that helped pay for the facility's maintenance. Among its students in 1922 were Willa Cather and Katharine Lee Bates, both veterans of college writing courses.

Under the directorship of John Farrar, editor of *The Bookman* and founding member of Farrar and Rinehart, the college opened its summer Writers' Conference in 1926, a non-credit program focused on writing skills and careers. Advising the first thirty-five students, who paid one hundred dollars each, was a staff of six, which included Harriet Monroe and Doris Hallman, reader for the American Play Company of New York. The four visiting speakers that year included Honorée Willsie Morrow, former editor of *The Delineator* and author of historical novels. Coming in 1927 and anchoring the study of fiction until World War II was Edith Mirrielees, who had already spent a quarter of a century as a Stanford writing professor. Her textbook *Story Writing* appeared in 1939, with a preface by her Stanford student John Steinbeck. Margaret Widdemer, poet and novelist who had won a Pulitzer Prize, joined the staff in 1928. After starting out as a librarian, she wrote collections of poems such as *Tree with a Bird in It* and *Ballads and Lyrics* as well as novels such as *More than Wife* and *Charis Sees It Through*. In 1934, Fanny Butcher, who had studied with Edwin Lewis at the Lewis Institute in Chicago and was then on the staff of the *Chicago Tribune*, joined the workshop staff along with Julia Peterkin, an author who chronicled the African American experience in the South. The visiting speakers that year included Shirley Baker, Helen Grace Carlisle, Allene Corless, Eleanor Chilton, and Josephine Johnson. Dorothy Canfield Fisher, an Ohio State graduate who had collaborated with Willa Cather when Cather was attending the University of Nebraska and Fisher's father was chancellor, came in 1932 to speak about the taste of the American reading public. Her job as book reviewer and selector for the Book of the Month Club enabled her to offer assistance to workshop attendees as well as many other young writers, such as Pearl Buck, Isak Dinesen, Anna Yezierka, and Richard Wright (Bain and Duffy 12–38).

When Ted Morrison, poet and magazine editor who had just joined the Harvard English department, became director in 1932, he changed the earlier curriculum of lectures to a week of lecture and a week of workshops, called "manuscript clinics," for a better balance of theory and practice that paralleled the workshop method from the colleges. With Bernard DeVoto, Harvard English professor and then editor of the *Saturday Review of Literature*, generally at its helm, the fiction faculty met each morning to assess the students' progress and plan the day's work of group clinics and individual appointments. Although teachers certainly had different methodologies, they often followed DeVoto's teaching plan: teaching movement, relationship to readers ("Write for the reader, never for yourself"), point of view, the fitting of style to character, structural revision ("Throw away the first five chapters" which often clarify the writer's thinking but may not involve the reader), and stylistic revision ("Murder your darlings!") (Stegner 130–31). Such "hardheaded, commonsensical, practical" advice, dispensed in lectures and individualized in clinics and conferences, as Wallace Stegner commented, may have been standard or even conservative but it "cured a good many of the half-baked astheticism that so often accompanied talent, and it made better writers of some, and it probably harmed or discouraged only a few" (132).

Like college students, these workshop attendees commented frequently on the difference that this environment and instruction made in their work. Within the first group of five students in the fellowship program—which Morrison initiated to provide financial help for some attendees—was Catherine Drinker Brown, a Pennsylvanian who had published a novel and was seeking a publisher for a volume of essays on poetry. DeVoto helped her get a contract with Little, Brown. In 1933, she wrote of his kindness and concern for craftsmanship:

> Bernard DeVoto was my valued friend. . . . I am among the host of writers who came to him for advice, for criticism, and for general renewal of spirit.

> In letters and by word of mouth DeVoto and I shouted at each other. But always, in the end, I sat still and listened to what he had to say. And after each encounter, I came away rejoicing in the existence of the vivid, generous, and diabolically intelligent presence. (Bain and Duffy 28–29)

In 1933, DeVoto also befriended fellow Josephine Johnson, for whose 1934 novel of Missouri farm life, *Now in November*, he wrote the preface. She returned in 1936 as a member of the faculty. In 1938, Frances Sandmel, who had also worked with the Carolina Playmakers, wrote to a friend about the excitement and commitment of working with DeVoto as well as Ted Morrison and Gorham Munson, who had written several books on American literature, edited the literary magazine *Secession*, and served on the editorial staff of both Doubleday and Thomas Crowell:

> Mr. Morrison, Mr. DeVoto, and Mr. Munson are all brilliant and trenchant thinkers, with a "live and let very few others live" attitude, and a glorious intolerance for ineptitude and mediocrity. The atmosphere of the place was a strange mixture of incisive caustic canniness, and absolute acceptance of excellence where (if?) it can be found. (Bain and Duffy 40)

Although women remained a minority on the faculty—from 1926 to 1930, the faculty either consisted of two women and three men or one woman and four men—they were continually a majority among the students. Of the fellows from 1934 to 1940, the numbers were twenty-two women and twenty-one men; the non-scholarship students, whose tuitions provided most of the income, were generally two-thirds women.

In 1931, to serve this increasing population of writers who sought an extension of college groups, the English department of the University of Iowa began its first summer Conference on Creative Writing, which got its impetus not only from the success of Iowa's undergraduate and graduate programs in writing but also from the attendance of Norman Foerster, director of the School of Letters and a professor of English, at Bread Loaf. The summer program regularly involved guest speakers such as Zona Gale and Ruth Suckow, who had won the Pulitzer Prize for her novel *The Folks*. In 1935, Dorothy Pownall and Elizabeth M. Bray discussed magazine writing, and Josephine Donovan, who had written the novel *Black Soil* (1929) while a student at Iowa, spoke on fiction writing. In the summer of 1939, Professor Edwin Ford Piper invited eleven writers not just to give guest lectures but to teach in the summer seminar: giving talks, participating in small-group critique sessions, and holding conferences with students. Within this first group of instructors at the Iowa Workshop, as the summer conference was then renamed, were three women: Ruth Suckow; Josephine Johnson, Pulitzer prize winner for *Now in November*, and Winifred Van Etten, a novelist who had won the *Atlantic Monthly* prize for *I Am the Fox*. Besides students who came just for the summer sessions, the Workshop enrolled students seeking the M.F.A. or the Ph.D. with a creative dissertation.

Both Iowa's summer courses and degree programs involved women students from their beginning; in fact, between one-fourth and one-third of the degree-seeking students and nearly two-thirds of the noncredit summer attendees were women. Throughout the 1930s, the workshop provided a community for women writers and a link to professional publication, expanding on opportunities they had encountered in college. The first creative master's thesis, completed in 1931, was a book of poems entitled *Paisley Shawl*, by Mary Roberts. In 1940, Janet Piper wrote *The Bitter Root*, the first collection of poems accepted as a doctoral dissertation. In 1942, Margaret Walker won the Yale Series Award for *For My People*, a book of verse that began as her master's thesis at Iowa in 1940. There she also researched her family history to continue work on *Jubilee*, a project she began as a senior at Northwestern University as weekly assignments of 1,500 words turned into Professor E. B. Hungerford ("How I Wrote *Jubilee*" 51). Mildred Haun, who had studied at Vanderbilt with John Crowe Ransom and Donald Davidson, submitted as her master's thesis in 1931 a compiled collection of "Cocke County Ballads and Songs," which with help from Professor Wilbur Schramm, who directed the Iowa Workshop for two years after Edwin Ford Piper's death in 1939, she made into a novel of life in the mountains called *The Hawk's Done Gone*.

Many women took full advantage of workshops such as those at Bread Loaf and Iowa by attending more than one of them or returning to the same one, becoming regular members of writing communities and using the connections to establish and further careers. Louise McNeill, for example, grew up on a farm near Swago Crick, West Virginia, and went to the state university at sixteen, where she composed her first poem on a borrowed typewriter in the dormitory, as she later recalled:

> Though I had no boyfriend, it was a poem of love and passion: "When scarlet clouds fly by the moon, I'm always in my memories with you." I read the poem to myself and something happened to me. I had felt such joy in the writing itself and in the rhythms of the lines that I swore a vow that I would be a poet and write poems forever. (*The Milkweed Ladies* 106)

McNeill returned home in 1930 to teach in a one-room school with two privies out back, broken windows, no heat, and twenty-six students in eight grades:

"[T]hough I had studied 'educational methods' in college, I had learned nothing about teaching school" (*The Milkweed Ladies* 107). She began pursuing a literary career by sending out poetry to magazines and entering contests, and she
finished college at age twenty-five with help from a professor who encouraged
her to read widely and develop her writing:

> I had a degree in English, though I knew not a whit of grammar beyond
> the noun and the verb. But a magnetic professor there, S.L. McGraw, had
> helped me to discover the world of books and philosophical thought. I set-
> tled down, worked hard, and lived an almost inspired life that next year, in
> the company of William Thorndike, William James, and Paul Elmer More.
> (*The Milkweed Ladies* 110)

To continue that "almost inspired life," McNeill attended Bread Loaf as a
student in 1938, where she was given free tuition for having won first prize
in the *Atlantic Monthly* Poetry Contest for College Students (W. L. Cather
47). Then, at the Iowa workshop in 1939, she studied with Norman Foerster, whom she had met at Bread Loaf, as well as with Wilbur Schramm, and
began work toward the doctorate. At Iowa, she worked on a group of poems
that became *Gauley Mountain*, a verse history of mountain people in West
Virginia, which was published in 1939 with an introduction by Stephen
Vincent Benét and jacket comments by Louis Untermeyer and Archibald
MacLeish, all of whom she had met at Bread Loaf: MacLeish had taken the
manuscript to Harcourt Brace in New York. At Iowa, she also began a
poetry collection called *Time Is Our House*, which was published by Bread
Loaf in 1942.

   While the students' progress was the primary focus of summer workshops, they also provided an "almost inspired life" for teachers. Ruth Suckow
had been active in writing groups, drama club productions, and the literary
magazine while majoring in English at Grinnell College in Iowa. After studying dramatic performance at the Curry School of Expression in Boston, like
her character Marjorie in *The Odyssey of a Nice Girl*, she transferred to Denver
University, where there were no writing groups or publications. After she graduated, she worked as a teaching assistant—a student remembered her as "standing up before large classes of gawky ranch boys and girls, a slender small person, talking with great sincerity of Walt Whitman and Thoreau" (Kissane 21).
But she wanted to write, not to teach, and she wanted to reestablish the group
involvement that she had found at Grinnell. In 1918, along with a friend, she
wrote to Harriet Monroe at *Poetry*, a magazine they both admired, about their
isolation as writers:

> We both attempt to write—but we are so far away from the centers of writing and there is so little encouragement for original work in school life that we feel the need of help. Is it possible to teach school and write? Is there anything that a young and exceedingly unaccepted writer can do to earn a living and still keep on with the kind of work that she feels is her best? There are so few openings here—almost none but teaching and clerking. Is there any hope for one who is not in Chicago or New York? (Kissane 22)

That year, she answered her own questions by abandoning teaching and moving home to Earlville, Iowa, where she could keep bees to earn the money she would need to write, a positive choice but one that further isolated her. But when she began sending stories to *Midland*, she started a friendship with the editor, John Frederick, that led to her spending winters in Iowa City helping to edit the magazine and meeting with his creative writing students as well as those at Iowa State, the University of Indiana, and the University of Wisconsin. Frederick introduced her to Henry Mencken and George Allen, who published her work in *Smart Set* and *American Mercury*, and to Alfred Knopf, who published her first novel, *Country People*. In an essay for a book celebrating Knopf's first ten years of publishing, John Frederick described the Iowa literary scene and Suckow's steady influence there, working to create for students the supportive atmosphere that she had also sought for herself:

> In the old house on the side street a dozen of us were sitting in the light around a book-strewn table, while a midwestern thunderstorm roared and beat against the windows. There was a Doctor of Philosophy who had not forgotten how to laugh; there was the demonically clever, externally sanctimonious young editor of a student literary magazine, and the calmly brilliant girl who piloted that magazine through its first year; there were the students who represent the true *literati* and *intelligentsia* of a huge midwestern University—clear-eyed, keen, lovable young men and women; and there was Ruth Suckow. Her clear skin was browned from days out of doors. She was small and cool and comradely. She talked genuinely and generously, and what she said crackled and burned with the fire of a tremendously vigourous intellect, ruthless and fearless, and yet tempered by profound understanding and sympathy. ("Literary Evening" 84)

As Suckow moved within this group of working writers, Frederick placed her "first among those of us who are trying to write about the middle west" for her vivid characterization and physical details and for her ability to lift a regional narration "into the realm of universal and permanent significance" ("Literary Evening" 85).

UNIVERSITY DRAMA ORGANIZATIONS

While summer workshops helped women writers to establish new groups of colleagues and hone their skills at poetry and fiction, university drama organizations helped them to continue their involvement in the theatre. Although the Carolina Playmakers began within an undergraduate course, like those at Harvard and Bryn Mawr, it quickly became a venue, like a writers' workshop, in which older writers and actors could adapt college structures to a professional sphere. Director Frederick H. Koch began his career as an instructor at the University of North Dakota and then went to Harvard to study drama with George Pierce Baker. In 1918 he came to the University of North Carolina and created English 31-32-33—Dramatic Composition, "a practical course in the writing of original plays. Emphasis is placed on the materials of tradition and folklore, and of present-day life." In this class, seated together at a long walnut table, "each student would read his play. Then his fellow students would discuss, criticize, make suggestions for improvement—all helping each other in plot, characterization, and dialogue" (Spearman 10). In that war year, Koch's first class had thirteen students, twelve women and one man, Thomas Wolfe, who had also studied with George Pierce Baker. After the first class, Wolfe came up to Koch's desk to explain the overabundance of women:

> "Proff," he said, "I don't want you to think that this Ladies Aid Society represents Carolina. We have a lot of he-men seriously interested in writing here, but they are all disguised in army uniforms now. I tried to get into one myself but they didn't have one long enough for me." (Spearman 11)

Although Koch's initial course was modeled on Baker's, his theatre soon followed the collaborative model of summer workshops for adults. The Carolina Playmakers began in January of 1919 as a university/community organization, sponsoring productions in Chapel Hill, on Southern tours, and on Broadway. The new organization announced itself in the campus newspaper, the *Tar Heel*, calling for "members of the community who show ability in any branch of dramatic art" to write and perform plays concerning "North Carolina life and people," the "beginnings of a new native theatre," as Koch stated in his first collection of the participants' plays:

> The *Carolina Folk-Plays* suggest the beginnings of a new native theatre. They are pioneer plays of North Carolina life. The stories and characters are drawn by the writers from their own tradition, and from their observation of the lives of their own people.
>   They are wholly native—simple plays of the locality, of common experience and of common interest. (xi)

With this theatre, Koch provided new opportunities for women as well as men. The first three plays selected for production were *The Return of Buck Gavin*, by Thomas Wolfe, *When Witches Ride*, by Elizabeth Lay, dramatizing on old legend of a witch who cast spells using a toad as a familiar, and *What Will Barbara Say?* by Minnie Sparrow, a comedy about college life in Chapel Hill. The second production of folk plays, in May 1919, included *The Fighting Corporal*, by Louisa Reid.

In these plays about daily life in the mountains and folk legends, women writers explored the complications of women's lives. Even in comedies, these Playmakers focused on the hard decisions facing women in restrictive rural communities: Gertrude Wilson Coffin, for example, describes the woman's view of a mail-order match in *Magnolia's Man* and of pregnancy and early marriage in *A Shotgun Splicin'* (Sandmel 70–74). In their dramas, these writers concentrated not on romanticizing rural life, but on portraying the limited choices of mountain women. In *Black Sheep*, for example, Marjorie Usher chronicles a white girl's tragic love for a black man. In *The Scarlet Petticoat*, Kate Porter Lewis tells the story of a young widow's ultimate escape from a dictatorial mother-in-law: she marries the stone cutter to whom she is sent to spend all her hard-earned money on a monument to her dead husband. One of the most moving of these plays was *Fixin's*, by Paul Green and his sister, Erma Green. It concerns a tenant farmer's wife who tries to create a little beauty, "life's fixin's," to ease the burdens of a harsh husband and unhappy marriage. When she is repeatedly ignored and treated as a laborer on his farm, she finally packs and leaves. As Koch insisted on new rules and traditions for an American theatre of the people, women playwrights, such as Coffin, Usher, Lewis, and Green, responded by discussing themes that were new to American drama.

In the 1920s and 1930s, Playmakers worked on productions that toured North Carolina and went from there to New York, enabling women to establish professional careers. Lula Vollmer's play with a North Carolina mountain background, *Sun-up* (1923), premiered on Broadway; she went on to write radio plays and weekly serial programs such as *The Widow's Sons* in 1936–1937 and *The American Story* in 1949. Her produced plays also included *Trigger* (1927), *Sentinels* (1931), *The Shame Woman* (1933), *Moonshine and Honeysuckle* (1934), and *The Hill Between* (1939). Another Playmakers member, Dorothy Kuhns Heyward, worked with her husband DuBose Heyward to successfully adapt two of his novels, *Porgy* (1927) and *Mamba's Daughters* (1939), into Broadway successes. They then teamed with George and Ira Gershwin on *Porgy and Bess*. After her short plays toured with the Playmakers, Dorothy DeJagers succeeded on Broadway with comedies such as *Hot Waffles* (1929). Frances Gray Patton accepted a Playmaker fellowship after graduating from Duke; the group produced her *The Beaded Buckle*, a comedy of village aristocracy, in 1923 and her *Out of the Past*, a college romance set as the Civil War begins, in 1925. During her career, she produced many prize-winning short stories as well as the popular novel and screenplay *Good Morning, Miss Dove*.

THE COMMUNIST PARTY AND THE
LEAGUE OF AMERICAN WRITERS

Like Francis Gray Patton in Chapel Hill, many women found space to write at workshops and in theatres, extending their habits from college. As women began to view themselves as writers, they attempted to move into groups where they could participate in the usually male tradition of influencing cultural values and public policy through writing. In the nineteenth century, women writers created heroines who mitigated against the harshest effects of a social and economic system that they could never really change; these twentieth-century writers, however, assumed the possibility of revolt and change. In the 1930s, the larger allegiance sought by many was with socialism and the Communist Party, then very influential in questioning the establishment and suggesting new roles for the dispossessed.

Ironically, in this social movement, the very assumption of the label of Writer made anyone suspect since intellectuals, and especially well-educated women, seemed too far removed from the fray. Genevieve Taggard felt that the Communist Party left most artists on the sidelines, as effetes who could not be truly involved:

> Practical men run revolutions, and there's nothing more irritating than a person with a long, vague look in his eye to have around, when you're trying to bang an army into shape, or put over a N.E.P. If I were in charge of a revolution, I'd get rid of every single artist immediately; and trust to luck that the fecundity of the earth would produce another crop when I had got some of the hard work done. (6)

Taggard discussed her feeling of inadequacy and marginalization in the *New Masses* by equating artists with children: "Being an artist, I have the sense that a small child has when its mother is in the middle of housework. I don't intend to get in the way, and I hope that there'll be an unmolested spot for me when things have quieted down" (6). Meridel Le Sueur also wrote in her journal about feeling isolated as an writer, standing at the side while activists changed the world:

> The strike is to be at midnight. I won't be held off from it. I won't be left out. I won't look at it lyrically. I'm afraid I won't be able to be IN it.... I must be part of it. That's the devil about being a writer in America.

> Reporting is objective observing, and writing is subjective and each is
> only half—without being a part so you become a special creature of a sort,
> neither fish nor fowl nor good red herring. So special and LOOKING
> ON, I am determined to get IN, to have an experience with it, and not
> just look at it. I am determined. (Coiner 103)

Within the movement, the call was for the few influential writers to be
blue-color laborers speaking honestly about America's low wages, poor working conditions, and meaningless repetitive work. Michael Gold, editor of the
New Masses, idealized working-class males such as lumberjacks and sailors who
could create tough confrontational prose. In "America Needs a Critic," he
points to the need for a speaker who "lives with the peasants, works side by side
with the factory workers, performs mighty social tasks," and he certainly is not
thinking of this speaker as a woman:

> Send a giant who can shame our writers back to their task of civilizing
> America. Send a soldier who has studied history. Send a strong poet who
> loves the masses, and their future. Send someone who doesn't give a damn
> about money. Send one who is not a pompous liberal, but a man of the
> street. Send no mystics—they give us Americans the willies. Send no cow-
> ard. Send no pedant. Send us a man fit to stand up to skyscrapers. A man
> of art who can match the purposeful deeds of Henry Ford. Send us a joker
> in overalls. Send no saint. Send an artist. Send a scientist. Send a Bolshe-
> vik. Send a man. (9)

Similarly, Gold's colleague Alfred Kreymborg apotheosized Carl Sandburg's
struggles with his material as a "slugging or wrestling match . . . I advise any-
body who is disturbed by this non-pretty theory to attend a prize-fight. That's
the game—something more than a boxing contest—a man undertakes with
art." In this environment, women might feel that anything they could write
would be unworthy, a waste of time in a world of male physical and mental
action. Meridel Le Sueur recorded in her journal a party organizer's attempts
to enlist her in office work because she was wasting time writing stories that
would not further the political goals:

> "We've got to collect money, we've got to make contacts here, we've got to
> hurry, we've got to be on the move, we've got to get busy. Organize the writ-
> ers' union, the office workers' union. We can't be subjective about this, about
> collecting money. . . . Listen, I don't want to interfere with your writing."

Le Sueur recognized that women's personal narratives seemed inconse-
quential to this group, yet they were "not expected to attempt to analyze

the formal or ideological concerns of proletarian writing. . . . Serious criticism was left to men" (Coiner 96).

With this emphasis on physical effort and male intellectual analysis, women often felt that their place within the group could only be as supporters or enablers, not as a true participants. For *Goodbye and Tomorrow*, written in 1931, Leane Zugsmith, a supporter of the socialist cause who had studied writing at the University of Pennsylvania, created Emmy Bishop as her central character, a woman who uses her house and money to support leftist artists and writers. Relying on a method Zugsmith described as "shamelessly derivative of Virginia Woolf," she enters her character's mind for one day as Emmy takes stock of her life. Emmy recognizes that what she has truly become is a facilitator for a group of opportunists. What she had envisioned as an avant-garde artistic and political quest has dwindled into another supportive and barren role for a woman: she has allowed others to feed off of her talents and energies but has set no artistic goals for herself. In this atmosphere, seemingly liberated and creative, Emmy had lost her compulsion "to do something herself, to learn to act, to try to dance, to attend lectures, to scribble *vers libre*" (55). At the end, to establish her own life, she asks all of these men to leave her house and begins, although falteringly, to consider her own creative needs.

Even with these restricted definitions of writer and of a woman's role, women did make their way into positive groups within the socialist movement, by drawing on their experience with collaboration, from college and after. In 1935 seventy writers signed a call for an American Writers' Congress to encourage colleagues who wanted to "depict the aspirations, struggles and sufferings of *the mass* of Americans" (H. Hart 9). These signers recognized the need for ongoing supportive groups:

> Many revolutionary writers live virtually in isolation, lacking opportunities to discuss vital problems with their fellows. Others are so absorbed in the revolutionary cause that they have few opportunities for thorough examination and analysis. Never have the writers of the nation come together for fundamental discussion. (H. Hart 10)

Nine women signed the call for a congress, among them Josephine Herbst, Meridel Le Sueur, Genevieve Taggard, and Tillie Lerner, along with their teachers and colleagues such as Robert Herrick, Robert Morss Lovett, Richard Wright, and Langston Hughes. For the first meeting, 216 delegates came from twenty-six states to join with 150 guests from other countries and 4,000 spectators. There were six sessions—a public one on the first day and then smaller sessions for delegates on the next two days—concerning the writer's position in a revolution. Women speakers especially stressed the need for a supportive environment as they crafted a literature of social change. Josephine Herbst, for example, spoke at the first session of the purpose and identity that writers could achieve within a revolutionary movement:

> The talk is the same though the language, inflection and rhythm vary. These men and women are becoming aware of the economic realities behind their troubles and they are beginning to fight. What has this to do with writing? So far as I am concerned, it has everything. It is impossible for me to stop myself from writing about anything so real. . . . We want to issue an invitation to these writers assembled to-night, to come down among the workers to find that life and to create a synthesis for it with their tools as writers. (H. Hart 14–15)

At the meeting, Meridel Le Sueur spoke of how a redirection of the American regionalist tradition, and its respect for the details of daily life, could provide a means for writers to help form a new "people's culture," thus enabling workers to examine their situations, to reevaluate their own worth in society, and to achieve liberation (Wald 25). Leane Zugsmith spoke about women's role in reaching the goals of congress members: "[W]e must take history in our hands and help write it from the creative point of view of those who labor and produce" (Ravitz 60). She argued that all women, whether at home or an outside job, are crucial members of the group who "labor and produce," and that women writers had to ensure that women's perspectives would be part of the ongoing planning for change.

Besides offering fellowship and a sense of purpose, these congress meetings included practical lectures on the craft of writing and on marketing manuscripts. At the second congress in 1937, for example, Joris Ivens lectured on political filmmaking; Henry Hart spoke on dealing with publishers. At the third congress in 1939, poets, dramatists, and fiction writers met in separate sessions to discuss their craft and review the participants' manuscripts, as was done in college classes and at summer workshops. Other sessions, led by leading writers and editors, concerned opportunities in and techniques of radio, filmmaking, and song writing.

The first congress meeting inaugurated a League of American Writers to promote a literature of the proletariat by supporting oppressed writers around the globe, opening new theatres, and sponsoring a literary magazine. Meridel Le Sueur, Agnes Smedley, Tillie Lerner, and Grace Lumpkin were among the members of the league's National Council, and Josephine Herbst and Genevieve Taggard were on the Executive Committee. From 1935 to 1942, the league sponsored many meetings for writers and established chapters in New York, Washington, Chicago, Connecticut, and Hollywood.

Most of the league's leaders and members were men, but the organization did include Meridel Le Sueur, Anna Louise Strong, Martha Gellhorn, and Genevieve Taggard; Dorothy Brewster, scholar and critic from Columbia University; Marjorie Fischer, author of children's books; poets Jean Starr Untermeyer, Muriel Rukeyser, and Ellen Conreid; and journalist Agnes Smedley, who was recording the process of revolution in Russia and China and working toward an international League of Leftist Writers. With their shared political goals, frequent meetings, league publications, and network of connections, these professional writers "felt a good deal more communal and friendly than the isolated writer of the past could ever have believed," commented Franklin Folsom, the executive secretary of the league (86).

Although these groups constrained the definition of writer, they also enabled women to write within networks of like-minded professionals. Trying to negotiate her way in the male-dominated Communist Party, Meridel Le Sueur relied on Zona Gale and Margery Latimer to keep her focused on their plan of forging a new literature about women's roles as workers:

> As we bonded together, escaping refugees along an unknown road, so they wrote for you not born yet. The three of us might not have survived without each other, without attacks on each other, even in the terrible web of our history. . . . I survived, maybe by camouflage. (233)

As a member of this group of like-minded women, Le Sueur was able to reap the benefits of allegiance to the Communist Party, which was certainly patriarchal but supportive of her work concerning women and labor: "I think I would go crazy without the communist party, which is like a father to me, something strong and paternal, and binds me to a large and tender family" (Coiner 95). Working within these structures, she wrote stories for *American Mercury*, *Scribner's*, and other magazines and documented the communist movement in the *Daily Worker* and the *New Masses*; a collection of her poetry and reportage, *Salute to Spring*, appeared in 1940.

The steady encouragement of reportage also led to *The Working Woman*, published as a monthly newspaper from 1929 to 1933 and as a monthly magazine from 1933 to 1935. For its readership, which peaked at 8,000, this journal provided investigative articles, interviews, and letters as well as some fiction. Here, for example, were published Mary Heaton Vorse's "Hard Boiled" on the Scottsboro trial and Vivian Dahl's "Them Women Sure Are Scrappers" about striking women farm workers. A further manifestation of this commitment to a workers' literature occurred in workers' theatres and the *New Theater* journal, which in January of 1935 had a circulation of 12,000 (H. Hart 182). At the first Writers' Congress, participants reported on three hundred groups that performed plays in factories, businesses, restaurants, lodges, and little theatres. Another product of this leftist involvement in writing occurred through adult education intended to enable working-class men and women to tell their own stories. The New York Writers' School, for example, involved in the late 1930s as teachers and students such writers as Helen Bergovoy, Vera Caspary, Joy Davidman, Mary Elting, Genevieve Taggard, Jean Starr Untermeyer, and Leane Zugsmith. At this site, students such as James Baldwin studied the short story with Mary Elting, children's writing with Marjorie Fischer, and poetry with Genevieve Taggard, who also started a poetry program in the schools.

WITH THE WPA: THE FEDERAL WRITERS' PROJECT AND FEDERAL THEATRE PROJECT

In the 1930s, other groups appeared that women writers could join to voice social critique, again with firm restrictions on the appropriate products. As Harry L. Hopkins, federal relief administrator for the New Deal, became overwhelmed with data coming to him from the Surplus Relief Corporation, the Civil Works Administration, the Works Progress Administration, the Temporary Emergency Relief Administration, and other governmental agencies whose conclusions he had to summarize for Congress and the president, he decided to send out investigators to give him a more human picture of the Depression and of the relief programs' impact. In 1933, he hired Lorena Hickok to travel around the country and report on living conditions and on the impact of New Deal programs. Ruth Suckow took on a similar role for the Farm Tenancy Committee beginning in 1936. Martha Gellhorn, sent out as an investigator for nearly a year, used her findings in a novel, *The Trouble I've Seen* (1936). Gellhorn devoted much of this chronicle to the lives of women and their children in a North Carolina textile town where pellegra and syphilis were rampant and where people lived in dilapidated homes, with little money and food.

Many young women writers, just out of college, joined New Deal agencies to engage in professional writing and social critique. Eudora Welty first attended the Mississippi College for Women, where she worked as a reporter on the college newspaper, *The Spectator:* "I became a wit and humorist of the parochial kind, and the amount I was able to show off in print must have been a great comfort to me" (79). She then transferred to the University of Wisconsin, where she studied literature with Ricardo Quintana. Like many other women who wanted to write, she hoped that she would not have to teach to afford the habit: "As certain as I was of wanting to be a writer, I was certain of *not* wanting to be a teacher. I lacked the instructing turn of mind, the selflessness, the patience for teaching, and I had the unreasoning feeling that I'd be trapped" (82). After she left Wisconsin, Welty studied advertising at Columbia and then worked at an advertising agency, a job she quit "because it was too much like sticking pins into people to make them buy things that they didn't need or really much want" (Bain and Duffy 45). She then returned home where she worked in advertising and publicity and wrote a Sunday column on Jackson society for the Memphis *Commercial Appeal*. To reconnect herself with a larger group of writers, she joined the WPA as a Junior Publicity Agent, a job that required her to travel around the state and report on local conditions and various projects, such as the rebuilding of Tupelo after a tornado. This position enabled her to interact with her state's residents, meeting with them in their homes, churches, and businesses, and to collaborate with editors in Mississippi and in Washington.

Relief administrators also established ongoing programs to provide regular work for the large numbers of struggling artists, including writers. The Emergency Relief Act of 1935 included "a nation-wide program for useful employment of artists, musicians, actors, entertainers, writers . . . and others in these cultural fields" with its goal being "to integrate the artist into the mainstream of American life and make the arts both expressive of the spirit of a nation and accessible to its people" (Mangione 39). Funding from this act created the Federal Writers' Project (FWP), which was at least partially intended to keep radicals busy and beholden to the government instead of off sparking insurrection: writers were not allowed to choose their own projects, as many artists in the Federal Art Project did, or to work at home. By 1936, the Federal Writers' Project had employed between 4,500 and 5,000 creative writers, researchers, and administrators (Ware 141).

Unlike the Federal Art Project, the Federal Writers' Project drew few famous professionals; the majority were young, struggling novelists, journalists, and editors of whom between 75 percent and 90 percent were on the relief rolls. In 1938, of the 1,722 employees, 551 had been reporters for a year or two, 339 had sold a few articles to newspapers and magazines, 165 had engaged in some minor form of scholarship, and 159 were absolute beginners, while 107 had held editorial posts, 105 were well-established journalists, scholars, educators, or researchers, and eighty-three were authors of one or more books (Mangione 100). Each state had the same number of paid positions allotted, a disadvantage for the many writers in New York City, certainly, but an advantage to those in other parts of the country.

To provide the positive and patriotic employment mandated in its goal statements, the FWP produced more than a thousand publications, the most well known being the WPA state guides, which combined tourism, folklore, and history. Other projects included regional guides such as *U.S. One, Maine to Florida;* ethnic and folklore studies such as *The Negro in Virginia;* and taped recordings of slave narratives. Although many writers objected to their restricted choices, Lewis Mumford in the *New Republic* stressed the value of working on the prescribed projects: "[T]his apprenticeship, this seeing of the American scene, this listening to the American voice may mean more for literature than the sudden forcing of stories and poems" (Mangione 247). He recognized that such chronicles presented a new view of American history, providing stories about the rich traditions and hard work of poor immigrants and slaves, and thus advanced a much wider definition of American hero.

In its mission of supporting struggling writers, the project provided another group involvement for women. Katharine Kellock of the Resettlement Administration took the job of field director; she had written for newspapers and magazines and the *Dictionary of American Biography.* Marianne Moore had proposed to Henry Alsberg, national director of the FWP, that state histories be the project's goal, but the specific plan for the guide series, to be modeled on the Baedeker guides to Europe, was Kellock's. As field director, she consulted frequently with each state's committees to ensure that the guides did not devolve into dull, formulaic pieces; she helped many directors who were behind schedule; and she created a separate group to collaborate on a Factbook Series. When a Hearst paper attacked her and her projects for being communist, an accusation shadowing all WPA efforts, she came into the Washington office from the field and supervised both the editing and the political battles from there. She then sent Stella Hanau, who had gone to Barnard and performed with the Provincetown Players and later worked as a freelance editor and publicist, to Alabama and Oklahoma to help complete their projects and deal with the conflicts between WPA administrators and state legislatures. Kellock and Hanau worked with many women who directed guidebook projects: Merle Colby (Massachusetts), Opal Shannon (Iowa), Louise DuBose and Mabel Montgomery (South Carolina), Irene Fuhlbruegge (New Jersey), and Jeannette Eckman (Delaware). Carita Corse, a historian, directed the Florida project for six years. Eudora Ramsay Richardson, writer and member of the Virginia State Board of Public Welfare, took over that state's project after it floundered for a year and a half, and she then oversaw the publication of *Virginia: A Guide to the Old Dominion, The Negro in Virginia,* and *Alexandria.* Dorris May Westall, who had worked on her hometown paper for twelve dollars a week until she was fired for smoking, took over an incompetent Maine project and brought out a guidebook ahead of schedule, in 1937. Miriam deAllen Ford, a poet, novelist, and social historian, worked on a guide to California's largest cities. Tillie Olsen recorded life stories of Mexicans, Slavs, and Filipinos on the California Project; Dorothy Canfield Fisher wrote for the Vermont guide.

Since in this federal initiative hiring was "often free of discrimination," the writers' project provided a collaborative opportunity for African American writers, such as Katherine Dunham, Margaret Walker, and Zora Neale Hurston as well as Arna Bontemps, Langston Hughes, Sterling Brown, Ralph Ellison, and Richard Wright (Hemenway 251). An Illinois research project provided Katherine Dunham, a University of Chicago anthropology student who had met Langston Hughes at the Little Theatre Group of Harper Avenue and was encouraged by him to join, with the chance to study Chicago cults. Zora Neale Hurston became an editor for the Florida state guide in 1938 while also collecting and editing material for another WPA project, *The Negro in Florida, 1528–1940*, for which she began visiting small Everglades communities to collect data. The resultant 200–page volume, including slave narratives, a study of slave spirituals and religion, and tall tales about Florida history and climate, was not published by the WPA because it remained a compilation of the interviews and lacked a unifying theme or structure (Hemenway 252–53). Instead of staying with the project, Hurston went on to a teaching job at the North Carolina College for Negroes in Durham, North Carolina, where she began collaborating with Paul Green of the Carolina Playmakers.

Along with the guides, some state projects published fiction and poetry by their members and allowed a few writers to receive funding while they did their own work. Alsberg permitted ten New York writers, including Charlotte Wilder and Helen Neville, to spend their time in this way. Meridel Le Seuer joined the Minnesota unit to finish a novel while supporting two children. Margaret Walker, who applied to the Chicago office after Richard Wright urged her to do so, joined at the age of twenty, pretending that she was twenty-one, right after she had graduated from Northwestern: "I graduated from college to the WPA" ("How I Wrote *Jubilee*" 51). At first she worked on the *Illinois Guide Book*, creating a portrait of the north side of Chicago where increasing numbers of African Americans lived in slums. The job, which paid eighty-five dollars a month and carried the title of junior writer, helped her to support her family in New Orleans. She was then allowed, when she agreed to report in each week and demonstrate her progress, to work on a novel at home. Through her weekly critique sessions, she reentered the group workshop environment that she had experienced in college. Her supervisor, Jack

Sher, read her work carefully and advised her to not become caught up in the socialist movement since it might take her away from the stories she wanted to tell, a 1930s conundrum for writers, as we have seen. When she also shared her work with fellow project member Richard Wright, they became friends and collaborators; she showed him clippings from a murder case that he later used in *Native Son*.

Project publications could provide an outlet for creative pieces, written for the FWP or before. In the California project, Miriam de Allen Ford served on an editorial board that brought out an anthology of fiction called *Material Gathered*. Along with Charlotte Wilder and Dorothy Van Ghent, she produced the first and only issue of another project-sponsored literary magazine, *The Coast*. The Nebraska Writers' Project published a twenty-three-page compilation of poems, articles, and stories called *Shucks* and then encouraged Alsberg to establish a national literary magazine, *American Stuff*, in 1937, a collection of short stories, poems, and Americana by fifty project writers, including Margaret Lund, Helen Neville, Lola Pergament, Ida Faye Sachs, Dorothy Van Ghent, and Charlotte Wilder. Ruth Widen published her first short story in the magazine; Elizabeth Lomax published a composite slave narrative drawn from interviews sponsored by the project. Only one issue appeared because the Dies Committee cancelled the FWP in September 1938 because of its high cost and seemingly un-American leanings. Then other magazines, such as *Frontier*, *Midland*, *New Republic*, *Poetry*, and *New Masses*, featured compilations of writing from the project.

Through the FWP, other women in small towns far away from the literary life of Chicago and New York had a chance to write for a living and maintain group involvements. Alice Corbin Henderson had gone to the University of Chicago and joined Harriet Monroe in setting up *Poetry* in 1912; she continued as an associate editor even after tuberculosis caused her to move to New Mexico in 1916. Throughout her life, she worked within groups of artists, helping Carl Sandburg, Sherwood Anderson, and Edgar Lee Masters launch their careers through publication in *Poetry;* corresponding with Ezra Pound, who suggested changes to drafts of her poetry as he also did with Mary Barnard; and encouraging a group of poets, including her close friend Witter Byner, to meet together regularly in Santa Fe. In the WPA, she made group experiences available to younger New Mexican writers—and to herself—in regular meetings at her home as she helped to plan the state guide and critiqued the work of project members.

During the years that writers profited from the group involvement and publication opportunities offered by the FWP, they also had access to support from the Federal Theatre Project, established by the Relief Act of 1935 as the only federally funded national theatre in American history, one intended to bring to audiences the richness of American lives and traditions, as the Carolina Playmakers were attempting in Chapel Hill. Hallie Flanagan, who went to Grinnell and was by then a member of the Vassar faculty with a national reputation for her work in experimental theatre, served as its director. In four years, performances sponsored by the project played to more than twenty-five million people as it met its dual goals of helping theatre workers who were on the relief rolls and creating innovative theatre with a focus on cultural diversity and political reform (Ware 151). The funding of more than ten million dollars a year equipped and renovated theatres, paid professionals and administrators, and subsidized low ticket prices for underprivileged groups. University leaders in drama instruction, such as Flanagan, Frederick Koch of the Carolina Playmakers, Zona Gale of the Wisconsin Drama Society, and E. C. Mabie of the Iowa University Theatre, joined with professional theatre and little theatre leaders to guide the varied groups that might be focusing on experimental drama and dance, one-act plays, "living newspaper" dramatizations of the news, African American youth theatre, or Yiddish, German, or Anglo-Jewish productions. These ambitious efforts aimed at greatly expanding the audiences of theatre, the number of professionals involved, and the types of stories told there, a political plan for the dramatic arts regularly chronicled in the *Federal Theatre Magazine* (Flanagan 60).

Many women writers, both black and white, found opportunities in the federal theatres. Susan Glaspell directed the midwestern play bureau, from which post she encouraged young writers and found appreciative audiences for her own plays, including some that she had written much earlier. Her *Inheritors* (1921) was especially popular on the Florida circuit of Jacksonville, Tampa, and Miami; her *Suppressed Desires*, co-authored with George Cram Cook in 1917 for the Provincetown Players, was listed by Congress as an example of a popular but too salacious play, part of the evidence used to withdraw funding from the Federal Theatre Project in 1939. Marie M. Coxe's *If Ye Break Faith*, a call for peace, was reviewed after its New Orleans production as the "most impressive offering the Federal Theatre has had before the public" (Flanagan 87). This play was also well received in Miami, Jacksonville, and Denver. In 1931, Thelma Myrtle Duncan wrote *Black Magic*, a comedy about a husband who seeks a voodoo cure for his wife's unfaithfulness—he finds out that her absences have been caused not by an affair but by her need to find a job and supplement their income. When the project's Play Bureau gave *Black Magic* a highly favorable rating, a network of theatres began to produce this play, written in black dialect.

Duncan's successes that year encouraged her to devote her time to writing, and so she abandoned a career as a music teacher. Shirley Graham DuBois also got an opportunity in the project to establish a writing career; she left a teaching job at Tennessee State College in 1936 to serve as director of the Negro Unit of the Chicago Federal Theatre, which produced two of her plays. In 1938, she left that position to enroll as a Julius Rosenwald Fellow at the Yale School of Drama, an educational experience that led to her writing seven more plays and many works of nonfiction, including biographies of Frederick Douglass, George Washington Carver, Paul Robeson, and her husband, W. E. B. DuBois.

For women at the end of the nineteenth century and afterwards, college had involved workshops and extracurricular opportunities through which they worked together and with men at honing their work and beginning careers. In their own literature about writing careers, they recognized that when they left the school environment they would have to cope with the expectations of their families and communities, with financial hardship, and with the isolation of artistic commitment. As a means of coping with these serious ongoing pressures, they chose never to leave that collaborative environment. As this group of women left college, they created and entered an unprecedented array of groups to continue college habits while perhaps also furthering social or political goals. In group settings, women had to cope with prejudices against them, as in many college writing workshops, but their commitment and hard work created a space for them. These carefully formed connections led to many creative forms of collaboration: in choosing subjects and improving drafts, in finding publishers, in producing plays, and in creating audiences for the work. These groups enabled writers working within them to have a great impact on American writing and on American definitions of Writer.

CHAPTER SIX

REDEFINITIONS OF
WOMEN WRITERS

Women's stuff is pretty nearly everything except fires,
riots, and the duller cases in Criminal Courts—and at
any moment women may inject themselves into these.

—Emma Bugbee

I think of the cry of a farm woman.

—Zona Gale

As women left college, writers' groups enabled them to establish their identities as writers and to build professional careers. After 1920, as they began
to enter the profession in large numbers, their presence and products dramatically altered the field of writing itself, changing not only the definition
of who a woman writer might be but ultimately of who any writer might
be and what she or he might write. The older definition of Writer as a male
creating his culture could no longer remain intact as women posited new
visions of this craft and its influence. This group of women, with college
educations and supportive networks of colleagues, recreated both reportage
and creative writing.

Although they encountered many obstacles and their choices were
limited, women steadily increased their presence throughout the work force
at the beginning of the twentieth century. From Census Reports, women
constituted 6.4 percent of the full time work force in 1870, 10 percent in

1890, 11.6 percent in 1910, and 13.3 percent in 1920 (Hill 41). Between 1890 and 1920, women's participation in paid professions increased by 226 percent while men's increased by 78 percent, with the increase for males primarily reflecting their movement away from family farms (Breckinridge 112). In the 1920s and 1930s, the greater numbers of women attending college (283,000 in 1920, 480,000 in 1930, and 601,000 in 1940) did so with a clear goal of employment if only for a short time after graduation (Solomon 142). Many of these women worked for only a few years until marriage and children: in 1920, only 12.2 percent of professional women were married and 25 percent of Ph.D.s (Chafe 100). Thus, the working single woman, and to a lesser extent her married counterpart, was becoming a regular presence in American towns and cities. As recorded in Robert Lynd and Helen Lynd's 1929 study of Middletown, forty-three people out of every one hundred worked to earn a living, with one in five of those workers being a woman:

> "What has become of the useful maiden aunt?" asks a current newspaper advertisement of a women's magazine, showing a picture of a woman in her late thirties dressed in sober black, and bearing the date "Anno Domini 1900." "She isn't darning anybody's stockings," it adds succinctly, "not even her own. She is a draftsman or an author, a photographer or a real estate agent. . . . She is the new phenomenon of everyday life." (25)

As women's participation in occupations increased, so did their involvement in professional writing even though it was not primarily a woman-identified career. Although a few women had very successful careers in the nineteenth century, as we saw in chapter 1, their numbers were small, a negligible percentage not even recorded in Census data before 1900. By 1886, only about five hundred women had full time jobs at newspapers. But for college-educated women in the early twentieth century, writing appeared as a serious profession, a difficult but attractive and possible choice. And women moved into this career steadily. As we have seen, women represented 4 percent of journalists in 1890, 7.3 percent in 1900, and 12 percent in 1910. By 1920, however, in a new Census category of authors, editors, and reporters, their numbers were 8,736 or 21.3 percent; in 1930, 17,371 or 37 percent, 43 percent in the category of authors and 23 percent in the category of editors and reporters. Within this second category of editors and reporters in 1930, the highest percentage of participation occurred in the youngest age group, which included the early child-bearing years, as large numbers of recent college graduates entered the career:

Percentage of Editors and Reporters Who Were Women: 1930

18–24	28.7
25–34	22.5
35–44	23.2
45–54	23.0
55–64	17.7
65 and above	13.9

Abstract of the Fifteenth Census of the United States: 1930. 358–59

In 1940, even after the Depression had caused a decrease in opportunities, 32.1 percent of authors and 25.3 percent of editors and reporters were women, with little variation throughout the country: in the four main geographical regions, the percentages varied only from twenty-three to twenty-seven. These numbers were much higher than those for other professional fields that were not becoming woman-identified:

Percentage of Professional Employees Who Were Women: 1940

Civil Engineers	.2
Dentists	1.5
Architects	2.3
Lawyers and Judges	2.4
Physicians and Surgeons	4.6
Journalists and Editors	*25.3*
College Professors and Instructors	26.6
Authors	*32.1*
Social and Welfare Workers	64.3
Teachers	75.4
Librarians	89.5
Nurses	97.9

Sixteenth Census 75

The rapidly increasing number of women going to work at newspapers, magazines, and publishing houses, backed by the support of their own groups, took on a variety of jobs there. In 1925, a survey of eighty-four newspaper editors in thirty-nine states, conducted by students in a graduate seminar at the University of North Dakota, indicated that society reporting was still the most common job, but women's presence in other positions was becoming much more common. While the respondents listed 121 women employees as "women's page" writers, 205 were not: eighty-seven did general reporting, sixty-four did feature work, twenty-three were drama and music critics, seventeen were desk editors, seven were editorial writers, five were copy readers, one was a Sunday editor, and one was a sportswriter. The value of a separate women's page, in fact, was by then being debated: fifty-five respondents said it was of great value to its readers, but twenty-six said it was of no or negligible value because women avidly read the entire paper (Reinholt 40). The majority of women hired, these editors claimed, had college degrees, and these better-educated reporters made the move from women's pages to general reporting much more frequently than their high school-educated colleagues. The survey rated the performance of these college graduates quite highly: these editors found it in no way inferior to the men's.

Data from this survey reflected the larger picture of journalism and other writing careers: of women who succeeded as writers in the early twentieth century, the vast majority had attended college. The few professional women writers of the nineteenth century generally had no higher education: only 12 percent of those writers born in the first half of the nineteenth century and listed in the 1899 *Who's Who* had any college training. But in a sample of approximately two hundred authors born after 1900, taken from various biographical indexes issued in the early 1950s, four out of five had attended college, three out of five had graduated, and one in six had secured graduate training. Of the writers about whom biographical entries appear in Roses and Randolph's *Harlem Renaissance and Beyond: Literary Biographies of 100 Black Women Writers, 1900–1945*, women who were born between 1880 and 1910 and whose "work belongs primarily to the early half of the twentieth century," sixty-four had attended a four-year college and four had gone to a normal school: at a time when college education was still a rare opportunity for black women, more than two-thirds of these professional writers had attended college. Coeducational historically black colleges enrolled most of these African American writers; private women's colleges nurtured the largest numbers of white women writers. Perhaps because of their frequent workshop classes, theatre groups, and opportunities for student publication, private women's colleges produced fourteen times the number of writers that would be expected from the size of their enrollments. The top group was Barnard, Bryn Mawr, Radcliffe, and Vassar—with ratios of approximately twenty-five times the number to be expected (Newcomer 206–07). In a comprehensive survey of Bryn Mawr alumnae, 21.8 percent of women who graduated between 1921 and 1940 reported publications or performances. From 1921 to 1930, 11.9 percent reported books and 25.6 percent other publications or performance of some kind. Of those Bryn Mawr English majors who had paid full-time positions during that decade, 20 percent chose an editorial or writing job; and from 1931 to 1940, 40 percent (A. Miller 13, 151).

ENTERING THE JOURNALISM PROFESSION:
GOOD GIRLS AND BAD

Even as women entered writing careers in larger numbers, they found themselves physically marginalized, in part-time positions, as the single female employee, working outside of the regular city room routines. As a reporter at the New York *Tribune* in 1910, for example, Emma Bugbee was not allowed to have a desk in the all-male newsroom and thus worked in an alcove on another floor. Such physical separation materialized the prevailing belief that women could not really enter into this male career. When newspaperman Sam Wilkeson Wistrom wrote in the January 1889 *Journalist* that women would "never make newspaper men," he indicated that even though their writing might be superior ("No matter how potent a Dixon they wield"), they just couldn't survive in this physically and mentally taxing "field of tripod, brain, muscle and pen." With "journalist" seemingly emitting a male mystique, women generally entered the career only through two extremes, which might be labeled as "good girls" and "bad girls." But their education and group identifications, which their nineteenth-century counterparts had lacked, enabled these writers to create new options: to abandon these extremes or to transform them into more meaningful types of journalism.

As in the nineteenth century but in much larger numbers, many women began their writing careers as good girls on the women's page, not necessarily because of their love of homemaking but because there was no other entrance to the daily newspaper. After graduating from the University of Kansas, Florence Finch Kelly arrived in Chicago to seek work, armed with a letter of introduction to Helen Ekin Starrett, a successful reporter. Starrett told Kelly that as a woman she would not be able to sell social or political commentary or any other type of analytical writing:

> "My child," she adjured me, "those things will never do! No editor would touch them! You'll have to write about something you have seen, can describe, something no one else has done. Now, what have you seen that would be news?" (138)

While Kelly longed for other assignments, she found herself with only society news to report even though as "a crude girl from a prairie farm," she felt herself particularly unsuited for this work (140). Elizabeth Banks could only land a secretarial position when she sought a reporting job. Her supervisor helped her get "in" with the editors with this hint about opportunities in fashion writing, as Banks recalled in her autobiography:

> I hear they have a great fashion opening round at the Murrill Stores this
> afternoon. Suppose you go and see if you can write a funny piece about
> funny fashions. I don't know if they want anything like that upstairs, but if
> they do, and your piece is up to the mark, they might use it on Sunday. (9)

Although she had no great interest in clothes, she took this opportunity
because it was the only one.

In San Benito, Texas, during the Depression, Carol Lu Hayes began her
career by reporting bridge parties, high school graduations, teas, and suppers as
woman's editor, a part-time job that paid five dollars a week and that required
attention to local social traditions:

> I had to describe in detail what every woman wore, and they had to be
> listed in order, according to the town's social hierarchy. The wedding party
> came first, then the woman who presided at the punch bowl, then the
> woman at the guest book, and then the guests in order of their importance
> in town. Later on, I worked for a North Carolina newspaper, and there I
> had to list everybody's grandparents. But we didn't do that in Texas.
> (Westin 180)

To relieve the boredom, Hayes created a Mrs. J. C. Eddern who gave lavish parties and took exotic out-of-town trips.

While the majority of women came to the newspaper through part time
good girl jobs writing about fashion and cooking, as the very few had also done
in the nineteenth century, other women entered with a new image and purpose. In the Progressive era, journalists such as Lincoln Steffens, Upton Sinclair,
and David Graham Phillips thrived by writing exposés of corruption—on politics, railroads, patent-drug companies, and factory working conditions. Women
journalists were not generally accorded the respect given to these male "muckrakers," but instead received their own separate designation and reputation as
"stunt girls." Editors expected them to embark on daring adventures that
would expose corruption and lead to reform while astounding and titillating
the public. Before 1920, women also took on the label of "sob sister," hired to
write piteous reports concerning accident victims, abandoned children, and
murderers. In both styles of bad girl writing, the journalists became as much
the articles' subjects as the institutions being investigated or the criminals on
trial: their looks, costumes, and exploits dominated the story and contributed
to their fame while separating them publicly from "serious" or "real" journalists such as Lincoln Steffens and Upton Sinclair who operated with "tripod,
brain, muscle and pen." For the woman reporter, this role of dangerous adven-
turer was as much a pose as dutiful homemaker. In fact, the trade magazine *Jour-*

nalist recognized that the newspaper's good and bad girl was often the same reporter, coping each day with the foolishness of both extremes: "She would turn from the ghastly horrors of an afternoon reception and find new life in the glorious details of a murder case."

The first few bad girls had entered the newspapers without college training. In the 1890s, Winifred Black Bonfils, better known as Annie Laurie, was one of Hearst's star reporters in San Francisco. She pretended to faint on the street and was hauled by horse cart to a hospital where she exposed obsolete and inhumane treatment methods. She won an exclusive interview with President Benjamin Harrison by hiding under a table on his campaign trail. Her greatest scoop came in 1900 when, disguised as a man, she slipped through police lines in Galveston, Texas, and reported on the storm and tidal wave that killed 7,000 people.

Elizabeth Cochrane ("Nellie Bly") feigned insanity to do an exposé for Pulitzer on the infamous Blackwell's Island asylum, living there for ten days as a patient. Her other stunt articles involved entering a women's prison as an inmate, facing a masher's attack in Central Park, investing in fraudulent money-making schemes, assisting a fake mesmerist, touring with Buffalo Bill's Wild West Show, and embarking on a globe-circling tour by ship, train, burro, carriage, and cart to, in seventy-two days, beat Phileas Fogg's eighty-day record from Jules Verne's popular book. To all of these assignments, she brought a personal approach to investigative reporting, providing detailed descriptions of particular scenes, as in the harrowing beginning to her piece on Blackwell's Island, which appeared in the *New York World* in October 1887: "On the wagon sped, and I, as well as my comrades, gave a despairing farewell glance at freedom as we came in sight of the long stone buildings" (124). She also clearly analyzed this institution's tyranny over women:

> I would like the expert physicians who are condemning me for my action, which has proven their ability, to take a perfectly sane and healthy woman, shut her up and make her sit from 6 A.M. until 8 P.M. on straight-back benches, do not allow her to talk or move during those hours, give her no reading and let her know nothing of the world or its doings, give her bad food and harsh treatment, and see how long it will take to make her insane. Two months would make her a mental and physical wreck. (Belford 136)

Although, like Nellie Bly, the few other stunt girls excelled at investigative reporting, they had to write on only those subjects, such as circuses and asylums, that would lead to grotesqueries and sexual innuendo: exposing graft in dangerous locations in scanty clothes. In Bly's exposé of Blackwell's asylum, the headings point to this emphasis: "Scrubbed with Soft Soap and Put to Bed in a Wet Gown, "Combed with a Public Comb," "Unspeakable Scenes in the Yard."

As women began newspaper careers after graduating from college journalism programs, they did this exposé writing while covering murder trials and creating cozy portraits of brides and family suppers. After studying journalism at the University of Wisconsin, Miriam Ottenberg began her career at the Akron *Times-Press* as good girl, stunt girl, and sob sister:

> In those early days I did human interest features and handled public service campaigns like the Community Chest and the *Star's* annual Christmas campaign. What I wrote were sob stories to raise funds.
>
> Since I was the only girl in the newsroom until the war, if they wanted a story that required an impersonation (I was a ham actress as every good investigative reporter should be) I did it. . . . By the time the war came, I was covering every major murder and in those days, a murder was covered by several top reporters. (Marzolf 71)

Emma Bugbee started at the New York *Tribune* by investigating the Salvation Army in her pose as a volunteer, by taking a trial flight in a new fighter aircraft, and by covering the day-to-day progress of murder trials while also completing good girl assignments, such as stories about cat and flower shows.

Both good and bad girl roles certainly marginalized women as various sorts of nonjournalists, less serious than their male counterparts, and thus continued nineteenth-century prejudices about their inappropriate presence in the career. But the common acceptance of this dual definition was in fact a first step beyond nineteenth-century limitations. Even though women often had to conform to gender-defined roles, they did not as frequently have to claim that they were working because of temporary economic destitution or a moral necessity. As well-trained college graduates, increasingly with degrees from schools of journalism, they had a right to initiate a career without an excuse. And their numbers would soon allow them to abandon the limitations of women's page writer, sob sister, and stunt girl and to define themselves as journalists.

MOVING INTO NEW CONTENT AREAS/ TRANSFORMING THE OLD ONES

As college-educated women demonstrated their capacities, especially at small papers that had to send out all reporters during emergencies, they began to move from society news or sensationalized exposés to other types of stories, their education and determination allowing them, as their nineteenth-century counterparts could not, to move from good girl and bad girl to reporter. When Lorena Hickok, for example, reflected on her own career, she recognized that she had gotten her start by treading a path away from those extremes:

> When I first went into the newspaper business, I had to get a job as a society editor—the only opening available to women in most offices. Then I'd build myself up solidly with the city editor by volunteering for night assignments, get into trouble with some dowager who would demand that I be fired, and finally land on the straight reportorial staff, which was where I had wanted to be from the beginning. (xxvi)

In her reporting job with the Associated Press, beginning in 1928, Hickok found the variety and challenges that she sought: she was the first reporter to meet rescued passengers from a sinking steamship; she wrote a series on the corruption of the New York mayor, Jimmy Walker; she reported on effects of the Depression and on Franklin Roosevelt's 1932 campaign.

Doris Fleeson also began her career at both extremes, as a good and bad girl writer, and moved from there to a full career. After graduating from the University of Kansas in 1923, she took a job as society editor of the *Evanston News Index*, a suburban paper. In 1927 she came to the *New York Daily News*, at first reporting on crimes, trials, and society scandals but then moving on to political news. In 1933, she went to Washington to the *Daily News'* newly opened bureau there, where she wrote a column called "Capitol Stuff" on the New Deal. She then became a roving war correspondent for several magazines, reporting on battlefronts in France and Italy. In 1945, she began a twice-weekly political column for the United Features Syndicate, from which post she covered the terms of five presidents (Belford 258–64).

Although women encountered new opportunities by leaving the women's page and stunt writing, they also transformed those territories where they had begun. A second trend, then, was not to abandon the women's story, but to expand on what that term could mean—by asserting the wide range of women's interests, in religion, education, politics, science, and the social sciences. Writers pursuing this option recognized that the women's page or column could reach to any subject at all: and ultimately, their efforts would cause its subject matter to permeate all sections of the newspaper and become its vast majority. And during this process, the stylistic limitations that critics traditionally attributed to women—that they were naturally suited only to description, to the interview, to personal statements—would transform not just the column and feature but the very definition of reporting.

This enrichment of the women's page or women's stories began not at daily newspapers with their clearly delineated short sections for women, but at magazines and political journals. As was discussed in chapter 1, the campaign for suffrage and equal rights led to women's magazines focused on social and political issues. Susan B. Anthony and Elizabeth Cady Stanton's *The Revolution*, published from 1868 to 1870, supported women's suffrage, easy divorce, and prostitution laws and opposed the Fifteenth Amendment since it only extended suffrage to another group of men. Lucy Stone's *Woman's Journal*, in print from 1869 to 1914, took a more moderate stance toward legal changes and the Fifteen Amendment while advocating suffrage for women. These editors assumed that women wanted to be informed of contemporary events, and especially of political decisions that would have an impact on their lives, a definition of the women's story that moved it beyond the happy home, recipes, and fashion.

In *La Follette's Weekly Magazine*, Belle Case La Follette was perhaps the first journalist to vastly expand the definition of a single women's page within a "men's" journal. As a student at the University of Wisconsin from 1875 to 1879, she had developed a close friendship with the president, John Bascom, who impressed upon her the college graduate's responsibility to improve civic life: "Again and again he would tell us what we owed the State and impress upon us our duty to serve the State in return" (La Follette and La Follette 38). When she and her husband, Senator Robert La Follette, began publishing the magazine in 1909, they regularly advertised their new publication as "an aggressive advocate of legitimate business, of clean government in the interest of the common good, of the ennobling of farm life, of better conditions for workingmen, and of social upliftment." Belle La Follette's "Women and Education" section, its headnote declared, would cover "health, children, education, life in Washington and other topics of everyday interest to women, from the standpoint of personal observation and experience." Her first Washington pieces concerned receptions and the politicians' homes, but she soon began to comment on their decisions and allegiances. She ended an essay on Taft's inauguration speech by commenting caustically on her readers' willingness to accept this change in subject:

> Need I apologize for taking the space of this department for giving my impressions of the Inaugural Address instead of the Inaugural Ball? I do not believe so. I trust there is not a reader of *La Follette's Magazine*, who does not care more for my opinion of it than any description I could give of Mrs. Taft's gown. (10)

Although she discussed cooking and housekeeping, she did so not just to improve the middle-class home but to help all women increase their understanding of nutrition and safety. Her articles about fish and milk, for example, stressed sanitation and vitamins as well as tasty dishes. She discussed furnishings with an eye to equipping a home economically and avoiding unnecessary housework. Her purview of home and neighborhood stretched to include urban planning, pollution, and disease prevention. Her discussion of women's lives led to articles on equal pay, the women's club movement, the suffrage campaign, amd extension education as well as portraits of leaders such as Jane Addams, union organizer Lulu Holley, and sculptor Vinnie Ream Howe. After the first few months of publication, stories about nutrition, women's labor, and suffrage came to occupy other parts of the magazine as well.

Suffrage, in fact, was the major issue that expanded the newspapers' concept of women's news since demonstrations and legislative battles were appropriate matter for the front page. After 1890, when the Stanton–Anthony group merged with Lucy Stone's faction, this alliance worked to advance women's rights on both the state and federal levels, leading to the granting of suffrage in Colorado, Utah, Idaho, and Washington by 1910, in ten more states by 1918, and then to a federal campaign. As the marches, meetings, and legislative debate continued, this news moved from the back page to the front page and women writers, such as Emma Bugbee of the New York *Tribune*, went with it. The Prohibition movement similarly showed that what began ostensibly as women's news could rivet the attention of the entire newspaper audience. The Anti-Saloon League of America (ASL), first organized in Ohio from women's groups interested in curbing family violence and improving community life, endorsed like-minded candidates for state government and insisted that citizens be allowed to vote on the granting of each saloon license. As this movement spread to other states, local newspaper writers had to report on rallies, interview participants, and analyze American priorities. By 1916, this news reached the national level as ASL-supported Congress members began pushing for the Eighteenth Amendment, ratified in 1919. Then, the law's effects continued as a "running story which occupied more columns in the twenties than any other," with front page and feature stories that concerned speakeasies and homebrew, organized crime's involvement with bootlegging, and the continuous fight over enforcement (Mott, *American Journalism* 699). Further enlargement of "women's news" occurred during the 1930s through Eleanor Roosevelt's press conferences for women that, as we have seen, involved housekeeping, nutrition, and child care, but also education, scientific developments, and politics.

As a leader among journalists, Emma Bugbee hoped that new generations of women entering the profession would recognize the possibilities for enriching their own careers and the newspapers they worked for through an expanded definition of "women's page." In her first book about the profession, *Peggy Covers the News* (1936), the main character, a student intern on the New York *Tribune*'s women's page, writes an article about a speech at a women's college in which the governor had "launched into an analysis of his attitude toward the major political topics of the year" (96). Peggy's mentor, an experienced, generous professional much like Bugbee herself, encourages her to see this assignment as representative of new possibilities for women's topics:

> The smart thing is to disdain "women's stuff," but "women's stuff" includes everything about churches, charities, schools, flowers, hospitals, art, music and literature, parks, Santa Claus and Easter lilies. It includes all human interest stories—child prodigies and women celebrities in every field from murder to Congress. Women's stuff is pretty nearly everything except fires, riots, and the duller cases in Criminal Courts—and at any moment women may inject themselves into these.
>
> I could never understand this prejudice against women's assignments. By and large, so-called women's news is as much about world politics, balancing the national budget, combating crime, and other difficult topics as it is about cooking and fashions. I long ago learned that, year in and year out, there were as many good assignments in the women's field as anywhere else. Surely, it was woman's stuff when we went to Porto Rico with Mrs. Roosevelt, one of the prize assignments of all time, and it was woman's stuff for the first girl who flew around South America for her paper. The women reporters have been in every interesting news spot, from Siberia to Ethiopia, and have had their heads smashed in riots—well, if not as often as men, at least often enough to be interesting. (99–100)

An enlargement of women's news may have begun at radical journals, but it finally transformed the daily newspaper itself and enabled many women to extend their careers. This expanding subject matter reordered priorities and led to varied philosophies of reporting. At the Boston *Traveler* and in weekly letters printed in the Chicago *Inter-Ocean* and the New Orleans *Times-Democrat*, Lilian Whiting used the personal column, as a biographer commented, to advocate "the woman question, the temperance question, the purity movement, and all those growing reforms" (*Lilian Whiting* 10). In a paper on ethics that she delivered before the American Society of Social Science, Whiting developed a definition of reporting centered on humane themes:

> Reporting is in itself a liberal education in social economics, in conscience, in philanthropy and judgment. The ideal reporter is the interpreter of men and events. He must go sympathetically to the work; he must

respond to its best elements, to that soul of things which is found in every combination of human affairs. While he should strive for accuracy, let it be rather the ideal than the harshly realistic accuracy. Give people and their doings the advantage of the best light, of the largest and most liberal construction. (*Lilian Whiting* 2)

Interpretions of "people and their doings"—which might involve education, religion, marriage, child care, philanthropy, career choices, environmental safety, and other topics—should be the heart of the newspaper, she argued: readers responded to this content since they might be living "every combination of human affairs." And her values did seem to represent those of readers across the country and of editors who had to respond to their preferences. The increasingly lengthy and segmented paper of the late 1930s contained sections on local events, education, religion, features or "living," business, and women's issues as well as a front news section. By that time, at least 80 percent of the newspaper's subject matter had first appeared on the women's page.

Just as the women's page good girl option was so frequently transformed by those women involved with it, so too were the bad stunt girl and sob sister genres changed by college-trained journalists and social scientists: ultimately these women would begin to write about criminal psychology or corporate corruption not as gimmicky characters but as professionals. Ida Tarbell, who began working at *McClure's* after graduating from Allegheny College in 1880 and writing for *The Chautauquan*, proved that a woman could write investigative pieces without adopting any lurid disguise. For her nineteen essays on Standard Oil of New Jersey's evasion of antitrust laws, she conducted research for five years, concentrating especially on the public record, which revealed continuous federal and state legislation against this holding company, beginning at its creation by John D. Rockefeller in 1872. She also relied on testimony garnered from company insiders and from competitors. In a clear and thorough style, her essays document Rockefeller's control over oil production and railroad shipping and then move to his other corporate takeovers while also portraying the man himself. She comments, for example, on his church attendance, philanthropy, and love of family, but then concludes concerning his secret deals with the railroads:

Yet he was willing to strain every nerve to obtain for himself special and illegal privileges from the railroads which were bound to ruin every man in the oil business not sharing them with him. Religious emotion and sentiments of charity, propriety and self-denial seem to have taken the place in him of notions of justice and regard for the rights of others. (79)

Her painstaking research protected *McClure's* from litigation, convinced readers of the essays' veracity, and established Tarbell's career as a serious investigative journalist, a new model for women (Fitzpatrick).

Following Tarbell, other writers entered exposé writing as trained professionals, not stunt girls. Marie Louise Van Vorst, along with her sister-in-law Bessie Van Vorst, worked in several factories, including a cotton mill in Columbia, South Carolina, and a shoe factory in Lynn, Massachusetts, to create a portrait of "The Woman Who Toils," a magazine series that also appeared in book form in 1903 with a preface by Theodore Roosevelt. Bessie Van Vorst's magazine articles on child labor in textile mills appeared in book form as *The Cry of the Children* in 1908. Like Nellie Bly and Annie Laurie, these writers endeavored to use description to portray the reality of downtrodden people and the institutions that controlled them, but they did not have to make themselves into extreme characters to do so. In a section of *The Woman Who Toils* entitled "The Child in the Southern Mills," for example, Marie Van Vorst presents herself as a knowledgable observer of child labor:

> I watch the children crouch on the floor by the frames; some fall asleep with food in their mouths until the overseer rouses them to their tasks again. Here and there totters a little child just learning to walk; it runs and crawls the length of the mill. Mothers who have no one with whom to leave their babies bring them to the workshop, and their lives begin, and continue and end in the horrible pandemonium. (283)

In this section, Marie Van Vorst analyzes the factory system: Northern owners control the mill family's access to food and shelter, dictate their work hours, and require that all children join their parents at work in the mill. In addition to examining physical situations, both writers analyze the values and expectations of women workers and American definitions of them. In a section entitled "Making Clothing in Chicago," for example, Bessie Van Vorst comments that many young women have been taught to see themselves not as laborers contributing to the family's welfare, but as flighty consumers "idolizing of material things," for whom work is a "prostitution to sell the body's health and strength for gewgaws." Young women, she claims, have not learned to respect themselves as able and self-supporting workers (113). She developed her articles, as did her sister-in-law, by applying various theories of history and economics to her observations, not by parading herself as a scantily clothed character at a raucous scene.

Through the effort of journalists such as Bessie Van Vorst and Marie Van Vorst, exposé writing changed radically for women. What had been a sideshow event grew into a serious investigative genre. Redefinitions of this bad girl approach led in the 1930s to the social reportage of writers such as Meridel Le Sueur, who wrote for newspapers and for magazines such as *American Mercury* and *Scribner's*. Such reportage also enriched many newspapers as their news sections developed beyond basic reports of events and legislation to investigative stories on the kidnapping of the Lindbergh baby and the birth of the Dionne quintuplets as well as the Wall Street crash, gangster killings, Gandhi's non-resistance campaign, the overthrow of the Spanish throne, the Japanese conquest of Manchuria, and Hitler's progress in Europe. According to University of Iowa teacher and journalism historian Frank Luther Mott, "the big story, 'played for all it is worth'" was becoming in the 1920s and 1930s "a striking feature of our journalism." With reporters researching all the angles and creating "drama and suspense" in their presentations, such a story could "crowd other matters of more instrinsic value off the front page for days at a time" (*American Journalism* 696). This investigative and feature style of news writing was influenced by women who followed the sob sisters and stunt girls as well as by men who followed the muckrakers.

Before World War II, women redefined newspapers by extending the women's page, the feature story, community news, and the exposé. As women writers wrote for and transformed every section of the newspaper, they were frequently relying on the skills that men viewed as their weaknesses, thus reorienting judgments of appropriate and inappropriate writing techniques long before New Journalism reportage of the 1960s. As we saw in chapter 2, journalism teachers and textbooks that emphasized the limited abilities of women did grant their own special skills. In *Writing and Editing for Women* (1927), a typical text for courses on the women's page, Ethel M. Colson Brazelton of Northwestern University praised women's "natural" penchant for providing the "heart interest," through interviews and other feature stories. This assumed ability to conduct an interview, tell a personal story, describe scenes, and emphasize connections among people could apply to other assignments than interviewing socialites as news became redefined as more than the basic who, what, when, where, and why of elections and lawmaking.

Many women based highly successful and varied careers on exploiting the assumption that they had special skills—while extending these skills and writing styles into new topic areas and new definitions of women's subjects. When Dorothy Thompson left the Lewis Institute and her classes with Edwin Herbert Lewis, she went to Syracuse University where she became a vigorous suffrage campaigner and developed her public speaking skills. She spent the war years in New York writing for an advertising agency and then committed

herself to a freelance career, traveling to Europe in 1920 with her savings of
$150 and from there selling articles to the Associated Press, the International
News Service, the *London Star*, the *Westminster Gazette*, and the *Manchester
Guardian*—especially interviews, which editors judged as an appropriate genre
for her, but with the personal touch or heart interest turned toward breaking
political news. She had the last interview with Mayor Terence MacSwiney of
Cork, the Irish independence leader who died in jail after a seventy-four-day
hunger strike, and she covered riots in Milan of Fiat metalworkers. Then for
Cyrus H. K. Curtis's *Philadelphia Public Ledger*, she conducted an exclusive interview with Emperor Karl and Empress Zita who were trying to regain the
Hapsburg throne and had just been defeated in a second attempt. Because of
her fine record, she was sent to Berlin in 1925 as Central European Bureau
chief for the *Ledger* and for the *New York Evening Post*, another Curtis paper. In
1936 she came to the attention of Helen Rogers Reid, wife of the *Herald Tribune's* publisher Ogden Reid, and started "On the Record," a column of one
thousand words that appeared three times a week, alternating with Walter Lipp-
mann's "Today and Tomorrow." It appeared in 140 papers in 1936 and even
more by the end of the decade, with seven million readers in 1939 (Woloch
459). In a personal tone, using anecdotes as well as statistics, Thompson argued
for many unpopular positions, such as interventionism before World War II and
Arab rights in the Middle East after it. In an April 1939 New York *Herald Tribune* article analyzing the reasons for Neville Chamberlain's enduring popularity with the English, even after Hitler had seized Czechoslovakia, she imagina-
tively compared him to Alice in Wonderland whose qualities, "her niceness, her
reasonability and her incredible foolishness," have great appeal for the English:

> If Alice made a mistake it is because of her innocence, because she is really
> much too nice to live in a world full of falsely labeled bottles and boxes,
> perverted nursery rhymes, vicious old Father Williamses and ugly
> Duchesses. She is confused as misled, but in the end it all turns out to be
> a nightmare.
>
> And she wakes up in her secure nursery, comforted by her tea,
> recalling the shriek of the gryphon, the choking of the suppressed
> guinea pigs and the distant sob of the miserable mock turtle as a fantas-
> tic experience.
>
> Yes, Alice is beloved by England because of her unconquerable
> simplicity.
>
> And so, strange as it may seem to any type of mind except the Eng-
> lish, it is extremely probable that Mr. Chamberlain is stronger in his lead-
> ership because he turned out to be wrong than he would have been had
> he been always right. (229)

Because of her ability to exploit all writing styles—to talk about Alice as well as the specific treacheries of Nazi sympathizers—Thompson was featured on a *Times* magazine cover on June 12, 1939, along with Eleanor Roosevelt, as one of the two most influential women in America.

Anne O'Hare McCormick made her name in the 1920s and 1930s with her own innovative coverage of European developments, especially Mussolini's rise to power in Italy, journalistic opportunities she secured by emphasizing her ability to tell a personal story. McCormick was from Columbus, Ohio, where she went to the College of Saint Mary of the Springs. After graduation, her family moved to Cleveland where she and her mother worked for the weekly *Catholic Universe Bulletin*. They next moved to Dayton where she worked as a freelancer for a decade, writing articles for the *New York Times Magazine* and poetry for *Smart Set* and *Bookman*. After Carl V. Van Anda, managing editor, gave her a traveling columnist position, she sent dispatches to the *New York Times* from throughout Europe and then, in 1922, began a thrice-weekly column on foreign affairs called "In Europe" and later "Abroad," relying on personal experience and interviews as well as analysis. She wrote exclusively for the *Times* after 1925, except for a series on Europe published in the *Ladies Home Journal* in 1933 and 1934 in which, long before other journalists, she recognized the growing power of Mussolini and Hitler. When Arthur Hays Sulzberger became managing editor of the *Times* in 1935, he placed McCormick on the editorial board (Belford 165–74). In 1937, she was the first woman to win a Pulitzer Prize in journalism and the only winner in the history of the Pulitzer for a body of important work rather than a particular article. She stayed at the *Times* for thirty-two years, spanning the period between the wars and the Cold War. She interviewed Mussolini, Hitler, Chamberlain, Stalin, and Churchill, as well as the citizens affected by their decisions, and competed for readers with Dorothy Thompson.

In her pieces, McCormick frequently used dramatic physical description, as in this scene intended to show the complex possibilities for progress in a Southern town that had recently become the site of a cotton mill:

> Drenched peach trees blossomed on the hillsides, aslant like the cottages, which straggled like stilts along climbing rods of red clay, now wet and slippery. White bath tubs in wooden crates were dumped in front of the houses, while little ells, evidently intended to be bathrooms, were being hammered up at the back. (Sheehan 42)

She tried, as with this sample dialogue on the effects of the Depression in 1932, to explain clearly how people felt about their government and their lives:

> The nearest thing to a political revolution in this country is the tax revolt. For the first time in a generation taxpayers are wrought up to the point of willingness to give up public services. "We'll do without county agents," they say. "We'll give up the public health service. We can no longer pay the cost of government." In many districts taxes are practically non-collectible. (Sheehan 93)

McCormick conducted many interviews with Franklin Roosevelt, letting Americans into his priorities and his style, exploiting her skill at description to bring readers, for example, into the vitality of the Executive Mansion in New York where "people seem to wander in and out, glancing at the telegrams on the hall table, eavesdropping if they will, examining the books piled up on the tables in all the rooms, in variety like a circulating library of current publications" (Sheehan 129). But she also analyzed his immense appeal with the American public, providing this analysis on the eve of his first presidential election: "When all is said and done, the Lochinvar who rides out of the East will ride on his personality, on his zest and gusto and confidence, on his eighteen-carat American background, on the blind desire to punish and to change, which is the mood of crisis" (Sheehan 137). Her subsequent essays further analyzed Roosevelt's use of his connection with the electorate to manipulate Congress and create an aura of positive action.

On the front page and the women's page, and on every other page of a newspaper, women writers wrote about traditional men's and women's subjects, adopting accepted newspaper styles and exploiting the more personal and creative styles deemed as their special territory. Newspaper owners and editors might cling to the "newspaperman" aura, but women writers had redefined the content, style, and audience of the American daily.

FROM JOURNALISM TO FICTION AND BACK AGAIN

As they transformed their assigned good and bad girl genres, women changed the style and structure of the American newspaper. And, as they altered definitions of journalism and journalist, they frequently also began writing fic-. tion as well. In 1917, Helen M. Bennett, manager of the Chicago Collegiate Bureau of Occupations, remarked on this trend of moving from the newspaper to the novel in her study, *Women and Work*: "The number of recognized [women] writers in America today who have come from the newspaper group seems astonishingly large to one who has not realized the newspaper is a great training-school for writers" (265). This influence is more commonly noted in the careers of early twentieth-century male writers such as John Dos

Passos and Ernest Hemingway who learned at the newspaper to respond to political issues, work from specific details, and rely on a concise style, but the city room also served as a laboratory for women. Researchers for the Southern Woman's Educational Alliance in 1927 concluded that at least half of the women who wrote fiction and poetry had begun their careers with newspaper work (Hatcher 110).

At newspapers, women got a chance to study contemporary women's issues, such as equal rights and family law, that would find their way into fictional form. There, much more frequently than the men, they also experimented with various styles and genres, such as the feature story, interview, column, and review, that had close ties to fiction. Willa Cather, for example, began writing for the *Nebraska State Journal* during her junior year after Will Owen Jones, the young managing editor who taught journalism part-time at the university, recommended her to editor and publisher Charles Gere. She first wrote a column called "One Way of Putting It," creating short vignettes on daily life, and then she also began to contribute regular theatre reviews. In 1927, she wrote a tribute to Gere for the *Journal's* sixtieth anniversary, emphasizing the creative license she enjoyed there:

> I was paid one dollar a column, which was certainly all my high-stepping rhetoric was worth. Those out-pourings were pretty dreadful, but . . . he let me step as high as I wished. It was rather hard on his readers, perhaps, but it was good for me, because it enabled me to riot in fine writing until I got to hate it, and began slowly to recover. (Woodress 84)

After she left college, Susan Glaspell joined the staff of the *Des Moines Daily News* as a state house and legislative reporter. By 1900, she was writing regular human interest sketches, under the title "The News Girl," using a young narrator who with comic innocence reported on the circus, a farm, travels about town, and other events, columns in which she employed the style and structure of fiction. In 1901, she quit her job to write short stories: "After less than two years of newspaper reporting I boldly gave up my job and went home to Davenport to give all my time to my own writing. I say boldly, because I had to earn my living." She published short stories from 1903 to 1922 and then turned to the novel and play (Waterman 17–20).

Not all who tread the ground from journalism to fiction just did so once; many women established varied careers incorporating parts of both and moving back and forth. Mildred Gilman, who had served as the first woman editor of the *Wisconsin Literary Magazine* while she was an undergraduate, got a reporting job at the New York *Journal* in 1928 because the city editor assumed she had newspaper experience since her novel *Headlines* presented fictionalized accounts of stories that had appeared in newspapers, a mistake Gilman did not correct and a blurring of genres that continued throughout her career. After interviewing criminals and victims, she left the newspaper to write *Sob Sister* as well as two more novels before returning to daily journalism in 1934, covering Eleanor Roosevelt and the New Deal for the *Herald*, and contributing freelance pieces to magazines (Belford 243–53).

A SAMPLING OF TEXTS:
THE DEVELOPMENT OF NEW VOICES IN FICTION

As women moved from journalism into fiction and poetry, they again encountered restricted possibilities. As they had found in journalism, their major acceptable option with publishers and readers was a type of good girl fiction, a continuation of the nineteenth-century tradition of sentimental poetry and of prose tales about simple girls doing good deeds. While teaching at the Allegheny High School, Willa Cather began her professional career with *April Twilights* (1903), a collection of poetry containing stylized reflections on Greek and Roman mythology and on nature. Here she speaks, for example, of a romantic love occurring in meadows and in bowers:

> Across the shimmering meadows—
> Ah, when he came to me!
> In the spring time,
> In the night time,
> In the starlight,
> Beneath the hawthorn tree.
>
> Up from the misty marsh land—
> Ah, when he climbed to me!
> To my white bower,
> To my sweet rest,
> To my sweet breast,
> Beneath the hawthorn tree.
>
> ("The Hawthorn Tree" 1–12)

In eighty-three stories about her hometown of Portage, Wisconsin, published from 1908 to 1919, Zona Gale successfully launched her own career as a sentimental moralist. In her idyllic Friendship Village, sixty-year-old Calliope March serves as the wise advisor to younger people. Her amiable friend

Amanda Toplady sooths her husband Timothy who worries and talks inces-santly. The young minister Abel Halsey listens carefully to the problems of each parishioner, including humorous but kindly characters such as Dick Dasher, the train engineer, and Peleg Bemus, the woodcutter. As husbands leave for work and children for school, mothers happily shape their lives by their weekly cal-endar of Washday, Ironday, Mend-day, Bakeday, Freeday, Scrubday, and Sunday. In *East Wind: West Wind* (1930), a book formed from two short stories, Pearl Buck began her writing career by advocating traditional women's values even as she described an exotic locale. Fully described are her Chinese heroine Kwei-lan's love for her family home, her distress over misunderstandings with her new husband, and her joy over the birth of her son, all emotions and scenes that made both a Chinese story and a woman writer acceptable to the Ameri-can reading public.

Like college-educated women working at newspapers and magazines, these writers soon moved beyond a restricted set of choices regarding their content, genre, and style. They, in fact, chose the same two options being explored in journalism: to abandon the tradition of writing solely about women's lives and to retheorize what writing about women might be. With support from group allegiances, they experimented with political, social, and personal subjects and with various writing styles and genres, abandoning expected norms, as had Bugbee, Hickok, Fleeson, and so many other women journalists. And, as also happened at American newspapers, the public responded positively to such creative endeavors. Of the twenty-two Pulitzer Prizes given for fiction between 1918 and 1940, eleven went to women, including Willa Cather, Edna Ferber, Julia Peterkin, Margaret Ayers Barnes, Pearl Buck, Josephine Johnson, and Marjorie Kinnan Rawlings. And many of the other popular novels of this time period, such as *My Antonia, Miss Lulu Bett, The Good Earth, Death Comes for the Archbishop, Gone with the Wind*, and *The Yearling*, also came from women's pens and typewriters. Even as these books won readers and acclaim, however, critics often reacted with dismay over their departures from acceptable female fiction as well as from male literary tradi-tions, revealing an awareness, and even fear, of this breaking up of traditionally enscribed circles.

By the 1920s, many texts illustrated the wide range of new choices embraced by American women as they exercised the option of moving away from traditional women's subjects and forms. In *The Making of Americans*, writ-ten from 1906 to 1911 and published in 1925, Gertrude Stein worked more with abstractions than with the specific details that were supposedly a woman's milieu. Reflecting her interest in modern psychology and each individual's stream of consciousness, her focus ultimately concerns not plot or character, but the author's mind as she meditates on the subject. In this story of two migrating families, Stein frequently repeats the same character names, introduces characters and never returns to them again, and moves families to various cities, creating a swirl of people and places through which she can consider family and personality types in an abstract and philosophical manner, an emphasis furthered by the lack of dialogue and the use of long, contemplative sentences. The end of Book I and beginning of Book II extend her analytical perspective through discursions on human personality, on recognizing the "bottom nature" of people, in novels and in life. By Book III, the focus is almost entirely on the author's consciousness ruminating on her subject. Like her friends Matisse and Picasso, Stein wanted to work with a lack of temporal specificity, creating a story that readers would have to make into a whole, just as they had to "assemble" a composite personality for anyone they might meet.

In *Death Comes for the Archbishop* (1927)—written four years after she had bought and destroyed as many copies of *April Twilights* as she could find and had published a second edition without thirteen of the original poems—Cather shows the complexity of her own developing vision and style loosed from the traditional territories of women's writing. The story concerns Father Jean Marie Latour who came to New Mexico from Ontario in 1851 as vicar. In the novel, his story is told not chronologically but imagistically, interwoven with descriptions of desert country, Mexican customs, adobe towns, an often corrupt clergy, missionaries' journeys, Indian rituals and legends, and frontier heroes and bandits. Here, like Stein, Cather uses time as a stream to go fishing in as she considers the intricate connections between past and present and the rich process by which events become meaningful to individuals and to history.

In *Pity Is Not Enough* (1933), Josephine Herbst presents characters whose stories continue in two more novels, with the emphasis on tracing the historical impact of the capitalist system on a family and on America, not on creating one kindly woman character who would require protection from it. After the Civil War, Joe Trexler leaves his family in Philadelphia and goes out to seek his fortune. He becomes the scapegoat for a railroad scandal in Atlanta and must leave there and change his name; he fails to succeed as a gold miner in the Dakota Territories as corrupt mine owners cheat him of his profits. His brother David, however, settles in Oregon where he buys a drugstore and later becomes a powerful banker, turning his back on his destitute family as his fortunes increase. Throughout the novel, these brothers' stories are interspersed with moments in the future, such as when Joe and David's sister tells her four daughters about the adventurousness of Joe and the fine successes of David, creating a romantic past as the family faces impending bankruptcy and the loss of their small farm. As these girls grow older—Herbst intersperses details about them with the story of their uncles—their own experience makes them reevaluate this received picture of a romantic and glorious American past. When they come to Seattle toward the end of World War I and become involved in a general strike there, they begin to see both brothers as victims of a bankrupt American dream: they find no true success or glory in their family stories or in an expanding, materialistic America.

These texts might seemed allied with different literary movements—modernism, regionalism, symbolism, and social realism—but they share an emphasis not traditionally available to women writers, on the larger confluences of the mind, time, history, and cultural change. Such experiments with novelistic form often received a positive response. Marianne Moore, for example, commented in *The Dial* that *The Making of Americans* was one of the few "extraordinary interpretations of American life": as "a truly psychological exposition of American living," it exhibited "great firmness in the method" ("The Spare American Emotion" 46–47). Robert Lovett aptly described *Death Comes for the Archbishop* as containing an "interlacing of theme, a shifting of material, which breaks the flat surface of the narrative into facets from which the light is variously reflected" (Review). But other critics expressed their puzzlement over such new formations and claimed that what these women were writing might be interesting and new, but could not be classified as novels. *The Making of Americans*, for example, seemed to critic George Knox to be a parody of the Great American Novel, a "super-spoof of the tradition," not a serious effort (679). Biographer Michael J. Hoffman discussed another typical response: Stein had produced an analysis of history or of personality types but her text lacked the chronology and specific detail of a novel (44–45). *Death Comes for the Archbishop* received the same variety of marginalizing labels. Echoing a familiar refrain that women wrote too much about goodness to be taken seriously, Frances Robbins claimed that Cather could be called a hagiographer but not a novelist; Maxwell Geismar labeled this book and *Shadows on the Rock* as "tracts of divine love and of golden goodness" (200). The use of real historical events also seemed to disqualify this work from exhibiting real literary worth: R. A. Taylor in the *Spectator* claimed that "it's not really a novel; and since it seems left in a halfway condition, one wishes it were" (894). Seldon Rodman in the *Saturday Review of Literature* praised Herbst's trilogy of which *Pity is Not Enough* was the first installment for "the social vision which the author shares with her young friends"; he thought, however, that these texts would not qualify as novels but as one "historical document" that was "refreshingly unliterary," crafted without the stylistic creativity of the novel.

Willa Cather found this hedging and renaming to be preposterous and felt that she must restate basic genre definitions to remind critics that the circle of fiction could contain her work as well as the experimentations of Dos Passos, Fitzgerald, Hemingway, and other male authors. In a letter to *Commonweal* in November 1927, although she first indicates that she is willing to use a different term, she then asserts her right to "novel":

> I am amused that so many reviews of this book begin with the statement: "This book is hard to classify." Then why bother? Many more assert vehemently that it is not a novel. Myself, I prefer to call it a narrative. In this case I think that term more appropriate. But a novel, it seems to me, is merely a work of imagination in which a writer tried to present the experiences and emotions of a group of people by the light of his own. That is what he really does. ("On *Death Comes*" 962)

When writers of many diverse interests, such as Cather, Stein, and Herbst, experimented with new subjects and styles, the first reaction was that they were not entering the circle of novelists and could not enlarge that circle through their own work. Like the first women students that Robert Herrick and Rollo Brown observed at writing workshop tables, these writers were being judged as ineligible to join that privileged group of American writers, an anxious reaction to the fact that a broadening of American literature was indeed occurring.

As women expanded the purview of their writing, backed by the support of colleagues and clubs, they also reconceptualized the nature of a fiction about women, moving beyond the piteous good girl to many new portrayals. Zona Gale envisioned these transformations as creating "the novel of tomorrow": she called for women to abandon the traditional portrayal of love as "a matter of bright feathers, of the *pas de seul* before the cave door, our only advance from that cave door courting being that there are antiphonal feathers and dancing instead of masculine antics alone" ("The Novel of Tomorrow" 68). To replace simplistic and demeaning formulations, she posited a fiction that would feature women as not just possessions to deck out and admire. She wanted to look at the heroic and tragic as they appeared in women situated in their own locales, leading "ordinary" lives whose physical details could reach to emotional truth:

> I think of the cry of a farm woman: "The grain burned up, the clover didn't catch, the corn hung small in the ear." Hebraic that, biblical in its

bitter cry against her lot—Greek, rather, in her woe before fate. I think
of the Winnebago Indian woman who, at fifty-odd, had a wish to live in
a house. She, who had never lived save in a wigwam, had a wish a raise
her standard of living, to have a sewing machine and curtains. Once one
gave her a yellow rose, and she threw back her head and said in the Winnebago tongue and with half-closed eyes: "Last night I dreamed of flowers." Material for fiction—but no more truly so than when this Indian
woman asked a neighbor to telephone to a friend: "We don't want my
son-in-law here no more. If you would please take him away." In any of
these multiple incidents it is not—and here lies the magic—it is not the
incident itself which is the material for fiction; no one could make a *tale*
of any of these. But it is that which lies within, and it is the comple-
menting power to be amazed and bemused by them, to be thrown into
a mood and then to induce a mood in others—in a current of emotion.
("Writing as Design" 33)

Gale is discussing the creation of a literature not determined by the genres and
subjects of a male literary elite, but one that might spring from women's own
experience, expressed through complex combinations of dialogue, description,
and analysis as in the developing "women's page" journalism. While literary historians frequently discuss American literature by referring to movements such
as realism and naturalism and to the male writers that inhabit these categories,
this first group of women who graduated from college and began writing
careers created literature that was very successful and influential but did not
adhere to accepted forms and labels. With substantial training and with their
own networks of mentors and colleagues, these writers did not have to conform to the avant-garde literary movements or to older traditions of what
women's writing should be.

   Many women created characters who were undergoing the same steps
toward growth and independence that the authors themselves had trod, involving them in a variety of situations and decisions not encountered in the
woman-as-saintly-victim literature of the nineteenth century. Like those texts
concerning the choice of a writing career that we examined in chapter 4, these
books emphasize for readers the ways in which women have been repressed
and the independent steps they have taken to end that repression. These are stories that investigate patriarchal society and talk plainly about women's limited
choices while also aiming to portray the magic of "that which lies within,"
Gale's goal for the "novel of tomorrow."

   Gale's best-selling novel, *Miss Lulu Bett* (1920), as well as the subsequent
play adaptation of the same name, presents the woman character fully entwined
in family bonds and small-town propriety and investigates the possible means

of escape. Unmarried at thirty-three, Lulu, along with her senile mother, must live in the home of her sister, whose husband, Dwight Deacon, expects her to do all the household chores in return for financial support. Her sister's complete dependence and sense of insecurity have made her ineffectual in handling even the daily decisions of a household. Lulu's own desire for rebellion and independence goes unsatisfied, however, for she finds no choice other than the endless household routine that she well understands: "Nobody cares what becomes of me after they're fed." In a mock ceremony during a rare trip to town, Lulu is married to Dwight's brother, a union that is legal because Dwight is a justice of the peace. When Lulu finds out that the brother has another wife, she must return home and face public humiliation. Lulu finally leaves the household through marriage to a music store owner who recognizes the terrible price that she paid in the traditional home. When Gale wrote the play adaptation for Broadway, she had Lulu leave the household on her own, with her mother saying to the sister, "Who's going to do your work now, I'd like to know?" as the final line.

Agnes Smedley's *Daughter of Earth* (1929) provides another complex picture of women's duty, respectability, and economic dependence. The child Marie grows up in poverty with a father who drinks his earnings, beats her mother, and often leaves the family destitute. Marie realizes that unless she rebels against her destiny, she will face a miserable future: "I might have remained in the mining towns all my life, married some working man, borne him a dozen children to wander the face of the earth, and died in my early thirties" (123). Her one role model is her mother's sister Helen, who becomes a prostitute to earn money for the family, a choice that gives her a type of independence not found in marriage. Helen's hard path enables Marie, and Smedley's readers, to consider the dependencies and degradation of women:

> The "respectability" of married women seemed to rest in their acceptance of servitude and inferiority. Men don't like free, intelligent women. I considered that before marriage men have relations with women, and nobody thought it wrong—they were but "sowing their wild oats." Nobody spoke of "fallen men" or men who had "gone wrong" or been "ruined." Then why did they speak so of women? I found the reason! Women had to depend upon men for a living; a woman who made her own living, and would always do so, could be as independent as men. That was why people did not condemn men. (189)

In marrying twice, Marie strives for an equitable type of companionship but finds that daily interactions even with supposedly liberated men, one Scandinavian and one Indian, do not allow for such a possibility. In both cases, the husband's reactions to sexual realities—her exhaustion after an abortion and her rape by one of the husband's comrades—end the relationship. Marie finally walks away from all family duties, forcing her father to care for her younger brothers. Freed from her father and husbands, she finds the freedom to work among comrades, become a journalist, and to get, as the final lines indicate, "out of this house . . . out of this country . . ." (406).

In *The Good Earth* (1931), another Pulitzer Prize winner, Pearl S. Buck also created a complex woman character in O-lan, providing details that the readers must make into a whole and judge for themselves. O-lan begins as a slave working in the kitchen of the Hwang estate, and from there she is married to Wang Lung, a poor farmer. She works in the fields, gathers wood for fuel, and keeps his clothing mended. She wants her first son to be dressed in finery and makes special cakes for their return to the Hwang household during New Year's festivities; she feels vengeful toward those who were once her owners as well as proud of her new life. When her family has to abandon their home during a drought, she strangles her newborn daughter because she knows that she cannot feed and protect the infant on the road. In the city, along with her husband, she steals jewels from an abandoned home to get money to return to the farm. O-lan is realistic and tries to move her family forward; she attempts to manipulate her husband through long campaigns of silence since she has no other real means of influencing him, especially after he brings his concubine into their home. Of her, critic Oscar Cargill wrote: "Earth of the earth-earthy, she triumphs in the end over her rivals, though her ugliness goes clear to the bone" (149).

In *Their Eyes Were Watching God* (1937), Zora Neale Hurston uses layers of narration to tell a story about a woman silenced and about her final entrance into a community of speakers and listeners. As a little girl, Janie is named and renamed by others on the farm so often that she is called Alphabet; her grandmother, who has been a slave, tells her that she will not achieve a separate identity but instead will become, like all black women, "de mule uh de world," responding to any name or need that a man utters (29). Janie tells stories to her friend Phoeby concerning her first husband, a landowner whom she was forced to marry, and her second husband, the "big voice" mayor of an African American town, both of whom had renamed Janie as the silent, dutiful wife. The mayor speaks for her when she is asked to talk at a town dedication ceremony; she talks only to herself when other people swap tales on a store porch. When she finally gives her own speech in which she compares her husband to Abraham Lincoln, the townspeople recognize her linguistic skills and thus her possibilities for involvement in the town: "Yo wife is uh born orator, Starks. Us never knowed dat befo'" (92). Her confidence growing, she then uses insults to publicly humiliate her tyrannical husband and runs away with Tea Cake, a younger man who introduces her to a new language of emotion. As Janie speaks to Phoeby, Hurston at times provides an omniscient narration, as though she is entering into a community with these two women, a group whose interactions are enriched by stories told by Janie's grandmother. At the novel's end, Phoeby and other women have heard Janie's story, and she reenters the town through her own voice.

Like women journalists who expanded the subject and style of newspapers, these novelists have been highly influential in expanding the scope of American fiction, although their influence has not been frequently acknowledged. Gertrude Stein's experiments with "no plot, no representationalism, no causal sequence of events, and non-referential, therefore self-contained movement" certainly influenced the "Lost Generation," as Hemingway recognized in *The Sun Also Rises*, but also authors of the "Beat Generation" such as Allen Ginsberg and Jack Kerouac as well as French "New Novelists" such as Alain Robbe-Grillet and Marguerite Duras (Knapp 10). Pearl Buck's multicultural lens has also been employed by Maxine Hong Kingston, Amy Tan, Toni Morrison, and other authors. The social reform message and feminist analysis of power structures found in Smedley's *Daughters of Earth* reached fruition again in Alice Walker, Doris Lessing, May Sarton, Adrienne Rich, and many other writers. The family and marriage traps laid in *Miss Lulu Bett* echo in the work of Anne Tyler, Ann Beattie, and Gloria Naylor. The new more complex regionalism of Willa Cather continued in Carson McCullers, Flannery O'Connor, and Louise Erdrich. And Hurston, as Alice Walker claimed, pointed the way for African American authors to represent the fullness of their experience, not just an intellectualized portion that white readers might find reassuring. After World War II, as women and men formed their new networks of professionals, they had before them an expanding palette of possibilities with which to begin making their own strokes.

As the first generations of college-educated writers developed their careers, both in journalism and the creative genres, they took on many themes and topics and did not limit themselves to any one view of women—or of anything. As they created portraits of women and of men, of society and of human rights, women writers reversed earlier conclusions about the writing styles appropriate to them. At first, as women's page writers, they could only provide fashion, home, or love advice laced with private details and "heart interest." Analysis of politics or cultural history, consideration of motives, intricate symbolism—these were best left to the men. In early fiction, women were expected to write solely about the moral woman reforming the home; creation of other types of culturally influential literature was best left to the men. But women writers who succeeded in their careers after World War I, however, worked diligently to remove such limited expectations and definitions from their work. The criticism they faced could be strident: their work, in fact, was marginalized as "not a novel" or "not a newspaper story" when it did not correspond to accepted genre definitions, and thus the woman could be portrayed as not a "real" novelist or journalist. But these small circles of right and wrong, of male and female, did not hold as these writers worked within groups to experiment with all topics and styles and thus to recreate American writing.

CONCLUSION

It's women who demand things of each other;
women who accomplish do it because they are dri-
ven by sisters or aunts or frank and brutal female
friends—like you!

—Julia Schwartz, *Elinor's College Career*

As we have seen, *A Room of One's Own* and *The Second Sex* provide a bleak picture of the early twentieth century, of women cast as the Other, outside of circles of influence and separated from their own experiences and talents. These
texts describe women writers as unable to discover or express their ideas fully
because of the patriarchal constraints on their education, their time, and their
reputations. The bleak pictures in these two books, however, do not fully apply
to the American situation. Before World War II, women writers were very
influential in both creative writing and journalism; in both arenas, by adopting
a working method derived from college experiences, they carved out a space
to explore new topics and genres and thereby to challenge accepted definitions
of what writing might be.

Since the publication of these two books, their depiction of woman as
Other has informed many feminist arguments. In *The Feminine Mystique* (1963),
for example, Betty Friedan discussed American women's involvement in the
suffrage movement as a temporary movement beyond the restrictive circles
described by Woolf and de Beauvoir, one that ended with their gaining the
vote. Then, women assumed active work roles during World War II but had to
return home when veterans needed jobs and rapidly growing industries needed
placid but shopping-ready suburban housewives to buy their new products. The
isolation of these two brief moments—the suffrage campaign and World War
II—during which women altered their identification as Other gave Friedan a

clear history to discuss, with moments to celebrate and to war against: women had twice shown their abilities and needs and they needed to regain their drive and fight against the suburban "problem with no name," finding a means of achieving not another high point but a lasting public role and continuing opportunities for personal development.

In 1970 in *The Female Eunuch*, Germaine Greer reconstructed this history, arguing that the suffragists' influence continued into the 1920s but that in every other decade women acquiesced to male structures and priorities. On the first page of the introduction, to state this thesis, she makes the following claim:

> After the ecstasy of direct action, the militant ladies of two generations ago settled down to the work of consolidation in hosts of small organizations, while the main force of their energy filtered away in post-war retrenchments and the revivals of frills, corsets and femininity after the permissive twenties, through the sexual sell of the fifties, ever dwindling ever more respectable. (1)

With this version of the past established, Greer can label her own generation as heroes of a clearly demarcated "second feminist wave" and, through comparison to suffrage, focus on the best means of keeping the 1960s movement alive.

As feminist theorists of the 1970s and 1980s proposed more radical cultural critiques, they reread the past without admitting to any moments of influence and growth. Instead, this group of theorists posited a history in which women had never been able to tell their own truths, never been able to influence others. In their call for a new *écriture féminine*, Hèléne Cixous and Catherine Clément argued that

> we are not culturally accustomed to speaking, throwing signs out toward a scene, employing the suitable rhetoric. . . . It is in writing, from woman and toward woman, and accepting the challenge of the discourse controlled by the phallus, that woman will affirm woman somewhere other than in silence, the place reserved for her in and through the Symbolic. May she get out of booby-trapped silence! (92–93)

Recognizing her indebtedness to Simone de Beauvoir, Cixous calls for women to abandon their attempts to identify with the male Self and to "write her self":

> I shall speak about women's writing: about *what it will do*. Woman must write her self: must write about women and bring women to writing, from which they have been driven away as violently as from their bodies—for the same reasons, by the same law, with the same fatal goal. Woman must put herself into the text—as into the world and into history—by her own movement. (245)

In response, many social-constructionist theorists have questioned Cixous's val-
orization of the relationship between the individual woman's body and her creation of texts. Toril Moi criticizes Cixous for naively asserting some unclearly
defined body-derived voice, but she doesn't deny Cixous's argument that generations of women have been inured in a "booby-trapped silence." Teachers
who advocate the collaborative writing class as a means of allowing women
access to a community of thinkers and learners, like those discussed in the
introduction, also seem to assume that they have not frequently had such experiences before.

　　While feminists continue to debate the reasons for women's silence and
the best means of seeking change, they have recognized that American women
did write many fine texts before 1940. The Feminist Press, for example,
reprinted Smedley's *Daughter of Earth*, Margaret Walker's *How I Wrote Jubilee and
Other Essays on Life and Literature*, and Josephine Herbst's *Rope of Gold* as well
as anthologies of stories by Zora Neale Hurston, Margery Latimer, and Meridel
Le Sueur. These texts, however, are presented within a discussion of the terrible isolation the authors felt, their difficulty in finding publishers, their role as
singular voices crying in the wilderness. Although the afterword of the Feminist Press' edition of *Daughter of Earth* details the many groups within which
Agnes Smedley developed her political theory and her writing, Alice Walker's
introduction claims that the desperate and isolated heroine Marie in this novel
"*is* Agnes Smedley, and through her story we glimpse the stories of countless
others who could not speak and who, in any event, were never intended to be
heard." Smedley's "acuteness of perception," Walker argued as did Virginia Woolf
concerning Shakespeare's sister, caused her "unrelieved pain, a sign of an
extremely loving and sensitive soul—virtually helpless before the forces
destroying all around it—being tortured to death" (2–3). Given the feminist
metaphors used to describe the decades in which Smedley worked, she had to
be portrayed as a mistreated waif voyaging on alone.

　　Although historians and theorists needed to stress the past isolation of
women and the lack of respect for their work—and they certainly pointed to
difficulties that did exist—we should not let rhetorical strategies blind us to a
larger picture of these years, and to the impact of women writers and their
texts. We can learn not just from their products but from their processes, from
women working as individual writers and within a variety of groups, a successful means of breaking through the accepted circles of earlier generations.

　　For what these women really did was define collaboration for women.
In *Elinor's College Career* (1906), Julia Schwartz focused on the group's role in
providing the motivation for creative work. In this novel, the four roommates

discuss reasons that so many women had given up on writing: the needs of families, the control of men, the inadequacy of their professional training. But Derrick, their leader, posits that what women have lacked is an ongoing form of group commitment, similar to what these roommates experienced in college:

> Why do you write poetry, Fran?—Al? Because you're simply bursting with something that has to be said? Pooh! You write it because you want my approval, I write it because I want yours—or because I want to surprise my family pleasantly some day. . . . It's women who demand things of each other; women who accomplish do it because they are driven by sisters or aunts or frank and brutal female friends—like you! (150)

Her friends are dismayed that she gives them no higher motive than writing for approval, but she has isolated the importance of the group in their own lives, and in the lives of so many other writers of their generation.

Whether they went to college to seek training or developed an interest in writing there, many women like Schwartz found this community in college. While they were still in school and immediately after, they envisioned, for readers and for themselves, what a writing life would be like if they faced the struggles alone, without the continuing support of such groups. But, even as they wrote about that bleak reality, they set out to avoid it, with the cushion, the connection, the identification of group involvements. In networks of friends and colleagues, in clubs, in graduate workshops, and in political organizations, they forged a method from which they never retreated. With the support of such groups, they assumed voices of authority without denying the isolation of writing and the dedication it requires. And, although definitions of women's writing—of an *écriture féminine*—have been debated recently, we see its actual creation here in women's claiming as their territory all of history, politics, religion, social mores, and individual consciousness, described through many forms of narrative and analysis. The paths of these writers, and the products they created, reveal the great energy and creativity of the collaborative environment—in classrooms and club meetings, with teachers who fully understood the method's purposes and those who did not, with women only and both women and men, with college students and older groups—for expanding the circles of expression and influence, for expanding the circle of Writer.

WORKS CITED

Abstract of the Fifteenth Census of the United States: 1930. Washington: GPO, 1933.

Abstract of the Fourteenth Census of the United States: 1920. Washington: GPO, 1923.

Adams, Hannah. *The History of the Jews from the Destruction of Jerusalem to the Nineteenth Century.* 2 vols. Boston: Eliot, 1812.

———. *Memoir of Miss Hannah Adams Written by Herself with Additional Notices by a Friend.* Boston: Gray and Bowen, 1832.

———. *A Summary History of New-England.* Dedham, MA: Mann and Adams, 1799.

———. *The Truth and Excellence of the Christian Religion Exhibited.* Boston: West, 1804.

Adams, Katherine H. *A History of Professional Writing Instruction in American Colleges.* Dallas: Southern Methodist UP, 1993.

———. *Progressive Politics and the Training of America's Persuaders.* Mahwah, NJ: Erlbaum, 1999.

Aldrich, Bess Streeter. *A Lantern in Her Hand.* New York: Grosset & Dunlap, 1928.

———. *Miss Bishop.* New York: Grosset & Dunlap, 1933.

———. *The Rim of the Prairie.* New York: Appleton, 1925.

———. *A White Bird Flying.* 1931. Lincoln: U of Nebraska P, 1988.

Alexandria. Alexandria, VA: Williams, 1939.

Allen, Annie Ware Winsor. *Home, School and Vacation: A Book of Suggestions.* Boston: Houghton, 1907.

———. *Without and Within.* New York: Vantage, 1952.

Ammons, Elizabeth. *Conflicting Stories: American Women Writers at the Turn into the Twentieth Century.* New York: Oxford UP, 1991.

Anderson, George K. *Bread Loaf School of English: The First Fifty Years.* Middlebury: Middlebury College, 1969.

Annas, Pamela J. "Silences: Feminist Language Research and the Teaching of Writing." *Teaching Writing: Pedagogy, Gender, and Equity.* Ed. Cynthia L. Caywood and Gillian R. Overing. Albany: State U of New York P, 1987. 3–17.

Anthony, Katharine Susan. *Catherine the Great.* New York: Knopf, 1925.

———. *Dolly Madison: Her Life and Times.* Garden City, NY: Doubleday, 1949.

———. *Feminism in Germany and Scandinavia.* New York: Holt, 1915.

———. *Louisa May Alcott.* New York: Knopf, 1938.

———. *Margaret Fuller: A Psychological Biography.* New York: Harcourt, 1920.

———. *Marie Antoinette.* New York: Knopf, 1933.

———. *Mothers Who Must Earn.* New York: Survey, 1914.

———. *Queen Elizabeth.* Garden City, NY: Garden City Publishing, 1929.

———. *Susan B. Anthony: Her Personal History and Her Era.* Garden City, NY: Doubleday, 1954.

Arnow, Harriette. *Mountain Path.* New York: Convici-Friede, 1936.

Ashton-Jones, Evelyn. "Collaboration, Conversation, and the Politics of Mankind." *Feminine Principles and Women's Experience in American Composition and Rhetoric.* Ed. Louise Wetherbee Phelps and Janet Emig. Pittsburgh: U of Pittsburgh P, 1995. 5–26.

Atherton, Gertrude. *Adventures of a Novelist.* New York: Liveright, 1932.

———. *California, The Land of Dreams.* Hollywood: Hollywood Print Shop, 1921.

Ault, Warren O. *Boston University: The College of Liberal Arts, 1873–1973.* Boston: Boston U, 1973.

Bain, David Haward, and Mary Smyth Duffy. *Whose Words These Are: A History of the Bread Loaf Writers' Conference, 1926–1992.* Hopewell, NJ: Ecco, 1993.

Banks, Elizabeth L. *The Autobiography of a "Newspaper Girl."* London: Methuen, 1902.

Barnard, Mary. *Assault on Mount Helicon: A Literary Memoir.* Berkeley: U of California P, 1984.

Bates, Arlo. *Talks on Teaching Literature.* Boston: Houghton, 1906.

Bates, Esther Willard. *Pageants and Pageantry.* Boston: Ginn, 1912.

Bates, Katharine Lee. *American Literature.* New York: Macmillan, 1900.

———. *Ballad Book.* Boston, Sanborn, 1924.

———. *The College Beautiful and Other Poems.* Cambridge, MA: Norumbega Fund, 1887.

———. *The English Religious Drama.* New York: Macmillan, 1893.

———. *Outlines of Lectures on Modern English Literature.* Boston: Bliss, 1895.

———. *The Retinue, and Other Poems.* New York: Dutton, 1918.

Baym, Nina. *Woman's Fiction: A Guide to Novels by and about Women in America, 1820–1870.* Ithaca, NY: Cornell UP, 1978.

Beasley, Maurine Hoffman. *Eleanor Roosevelt and the Media: A Public Quest for Self-Fulfillment.* Urbana: U of Chicago P, 1987.

———. *The First Women Washington Correspondents.* G.W. Washington Studies 4. Washington: George Washington U, 1976.

Belford, Barbara. *Brilliant Bylines: A Biographical Anthology of Notable Newspaperwomen in America.* New York: Columbia UP, 1986.

Bennett, Helen M. *Women and Work: The Economic Value of College Training.* New York: Appleton, 1917.

Berelson, Bernard. *Graduate Education in the United States.* New York: McGraw, 1960.

Berlin, James. *Rhetoric and Reality: Writing Instruction in American Colleges, 1900–1985.* Carbondale: Southern Illinois UP, 1987.

———. *Writing Instruction in Nineteenth-Century American Colleges.* Carbondale: Southern Illinois UP, 1984.

Bernays, Edward L. *Propaganda.* New York: Liveright, 1928.

Biggs, Walter K. *Education of Teachers.* New York: Center for Applied Research in Education, 1965.

Bishop, Elizabeth. *North and South.* Boston: Houghton, 1946.

———. *One Art.* Ed. Robert Giroux. New York: Farrar, Straus, Giroux, 1994.

Bizzell, Patricia. Review of *Invention as a Social Act*, by Karen Burke Lefevre. *College Composition and Communication* 38 (1987): 485–86.

Black, Ruby. *Eleanor Roosevelt.* New York: Duell, 1940.

Blair, Karen J. *The Clubwoman as Feminist: True Womanhood Redefined, 1868–1914.* New York: Holmes and Meier, 1980.

———. *The Torchbearers: Women and Their Amateur Arts Associations in America, 1890–1930.* Bloomington: Indiana UP, 1994.

Blake, Mabelle Babcock. *Guidance for College Women: A Survey and a Program for Personnel Work in Higher Education.* New York: Appleton, 1926.

Bleecker, Ann Eliza. *Posthumous Works of Ann Eliza Bleecker.* Ed. Margaretta V. Faugeres. New York: Swords, 1793.

Bleyer, Willard. Letter to Reading Publishers, 1910. ms. Archives, U. of Wisconsin, Madison.

Bok, Edward. *The Americanization of Edward Bok: The Autobiography of a Dutch Boy Fifty Years After.* New York: Scribner's, 1920.

Bonner, Marita Odette. "The Hands." *Opportunity* Aug. 1925: 235–37.

———. "Nothing New." *Crisis* Nov. 1926: 17–20.

———. "The Prison Bound." *Crisis* Sept. 1926: 225–26.

Bowles, Frank, and Frank A. DeCosta. *Between Two Worlds: A Profile of Negro Higher Education.* New York: McGraw-Hill, 1971.

Bradstreet, Anne. "The Author to Her Book." *The Complete Works of Anne Bradstreet.* Ed. Joseph R. McElrath, Jr. and Allan P. Robb. Boston: Twayne, 1981. 177–78.

———. *Several Poems Compiled with Great Variety of Wit and Learning, Full of Delight.* Boston: Foster, 1678.

———. *The Tenth Muse Lately Sprung Up in America.* London: Pratt, 1650.

Brandt, H. C. G. "How Far Should Our Teaching and Text-books Have a Scientific Basis?" *The Origins of Literary Studies in America: A Documentary Anthology.* Ed. Gerald Graff and Michael Warner. New York: Routledge, 1989. 28–33.

Brazelton, Ethel M. Colson. *Writing and Editing for Women.* New York: Funk and Wagnalls, 1927.

Breckinridge, Sophonisba P. *Women in the Twentieth Century: A Study of Their Political, Social and Economic Activities.* New York: McGraw, 1933.

Brittin, Norman A. *Edna St. Vincent Millay.* New York: Twayne, 1967.

Brown, Rollo Walter. "Coeducation versus Literature." *Harper's Magazine* 148 (May 1924): 784–90.

———. *Dean Briggs.* New York: Harper, 1926.

Bruce, Harold Lawton. *Voltaire and the English Stage.* Berkeley: U of California P, 1918.

Buck, Gertrude. *A Course in Narrative Writing.* New York: Holt, 1906.

Buck, Pearl S. *East Wind: West Wind.* New York: Grosset and Dunlap, 1930.

———. *The Good Earth.* New York: Grosset and Dunlap, 1931.

Bugbee, Emma. *Peggy Covers the News.* New York: Dodd, Mead, 1936.

———. *Peggy Covers Washington.* New York: Dodd, Mead, 1937.

Bullock, Penelope L. *The Afro-American Periodical Press, 1838–1909.* Baton Rouge: Louisiana State UP, 1981.

Butcher, Fanny. *Many Lives—One Love.* New York: Harper, 1972.

Campbell, Barbara Kuhn. *The "Liberated" Woman of 1914: Prominent Women in the Progressive Era.* Ann Arbor, MI: UMI Research Press, 1979.

Canfield, Dorothy. *The Home-Maker.* New York: Harcourt, 1924.

Capper, Charles. *Margaret Fuller: An American Romantic Life.* Vol. 1. New York: Oxford UP, 1992.

Cargill, Oscar. *Intellectual America: Ideas on the March.* New York: Macmillan, 1941.

Carroll, Gladys Hasty. *To Remember Forever: The Journal of a College Girl 1922–23.* Boston: Little, Brown, 1963.

Carruth, William. *Verse Writing.* New York: Macmillan, 1917.

Caspary, Vera. *The Secrets of Grown-ups.* New York: McGraw, 1979.

Cather, Willa. "Concerning Thomas Carlyle." *The Kingdom of Art: Willa Cather's First Principles and Critical Statements, 1893–1896.* Ed. Bernice Slote. Lincoln: U of Nebraska P, 1966. 421–25.

———. *Death Comes for the Archbishop.* New York: Knopf, 1927.

———. "Edgar Allan Poe." *The World and the Parish: Willa Cather's Articles and Reviews, 1893–1902.* Ed. William M. Curtin. Vol. I. Lincoln: U of Nebraska P, 1970. 157–63.

———. "The Hawthorn Tree." *April Twilights.* 1903. Ed. Bernice Slote. Lincoln: U of Nebraska P, 1968. 13.

———. *My Antonia.* Boston: Houghton, 1918.

———. "On *Death Comes for the Archbishop.*" *Willa Cather: Stories, Poems, and Other Writings.* New York: Library of America, 1992. 958–62.

———. "Peter." *Mahogany Tree* 21 May 1892: 323–24.

———. "Shakespeare and Hamlet." *The Kingdom of Art: Willa Cather's First Principles and Critical Statements, 1893–1896.* Ed. Bernice Slote. Lincoln: U of Nebraska P, 1966. 426–36.

————— . *The Song of the Lark*. Boston: Houghton, 1915.

Cather, Willa Louise. "Portrait of Dr. Louise McNeill Pease, West Virginia Educator." Diss. West Virginia U, 1988.

Caywood, Cynthia L., and Gillian R. Overing. "Writing across the Curriculum: A Model for a Workshop and a Call for Change." *Teaching Writing: Pedagogy, Gender, and Equity.* Ed. Caywood and Overing. Albany: State U of New York P, 1987. 185–200.

Chadakoff, Rochelle, ed. *Eleanor Roosevelt's My Day: Her Acclaimed Columns 1936–45.* New York: Pharos, 1989.

Chafe, William. *The American Woman: Her Changing Social, Economic, and Political Roles, 1920–1970.* New York: Oxford UP, 1972.

Chekhov, Anton. *The Seagull: A Play in Four Acts.* London: Hendersons, 1915.

Child, Lydia Maria. *The American Frugal Housewife.* Boston: Carter and Hendee, 1832.

————— . *The Frugal Housewife.* Boston: Marsh and Capen, 1829.

Cixous, Hélène. "The Laugh of the Medusa." Trans. Keith Cohen and Paula Cohen. *Signs* 1–4 (1976): 875–93.

Cixous, Hélène, and Catherine Clément. *The Newly Born Woman.* Trans. Betsy Wing. Minneapolis: U of Minnesota P, 1986.

Cochrane, Elizabeth ("Nellie Bly"). "Inside the Madhouse." *Brilliant Bylines: A Biographical Anthology of Notable Newspaperwomen in America.* Ed. Barbara Belford. New York: Columbia UP. 124–49.

Coffin, Gertrude Wilson. *Magnolia's Man, A Mountain Comedy. Carolina Folk Comedies. Carolina Folk-Plays* Ser. 4. Ed. Frederick H. Koch. New York: French, 1931. 1–43.

————— . *A Shotgun Splicin', A Mountain Comedy. Carolina Folk-Plays* Ser. 3. Ed. Frederick H. Koch. New York: Holt, 1928. 121–57.

Coiner, Constance. *Better Red: The Writing and Resistance of Tillie Olsen and Meridel Le Sueur.* New York: Oxford, 1995.

Cole, Arthur C. *A Hundred Years of Mt. Holyoke College: The Evolution of an Educational Ideal.* New Haven: Yale UP, 1940.

Compendium of the Eleventh Census: 1890. Part 3. Washington: GPO, 1897.

Cone, Helen Gray. "Woman in Literature." *Woman's Work in America.* Ed. Annie Nathan Meyer. New York: Holt, 1891. 107–27.

Conrad, Lawrence H. *Teaching Creative Writing.* New York: Appleton, 1937.

Cooper, Lane. *Two Views of Education with Other Papers Chiefly on the Study of Literature.* New Haven: Yale UP, 1922.

Coultrap-McQuin, Susan. *Doing Literary Business: American Women Writers in the Nineteenth Century.* Chapel Hill: U of North Carolina P, 1990.

Cowan, Louise. *The Fugitive Group: A Literary History.* Baton Rouge: Louisiana State UP, 1959.

Croly, Jane Cunningham ("Jennie June"). *Jennie June's American Cookery Book.* New York: American News, 1866.

Cummins, Maria. *The Lamplighter.* Boston: Jewett, 1854.

Davis, Deborah. *Katharine the Great: Katharine Graham and the Washington Post*. Bethesda, MD: National P, 1987.

Davis, Linda. *Onward and Upward: A Biography of Katharine S. White*. New York: Harper, 1987.

de Beauvoir, Simone. *The Second Sex*. 1949. Trans. H. M. Parshley. New York: Knopf, 1952.

DeJagers, Dorothy. *Hot Waffles: A Comedy in One Act*. New York: French, 1929.

Derleth, August. *Still Small Voice: The Biography of Zona Gale*. New York: Appleton, 1940.

Dewey, John, and Evelyn Dewey. *Schools of To-morrow*. New York: Dutton, 1915.

Dickinson, Thomas H. *The Case of American Drama*. Boston: Houghton, 1915.

Dinger, Ed. *Seems Like Old Times*. Iowa City: n.pub., 1986.

Donnelly, Lucy Martin. "The Heart of a Blue Stocking." *Atlantic Monthly* 102 (1908): 536–39.

Donovan, Josephine. *Black Soil*. Boston: Stratford, 1929.

Dorr, Rheta Childe. *A Woman of Fifty*. 1924. New York: Arno, 1980.

Douglas, Ann. *The Feminization of American Culture*. New York: Knopf, 1978.

DuBois, Shirley Graham. *Dr. George Washington Carver, Scientist*. New York: Messner, 1944.

———. *His Day is Marching On: A Memoir of W.E.B. DuBois*. Philadelphia: Lippincott, 1971.

———. *Paul Robeson: Citizen of the World*. New York: Messner, 1946.

———. *There Was Once a Slave: The Heroic Story of Frederick Douglass*. New York: Messner, 1947.

———. *Tom-Tom*. Cleveland: Laurence, 1932.

Duchen, Claire. *Women's Rights and Women's Lives in France, 1944–1968*. London: Routledge, 1994.

Eckley, Wilton. *Harriette Arnow*. New York: Twayne, 1974.

Ede, Lisa, and Andrea Lunsford. "Let Them Write—Together." *English Quarterly* 18 (1985): 119–27.

———. *Singular Texts/Plural Authors: Perspectives of Collaborative Writing*. Carbondale: Southern Illinois UP, 1990.

Emerson, William. Reviews of Hannah Adams's *A Summary History of New England* and of Jedidiah Morse and Elijah Parish's *A Compendious History of New England*. *Monthly Anthology* 2 (1805): 538–49.

Emery, Edwin, and Michael Emery. *The Press and America: An Interpretative History of the Mass Media*. 1954. 4th ed. Englewood Cliffs, NJ: Prentice, 1978.

Emery, Edwin, and Joseph P. McKerns. *AEJMC: Seventy-Five Years in the Making—A History of Organizing for Journalism and Mass Communication Education in the United States*. Journalism Monographs 104. ED 292 091.

Faber, Doris. *The Life of Lorena Hickok: E.R.'s Friend*. New York: Morrow, 1980.

Ferber, Edna. *Dawn O'Hara: The Girl Who Laughed*. New York: Stokes, 1911.

———. *A Peculiar Treasure.* New York: Doubleday, 1939.

Ferguson, Alfred Riggs. *Edward Rowland Sill: The Twilight Poet.* The Hague: Martinus Nijhoff, 1955.

Fern, Fanny. *Fern Leaves from Fanny's Portfolio.* Vol. 1. Auburn: Derby and Miller, 1853.

———. *Rose Clark.* New York: Mason Brothers, 1856.

Fitzpatrick, Ellen. "Tarbell and 'The Oil War of 1872.'" *Muckraking: Three Landmark Articles.* Ed. Ellen Fitzpatrick. Boston: St. Martin's, 1994. 23–27.

Flanagan, Hallie. *Arena: The History of the Federal Theatre.* New York: Benjamin Blom, 1940.

Fletcher, Robert Samuel. *A History of Oberlin from Its Foundation through the Civil War.* 2 vols. Oberlin: Oberlin College, 1943.

Folsom, Franklin. *Days of Anger, Days of Hope: A Memoir of the League of American Writers, 1937–1942.* Niwot, CO: UP of Colorado, 1994.

Foster, Frances Smith. "Adding Color and Contour to Early American Self-Portraitures: Autobiographical Writings of Afro-American Women." *Conjuring: Black Women, Fiction, and Literary Tradition.* Ed. Marjorie Pryse and Hortense J. Spillers. Bloomington: Indiana UP, 1985. 25–38.

Fountain, Gary, and Peter Brazeau. *Elizabeth Bishop: An Oral Biography.* Amherst: U of Massachusetts P, 1994.

Frederick, John T. "Literary Evening—Iowa Style." *The Borzoi, 1925: Being a Sort of Record of Ten Years of Publishing* New York: Knopf, 1925. 84–87.

———. "A Maker of Songs." *American Prefaces* 2 (March 1937): 83–84.

Freire, Paulo. *Pedagogy of the Oppressed.* Trans. Myra Bergman Ramos. New York: Seabury, 1974.

Friedan, Betty. *The Feminine Mystique.* New York: Norton, 1963.

Fuller, Margaret. *Woman in the Nineteenth Century.* 1845. Ed. Bernard Rosenthal. New York: Norton, 1971.

Gale, Zona. *Faint Perfume.* New York: Appleton, 1923.

———. *Friendship Village.* New York: Macmillan, 1908.

———. *Friendship Village Love Stories.* New York: Macmillan, 1909.

———. *Miss Lulu Bett.* New York: Appleton, 1920.

———. *Miss Lulu Bett: An American Comedy of Manners.* New York: Appleton, 1921.

———. *Neighborhood Stories.* New York: Macmillan, 1914.

———. "The Novel of Tomorrow." *The Novel of Tomorrow and the Scope of Fiction.* Indianapolis: Bobbs-Merrill, 1922. 65–72.

———. *Peace in Friendship Village.* New York: Macmillan, 1919.

———. *When I Was a Little Girl.* New York: Macmillan, 1913.

———. "Writing as Design." *The Writer and His Craft.* Ed. Robert Morss Lovett. Ann Arbor: U of Michigan P, 1954. 30–38.

Gavf, Emma, pseud. *A Comedy of Circumstance.* Garden City, NY: Doubleday, 1911.

Geismar, Maxwell. *The Last of the Provincials: The American Novel, 1915–1925*. Boston: Houghton, 1943.

Gelderman, Carol W. *Mary McCarthy: A Life*. New York: St. Martin's, 1988.

Gellhorn, Martha. *The Trouble I've Seen*. New York: Morrow, 1936.

——— . *What Mad Pursuit, A Novel*. New York: Stokes, 1934.

Gere, Ann Ruggles. *Intimate Practices: Literacy and Cultural Work in U.S. Women's Clubs, 1880–1920*. Urbana: U of Illinois P, 1997.

——— . *Writing Groups: History, Theory, and Implications*. Carbondale: Southern Illinois UP, 1987.

Gilman, Mildred. *Fig Leaves*. New York: Siebel, 1925.

——— . *Headlines*. New York: Liveright, 1928.

——— . *Sob Sister*. New York: Cape and Smith, 1931.

Glaspell, Susan. *Inheritors*. New York: Dodd, 1921.

——— . *The Road to the Temple*. New York: Stokes, 1927.

Glaspell, Susan, and George Cram Cook. *Suppressed Desires*. New York: Shay, 1917.

Gold, Michael. "America Needs a Critic." *New Masses* Oct. 1926: 7–9.

Gordon, Lynn D. "Co-Education on Two Campuses: Berkeley and Chicago, 1890–1912." *Woman's Being, Woman's Place: Female Identity and Vocation in American History*. Ed. Mary Kelley. Boston: Hall, 1979. 171–93.

Graff, Gerald. *Professing Literature: An Institutional History*. Chicago: U of Chicago P, 1987.

Green, Erma, and Paul Green. *Fixin's*. New York: French, 1934.

Greenwood, Grace. *Greenwood Leaves: A Collection of Sketches and Letters*. Boston: Ticknor, 1850.

Greer, Germaine. *The Female Eunuch*. New York: McGraw-Hill, 1971.

Harland, Marion. *Common Sense in the Household: A Manual of Practical Housewifery*. New York: Scribner's, 1871.

——— . *Marion Harland's Autobiography: The Story of a Long Life*. New York: Harper, 1910.

Hart, Henry. *American Writers' Congress*. New York: International, 1935.

Hart, James Morgan. "The College Course in English Literature, How It May Be Improved." *The Origins of Literary Studies in America: A Documentary Anthology*. Ed. Gerald Graff and Michael Warner. New York: Routledge, 1989. 34–37.

Hart, Sophie Chantal. "English Composition—An Interpretation." *Wellesley Magazine* June 1937: 372–74.

Hatcher, O. Latham. *Occupations for Women: A Study Made for the Southern Woman's Educational Alliance*. Richmond: Southern Woman's Educational Alliance, 1927.

Haun, Mildred. *The Hawk's Done Gone*. New York: Bobbs Merrill, 1940.

Hemenway, Robert E. *Zora Neale Hurston: A Literary Biography*. Urbana: U of Illinois P, 1978.

Herbst, Josephine. *Pity is Not Enough*. 1933. Urbana: U of Illinois P, 1998.

——— . *Rope of Gold*. New York: Harcourt, 1939.

Herrick, Robert. "Barrett Wendell." *New Republic* 10 Dec. 1924: 6–7.

——— . *Chimes.* New York: Macmillan, 1926.

——— . *The Common Lot.* New York: Macmillan, 1904.

——— . *A Life for a Life.* New York: Macmillan, 1910.

——— . *The Memoirs of an American Citizen.* New York: Macmillan, 1905.

——— . "The New Novel." *The Novel of Tomorrow and the Scope of Fiction.* Indianapolis: Bobbs-Merrill, 1922. 91–102.

Heyward, Dorothy Kuhns, and DuBose Heyward. *Mamba's Daughters; A Play.* New York: Farrar and Reinhart, 1939.

——— . *Porgy: A Play in Four Acts.* Garden City, NY: Doubleday, 1927.

Hill, Joseph. *Women in Gainful Occupations, 1870–1920.* Census Monograph 9. Washington: GPO, 1929.

Historical Statistics of the United States: Colonial Times to 1970. Part I. Washington: U.S. Department of Commerce, Bureau of the Census, 1975.

Hobson, Laura Z. *Gentleman's Agreement: A Novel.* New York: Grosset and Dunlap, 1947.

——— . *Laura Z: The Early Years and Years of Fulfillment.* New York: Fine, 1987.

Hoffman, Michael J. *Gertrude Stein.* Boston: Twayne, 1976.

Howard, Lillie P. *Zora Neale Hurston.* Boston: Twayne, 1980.

Hudson, Frederic. *Journalism in the United States, from 1690 to 1872.* 1873. New York: Haskell, 1968.

Hull, Helen R. *A Circle in the Water.* New York: Coward-McCann, 1943.

——— . *Hardy Perennial.* New York: Coward-McCann, 1933.

——— . *Hawk's Flight.* New York: Coward-McCann, 1946.

——— . *Islanders.* New York: Macmillan, 1927.

——— . *Labyrinth.* New York: Macmillan, 1923.

——— . *Mayling Soong Chiang.* New York: Coward-McCann, 1943.

——— . *Octave: A Book of Stories.* New York: Coward-McCann, 1947.

Hunt, Percival. *The Gift of the Unicorn.* Pittsburgh: U of Pittsburgh P, 1965.

Hunt, Theodore W. "The Place of English in the College Curriculum." *The Origins of Literary Studies in America: A Documentary Anthology.* Ed. Gerald Graff and Michael Warner. New York: Routledge, 1989. 38–49.

Hurston, Zora Neale. *Dust Tracks on a Road.* 1942. Urbana: U of Chicago P, 1984.

——— . *Their Eyes Were Watching God.* Philadelphia: Lippincott, 1937.

Hyde, Grant Milnor. "Raising the Quality of Students." *Journalism Bulletin* 4.1 (1927): 15–22.

——— . "Taking Stock after Twenty-Four Years." *Journalism Quarterly* 6 (Mar. 1929): 8–12.

Ings, Marvel. *Our Own Wisconsin.* Madison: State Historical Society of Wisconsin, 1945.

Interview with Louisa Knapp. *Journalist* Jan. 1889: 2.

James, Edward T., ed. *Notable American Women, 1607–1950: A Biographical Dictionary*. 3 vols. Cambridge, MA: Harvard UP, 1971.

James, Henry. *Roderick Hudson*. Boston: Osgood, 1875.

Johnson, Alvin. *Pioneer's Progress: An Autobiography*. New York: Viking, 1952.

Johnson, Josephine. *Now in November*. New York: Simon and Schuster, 1934.

Johnston, Annie Fellows. *The Little Colonel*. Boston: Page, 1895.

Jones, Ann Rosalind. "Writing the Body: Toward an Understanding of *L'Ecriture Féminine*. *Feminist Studies* 7.2 (1981): 247–63.

Kelley, Mary. *Private Woman, Public Stage: Literary Domesticity in Nineteenth-Century America*. New York: Oxford, 1984.

Kelly, Emma Dunham. *Megda*. Boston: Earle, 1891.

Kelly, Florence Finch. *Flowing Stream: The Story of Fifty-Six Years in American Newspaper Life*. New York: Dutton, 1939.

Kenne, Helen. "The Field of Domestic Science." *Vocations for the Trained Woman: Opportunities Other than Teaching*. New York: Longmans, 1910. 81–85.

Kessler-Harris, Alice. *Out to Work: A History of Wage-Earning Women in the United States*. New York: Oxford UP, 1982.

King, Georgiana Goddard. *The Way of Perfect Love*. New York: Macmillan, 1908.

Kirkland, Caroline. Review of *The Wide, Wide World* and *Queechy*. *The North American Review*. 1853. *Nineteenth-Century Literary Criticism*. Vol. 31. Ed. Paula Kepos. Detroit: Gale Research, 1991. 332–37.

Kissane, Leedice McAnelly. *Ruth Suckow*. New York: Twayne, 1969.

Kitchel, Anna. *George Lewes and George Eliot: A Review of Records*. New York: Day, 1933.

Knox, George. "The Great American Novel: Final Chapter." *American Quarterly* 21 (Winter 1969): 679.

Koch, Frederick H. "Folk-Play Making." *Carolina Folk-Plays* Ser. 1. Ed. Frederick H. Koch. New York: Holt, 1922. xi–xxix.

Kolodny, Annette. "Inventing a Feminist Discourse: Rhetoric and Resistance in Margaret Fuller's *Woman in the Nineteenth Century*. *Reclaiming Rhetorica: Women in the Rhetorical Tradition*. Ed. Andrea A. Lunsford. Pittsburgh: U of Pittsburgh P, 1995. 137–66.

Knapp, Bettina L. *Gertrude Stein*. New York: Ungar, 1990.

Knox, George. "The Great American Novel: Final Chapter." *American Quarterly* 21 (Winter 1969): 667–82.

Kurth, Peter. *American Cassandra: The Life of Dorothy Thompson*. Boston: Little, Brown, 1990.

La Follette, Belle Case. "The Inauguration." *La Follette's Magazine* 1.10 (1907): 10.

La Follette, Belle Case, and Fola La Follette. *Robert M. La Follette: June 14, 1855–June 18, 1925*. Vol. 1. New York: Macmillan, 1953.

La Follette, Robert. Address Given at the University of Wisconsin. 1904. ms. Archives, U. of Wisconsin, Madison.

Langer, Elinor. *Josephine Herbst*. Boston: Little, Brown, 1983.

Latimer, Margery. "Guardian Angel." *Guardian Angel and Other Stories*. Old Westbury, NY: Feminist P, 1984. 76–164.

———. *We Are Incredible*. New York: Sears, 1928.

Lay, Elizabeth A. *When Witches Ride*. *Carolina Folk-Plays* Ser. 1. Ed. Frederick H. Koch. New York: Holt, 1922. 1–23.

Leonard, Sterling. *English Composition as a Social Problem*. Boston: Houghton, 1917.

Leslie, Eliza. *The Behaviour Book: A Manual for Ladies*. Philadelphia: Hazard, 1853.

———. *Seventy-five Receipts for Pastry, Cakes and Sweetmeats*. Boston: Munroe, Francis, 1827.

Le Sueur, Meridel. "Afterword: A Memoir." *Guardian Angels and Other Stories*. By Margery Latimer. Old Westbury, NY: Feminist P, 1984. 230–35.

———. *Salute to Spring*. New York: International, 1940.

Lewis, Edwin Herbert. *Business English*. Chicago: LaSalle Extension University, 1911.

———. *A First Book in Writing English*. New York: Macmillan, 1897.

———. *A First Manual of Composition*. New York: Macmillan, 1899.

Lilian Whiting, Journalist, Essayist, Critic, and Poet. A Sketch. Boston: Little, Brown, 1900.

Little, Frances. *The Lady of the Decoration*. New York: Century, 1906.

———. *Little Sister Snow*. New York: Century, 1909.

Locke, Alain. "The New Negro." *The New Negro: An Interpretation*. Ed. Locke. New York: Boni, 1925. 3–16.

Loughridge, Nancy. "Afterword: The Life." *Guardian Angels and Other Stories*. By Margery Latimer. Old Westbury, NY: Feminist P, 1984. 215–29.

Lovett, Robert Morss. *All Our Years: The Autobiography of Robert Morss Lovett*. New York: Viking, 1948.

———. "Literature and Animal Faith." *The Writer and His Craft*. Ed. Lovett. Ann Arbor: U of Michigan P, 1954. 1–15.

———. Preface. *Collected Verse by the Poetry Club of the University of Chicago*. Ed. Lovett. Chicago: Covici-McGee, 1923. N.pag.

———. Review of *Death Comes for the Archbishop*. *New Republic* 26 Oct. 1927: 266.

Lynd, Robert, and Helen Lynd. *Middletown: A Study in Contemporary American Culture*. New York: Harcourt, 1929.

Macdougall, Allan Ross. *Letters of Edna St. Vincent Millay*. New York: Harper, 1952.

MacDougall, Curtis D. "Streamlining the Journalism Course." *Journalism Quarterly* 15 (1938): 282–88.

MacDuffie, Abby Parsons. *The Little Pilgrim: An Autobiography*. New York: Marchbanks, 1938.

MacKaye, Percy. *The Pilgrim and the Book*. New York: American Bible Society, 1920.

Maher, Frances. "Classroom Pedagogy and the New Scholarship on Women." *Gendered Subjects: The Dynamics of Feminist Teaching*. Ed. Margo Culley and Catherine Portuges. Boston: Routledge, 1985. 29–48.

Mangione, Jerre. *The Dream and the Deal: The Federal Writers' Project, 1935–1943*. Boston: Little, Brown, 1972.

Mann, Thomas. *Death in Venice*. Mattituck, NY: Amereon, 1900.

March, Francis. *Method of Philological Study of the English Language*. New York: Harper, 1865.

Martin, George Madden. *Emmy Lou: Her Book and Heart*. Garden City, NY: Doubleday, 1902.

Marzolf, Marion. *Up from the Footnote: A History of Women Journalists*. New York: Hastings, 1977.

McCarthy, Mary. *How I Grew*. San Diego: Harcourt, 1987.

McDowell, Frederick P. W. *Elizabeth Madox Roberts*. New York: Twayne, 1963.

McFetridge, Elizabeth. "The Point of View." *The Newcomb Arcade* 6.2 (1914): 40–43.

McIntosh, Maria. *The Children's Mirror: A Treasury of Stories*. New York: Nelson, 1887.

———. *Conquest and Self-Conquest; Or, Which Makes the Hero?* New York: Harper, 1839.

McNeill. Louise. *Gauley Mountain*. New York: Harcourt, 1939.

———. *The Milkweed Ladies*. Pittsburgh: U of Pittsburgh P, 1988.

———. *Time Is Our House*. Bread Loaf, VT: Middlebury College P, 1942.

Mearns, Hughes. *Creative Youth: How a School Environment Set Free the Creative Spirit*. Garden City, NY: Doubleday, 1930.

Millay, Edna St. Vincent. *Aria da Capo: A Play in One Act*. Boston: Baker's Plays, 1920.

Miller, Alice Duer, and Susan Myers. *Barnard College: The First Fifty Years*. New York: Columbia UP, 1939.

Miller, Ann, ed. *A College in Dispersion: Women of Bryn Mawr, 1896–1975*. Boulder, CO: Westview, 1976.

Miller, May. *Plays and Pageants from the Life of the Negro*. Washington: Associated, 1930.

Miller, May, and Willis Richardson, eds. *Negro History in Thirteen Plays*. Washington: Associated, 1935.

Mirrielees, Edith. *Story Writing*. Boston: Writer, 1939.

Mitchell, Margaret. *Gone with the Wind*. New York: Macmillan, 1936.

Moi, Toril. *Sexual/Textual Politics: Feminist Literary Theory*. New York: Methuen, 1985.

Molesworth, Charles. *Marianne Moore: A Literary Life*. New York: Atheneum, 1990.

Moore, Marianne. "The Discouraged Poet." *The Complete Prose of Marianne Moore*. Ed. Patricia C. Willis. New York: Viking, 1986. 8–10.

———. "A Pilgrim." *The Complete Prose of Marianne Moore*. Ed. Patricia C. Willis. New York: Viking, 1986. 10–12.

———. "The Plumet Basilick." *The Complete Poems of Marianne Moore*. New York: Viking, 1958. 20–24.

———. "Pym." *The Complete Prose of Marianne Moore*. Ed. Patricia C. Willis. New York: Viking, 1986. 12–16.

———. *The Selected Letters of Marianne Moore*. Ed. Bonnie Costello, Celeste Goodridge, and Christine Miller. New York: Knopf, 1997.

————. "The Spare American Emotion." *Critical Essays on Gertrude Stein*. Ed. Michael Hoffman. Boston: Hall, 1986. 46–49.

————. "Wisdom and Virtue." *The Complete Prose of Marianne Moore*. Ed. Patricia C. Willis. New York: Viking, 1986. 26–30.

Morison, Samuel Eliot. *The Development of Harvard University since the Inauguration of President Eliot, 1869–1929*. Cambridge: Harvard UP, 1930.

Mott, Frank Luther. *American Journalism: A History of Newspapers through 250 Years, 1690–1940*. New York: Macmillan, 1941.

————. *A History of American Magazines*. Vol. 2. Cambridge: Harvard UP, 1938.

Mowat, Charles Loch. *Britain between the Wars, 1918–1940*. Chicago: U of Chicago P, 1955.

Murray, Judith Sargent. *Virtue Triumphant. The Gleaner*. Vol. 3. Boston: Thomas and Andrews, 1798.

Murray, Pauli. *Song in a Weary Throat: An American Pilgrimage*. New York: Harper, 1987.

M.V.A. "How to Make a Daily Theme." *Radcliffe Magazine* 2 (1900): 31–32.

Myers, D. G. *The Elephants Teach: Creative Writing Since 1880*. Englewood Cliffs, NJ: Prentice, 1996.

The Negro in Virginia. New York: Hastings House, 1940.

Nevius, Blake. *Robert Herrick: The Development of a Novelist*. Berkeley: U of California P, 1962.

Newcomer, Mabel. *A Century of Higher Education for American Women*. New York: Harper, 1959.

"Notes of the Schools." *Journalism Bulletin* 1 (1924): 30–34.

O'Dell, De Forest. *The History of Journalism Education in the United States*. New York: Columbia University Teachers College Bureau of Publications, 1935.

Palmieri, Patricia A. "Here Was Fellowship: A Social Portrait of Academic Women at Wellesley College, 1895–1920." *Women Who Taught: Perspectives on the History of Women and Teaching*. Ed. Alison Prentice and Marjorie R. Theobald. Toronto: U of Toronto P, 1991. 233–57.

Parker, William Belmont. *Edward Rowland Sill: His Life and Work*. Boston: Houghton, 1915.

Pattee, Fred Lewis. *The Feminine Fifties*. New York: Appleton, 1940.

Patterson, Helen M. *Writing and Selling Special Feature Articles*. New York: Prentice, 1939.

Patton, Frances Gray. *The Beaded Buckle. Carolina Folk-Plays* Ser. 2. Ed. Frederick H. Koch. New York: Holt, 1924.

————. *Good Morning, Miss Dove*. New York: Dodd, Mead, 1946.

Piper, Edwin Ford. *Barbed Wire and Wayfarers*. New York: Macmillan, 1924.

————. *The Land of the Aiouwas*. Iowa City, IA: Midland, 1922.

————. *Paintrock Road*. New York: Macmillan, 1927.

Pitkin, Walter. *The Art and the Business of Story Writing*. New York: Macmillan, 1912.

"Playshop Laboratory Curtain Up." *Playshop Laboratory Plays.* Ed. Jeannette Marks. South Hadley: Mount Holyoke College, 1932. xiii–xxix.

Porter, Philip W., and Norval Neil Luxon. *The Reporter and the News.* New York: Appleton, 1935.

Price, Doris. *The Bright Medallion. University of Michigan Plays.* Ed. Kenneth T. Rowe. Ann Arbor: G. Wahr, 1932. 277–318.

———. *The Eyes of the Old. University of Michigan Plays.* Ed. Kenneth T. Rowe. Ann Arbor: G. Wahr, 1932. 319–38.

Rabinowitz, Paula. *Labor and Desire: Women's Revolutionary Fiction in Depression America.* Chapel Hill: U of N Carolina P, 1991.

Ransom, John Crowe. "The Poet as Woman." *Southern Review* 2 (Spring 1937): 783–806.

Ravitz, Abe. *Leane Zugsmith: Thunder on the Left.* New York: International, 1922.

Rawlings, Marjorie Kinnan. *The Yearling.* New York: Scribner's, 1933.

Rayne, Martha Louise. *What Can a Woman Do; Or, Her Position in the Business and Literary World.* 1886. New York: Arno, 1974.

Reinholt, Ferdina. "Women in Journalism." *Journalism Bulletin* 2.3 (1925): 38–41.

Review of *The Wide, Wide World. Holden's Dollar Magazine.* 1851. *Nineteenth-Century Literary Criticism.* Vol. 31. Ed. Paula Kepos. Detroit: Gale Research, 1991. 332.

Rice, Alice Caldwell Hegan. *The Inky Way.* New York: Appleton, 1940.

———. *Mrs. Wiggs of the Cabbage Patch.* New York: Grosset and Dunlap, 1901.

Riegel, Robert E. *American Women: A Story of Social Change.* Cranbury, NJ: Associated University Presses, 1970.

Roach, Abby Meguire. *Some Successful Marriages.* New York: Harper, 1906.

Robbins, Frances. Review of *Death Comes for the Archbishop. Outlook* 26 Oct. 1927: 251.

Roberts, Elizabeth Madox. *In the Great Steep's Garden.* Colorado, Springs, CO: Gowdy-Simmons, 1915.

———. *Jingling in the Wind.* New York: Viking, 1928.

———. *My Heart and My Flesh: A Novel.* New York: Grosset & Dunlap, 1927.

———. *The Sacrifice of the Maidens.* Garden City, NY: Doubleday, 1930.

———. *The Time of Man.* New York: Viking, 1926.

Robinson, William H., Jr. *Early Black American Poets: Selections with Biographical and Critical Introductions.* Dubuque, IA: William C. Brown, 1969.

Rodman, Seldon. "A Historical Novel of Modern America." *Saturday Review of Literature* 10 Nov. 1934: 273.

Roebuck, Julian B., and Komanduri S. Murty. *Historically Black Colleges and Universities: Their Place in American Higher Education.* Westport, CT: Praeger, 1993.

Rose, Christopher. "Dear Dorothy Dix." New Orleans *Times-Picayune* 26 May 1996: D1+.

Roses, Lorraine Elena, and Ruth Elizabeth Randolph. *Harlem Renaissance and Beyond: Literary Biographies of 100 Black Women Writers, 1900–1945.* Boston: Hall, 1990.

Rudolph, Frederick. *The American College and University: A History.* New York: Knopf, 1962.

Sanders, Marion K. *Dorothy Thompson: A Legend in Her Time.* Boston: Houghton, 1973.

Sandmel, Frances Fox. *The Conception and the Creation: A Critical Evaluation of the Work of the Carolina Playmakers.* Diss. U of North Carolina, 1941.

Santmyer, Helen Hooven. *Herbs and Apples.* 1925. New York: Harper, 1985.

Scarborough, Dorothy. *In the Land of Cotton.* New York: Macmillan, 1923.

———. *The Wind.* New York: Harper, 1925.

Schilpp, Medelon, and Sharon M. Murphy. *Great Women of the Press.* Carbondale: Southern Illinois UP, 1983.

Schwartz, Julia Augusta. *Elinor's College Career.* Boston: Little, Brown, 1906.

———. *Vassar Studies.* New York: Putnam's, 1899.

Scobie, Ingrid Winther. *Center Stage: Helen Gahagan Douglas, A Life.* New York: Oxford UP, 1992.

Semple, Ellen Churchill. *American History and Geographic Conditions.* Boston: Houghton, 1903.

———. *Influences of Geographic Environment.* New York: Holt, 1911.

Sharp, Dallas Lore. *Roof and Meadow.* New York: Century, 1904.

———. *A Watcher in the Woods.* New York: Century, 1901.

———. *Wild Life Near Home.* New York: Century, 1901.

Sheehan, Marion Turner, ed. *The World at Home: Selections from the Writing of Anne O'Hare McCormick.* New York: Knopf, 1956.

Shuman, Edwin L. *Practical Journalism: A Complete Manual of the Best Newspaper Methods.* New York: Appleton, 1903.

Sigourney, Lydia Huntley. *Water-Drops.* New York: Carter, 1848.

Simmons, Sue Carter. "Radcliffe Responses to Harvard Rhetoric: 'An Absurdly Stiff Way of Thinking.'" *Nineteenth-Century Women Learn to Write.* Ed. Catherine Hobbs. Charlottesville: UP of Virginia, 1995. 264–92.

Simonson, Harold P. *Zona Gale.* New York: Twayne, 1962.

Sixteenth Census of the United States: 1940. Part I. Vol. 3. Washington: GPO, 1943.

Smedley, Agnes. *Daughter of Earth.* 1929. New York: Feminist P, 1987.

Solomon, Barbara Miller. *In the Company of Educated Women.* New Haven: Yale UP: 1985.

Spearman, Walter. *The Carolina Playmakers: The First Fifty Years.* Chapel Hill, NC: U of North Carolina P, 1970.

Spencer, Cornelia. *The Exile's Daughter: A Biography of Pearl S. Buck.* New York: Coward McCann, 1944.

Spencer, Elizabeth. *Landscapes of the Heart: A Memoir.* New York: Random, 1998.

Stanton, Domna C. "Difference on Trial: A Critique of the Maternal Metaphor in Cixous, Irigaray, and Kristeva." *The Thinking Muse: Feminism and Modern French Philosophy.* Ed. Jeffner Allen and Iris Marion Young. Bloomington: Indiana UP, 1989. 156–79.

Stanton, Elizabeth Cady. "Address Delivered at Seneca Falls." *The Elizabeth Cady Stanton—Susan B. Anthony Reader*. Ed. Ellen Carol DuBois. Rev. ed. Boston: Northeastern UP, 1992. 27–35.

———. "Declarations of Sentiments and Resolutions." *Daughters of the Revolution: Classic Essays by Women*. Ed. James D. Lester. Lincolnwood, IL: NTC Publishing Group, 1996. 11–16.

Stegner, Wallace. *The Uneasy Chair: A Biography of Bernard DeVoto*. New York: Doubleday, 1974.

Stirling, Nora. *Pearl Buck: A Woman in Conflict*. Picataway, NJ: New Century, 1983.

Stein, Gertrude. *The Making of Americans*. Paris: Contact Editions, 1925.

Steinberg, Salme Harju. *Reformer in the Marketplace: Edward W. Bok and The Ladies' Home Journal*. Baton Rouge, LA: Louisiana State UP, 1979.

Stetson, Erlene. "Eighteenth- and Nineteenth-Century Poets." *Black Sister: Poetry by Black American Women, 1746–1980*. Ed. Stetson. Bloomington: Indiana UP, 1981.

Storr, Richard J. *Harper's University: The Beginnings*. Chicago: U of Chicago P, 1966.

Stowe, Harriet Beecher. *My Wife and I; or, Harry Henderson's History*. Boston: Houghton, 1861.

———. *Uncle Tom's Cabin, or, Life among the Lowly*. Boston: Jewett, 1851.

———. *We and Our Neighbors; Or, The Records of an Unfashionable Street*. Boston: Houghton, 1873.

Strong, Anna Louise. *The First Time in History: Two Years of Russia's New Life*. New York: Boni and Liveright, 1924.

Suckow, Ruth. *Country People*. New York: Knopf, 1924.

———. *The Odyssey of a Nice Girl*. New York: Knopf, 1925.

———. *A Part of the Institution. A Ruth Suckow Omnibus*. Iowa City: U of Iowa Press, 1988. 51–139.

Surbridge, Agnes. *The Confessions of a Club Woman*. New York: Doubleday, 1904.

Taggard, Genevieve. "Are Artists People?" *New Masses* Jan. 1927: 6–9.

Tarbell, Ida. "The Oil War of 1872." *Muckraking: Three Landmark Articles*. Ed. Ellen F. Fitzpatrick. Boston: St. Martin's, 1994. 60–80.

Taylor, R. A. Review of *Death Comes for the Archbishop*. *Spectator* 19 Nov. 1927: 894.

Thomas, M. Carey. "The Curriculum of the Woman's College." *Journal of the Association of Collegiate Alumnae* 10 (May 1917): 585–91.

———. "From *The Making of a Feminist*." *The Origins of Literary Studies in America: A Documentary Anthology*. Ed. Gerald Graff and Michael Warner. New York: Routledge, 1989. 179–89.

Thompson, Dorothy. "Let the Record Speak: Chamberlain and Alice." *Brilliant Bylines: A Biographical Anthology of Notable Newspaperwomen in America*. Ed. Barbara Belford. New York: Columbia UP. 228–30.

Thompson, Era Bell. *American Daughter*. Chicago: U of Chicago P, 1946.

Ticknor, Caroline. *Hawthorne and His Publisher*. Boston: Houghton, 1913.

Tompkins, Jane. *Sensational Designs: The Cultural Work of American Fiction, 1790–1860.* New York: Oxford UP, 1985.

U. S. One: Maine to Florida. New York: Modern Age, 1938.

Van Etten, Winifred. *I Am the Fox.* Boston: Little, Brown, 1936.

Van Vorst, Bessie McGinnis. *The Cry of the Children: A Study of Child-Labor.* New York: Moffat, Yard, 1908.

Van Vorst, Bessie McGinnis, and Marie Van Vorst. *The Woman Who Toils: Being the Experience of Two Gentlewomen as Factory Girls.* New York: Doubleday, 1903.

Vella, Michael. "Theology, Genre and Gender: The Precarious Place of Hannah Adams in American Literary History." *Early American Literature* 28.1 (1993): 21–41.

Virginia: A Guide to the Old Dominion. New York: Oxford UP, 1940.

Vollmer, Lula. *The Hill Between: A Folk Play in Three Acts.* New York: Longmans, Green, 1939.

———. *Moonshine and Honeysuckle: A Play in Three Acts.* New York: French, 1934.

———. *Sun-up: A Play in Three Acts.* New York: Brentano's, 1923.

Wagner, Joanne. "'Intelligent Members or Restless Disturbers': Women's Rhetorical Styles, 1880–1920." *Reclaiming Rhetorica: Women in the Rhetorical Tradition.* Ed. Andrea A. Lunsford. Pittsburgh: U of Pittsburgh P, 1995. 185–202.

Wald, Alan. "The Many Lives of Meridel Le Sueur (1900–1996)." *Monthly Review* 49.4 (1997): 23–31.

Walker, Alice. Forward. *Daughter of Earth.* By Agnes Smedley. New York: Feminist P, 1987. 1–4.

Walker, Margaret. *For My People.* New Haven: Yale UP, 1942.

———. "How I Wrote *Jubilee.*" *How I Wrote Jubilee and Other Essays on Life and Literature.* Ed. Maryemma Graham. New York: Feminist P, 1990. 50–65.

———. *Jubilee.* Toronto: Houghton, 1966.

Wall, Cheryl A. *Women of the Harlem Renaissance.* Bloomington: Indiana UP, 1995.

Wallace, Una. "A Singing Professor." *Daily Iowan* 6 December 1931, Sunday Magazine Section: 1+.

Ware, Susan. *Holding Their Own: American Women in the 1930s.* Boston: Twayne, 1982.

Warner, Susan. *Queechy.* New York; Putnam, 1852.

———. *The Wide, Wide World.* New York: Putnam, 1851.

Waterman, Arthur E. *Susan Glaspell.* New York: Twayne, 1966.

Watson, Carole McAlpine. *Prologue: The Novels of Black American Women, 1891–1965.* Westport, CT: Greenwood, 1985.

Wells, Anna Mary. *Miss Marks and Miss Woolley.* Boston: Houghton, 1978.

Welter, Barbara. "The Cult of True Womanhood: 1820–1860." *American Quarterly* 18 (Summer 1966): 151–74.

Welty, Eudora. *One Writer's Beginnings.* Cambridge, MA: Harvard UP, 1984.

Wendell, Barrett. Notes of Lectures in English 12, 1885–87, ms. Pusey Library, Harvard U.

Westin, Jean. *Making Do: How Women Survived the '30s.* Chicago: Follett, 1976.

Wheatley, Phillis. *Poems on Various Subjects, Religious and Moral.* London: Bell, 1773.

White, William Allen. *The Autobiography of William Allen White.* New York: Macmillan, 1946.

Widdemer, Margaret. *Ballads and Lyrics.* New York: Harcourt, 1925.

———. *Charis Sees It Through.* New York: Grosset and Dunlap, 1924.

———. *More than Wife.* New York: Harcourt, 1927.

———. *A Tree with a Bird in It.* New York: Harcourt, 1922.

Wilbers, Stephen. *The Iowa Writers' Workshop: Origins, Emergence, and Growth.* Iowa City: U of Iowa P, 1980.

Wilde, Oscar. *The Picture of Dorian Gray.* London: Ward, Lock, 1891.

Williams, Sara Lockwood. *Twenty Years of Education for Journalism.* Columbia, MO: Stephens, 1929.

Wilson, Harriet E. *Our Nig or, Sketches from the Life of a Free Black in a Two-Story White House, North; Showing that Slavery's Shadows Fall Even There.* Boston: Rand and Avery, 1859.

Wilson, Margaret. *The Able McLaughlins.* New York: Windsor, 1923.

———. *The Crime of Punishment.* London: Cape, 1931.

———. *Daughters of India, A Novel.* New York: Harper, 1928.

———. *One Came Out.* New York: Harper, 1932.

Winters, Ivor. "The Barnyard." *Collected Poems.* n.c.: Alan Swallow, 1960. 32.

Wolfe, Thomas. *The Return of Buck Gavin. Carolina Folk-Plays* Ser 2. Ed. Frederick H. Koch. New York: Holt, 1924. 33–44.

Woloch, Nancy. *Women and the American Experience.* New York: Knopf, 1984.

Woodress, James. *Willa Cather: A Literary Life.* Lincoln: U of Nebraska P, 1987.

Woody, Thomas. *A History of Women's Education in the United States.* 2 vols. New York: Science, 1929.

Woolf, Virginia. *A Room of One's Own.* New York: Harcourt, 1929.

Wozniak, John Michael. *English Composition in Eastern Colleges, 1850–1940.* Washington: UP of America, 1978.

Wroth, Lawrence C., and Rollo G. Silver. "Book Production and Distribution from the American Revolution to the War between the States." *The Book in America: A History of the Making and Selling of Books in the United States.* Ed. Hellmut Lehmann-Haupt, Wroth, and Silver. New York: Bowker, 1951. 61–136.

Young, Thomas Daniel. *Gentleman in a Dustcoat: A Biography of John Crowe Ransom.* Baton Rouge: Lousiana State UP, 1976.

Zimmerman, Joan G. "Daughters of Main Street: Culture and the Female Community at Grinnell, 1884–1917." *Woman's Being, Woman's Place: Female Identity and Vocation in American History.* Ed. Mary Kelley. Boston: Hall, 1979. 154–70.

Zugsmith, Leane. *Goodbye and Tomorrow.* New York: Liveright, 1931.

INDEX

A GROUP OF THEIR OWN

A GROUP OF THEIR OWN

College Writing Courses and
American Women Writers, 1880–1940

KATHERINE H. ADAMS

STATE UNIVERSITY OF NEW YORK PRESS

Published by
STATE UNIVERSITY OF NEW YORK PRESS
ALBANY

© 2001 State University of New York

For information, address
State University of New York Press,
90 State Street, Suite 700, Albany, NY 12207

Production and book design, Laurie Searl
Marketing, Anne M. Valentine

Library of Congress Cataloging-in-Publication Data

Adams, Katherine H., 1954–
    A group of their own : college writing courses and American women writers.
1880–1940 / Katherine H. Adams
        p. cm.
    Includes bibliographical references and index.
    ISBN 0-7914-4935-1 (alk. paper) — ISBN 0-7914-4936-X (pbk. : alk. paper)
        1. Women authors, American—Education. 2. American literature—Women
authors—History and criticism. 3. English language—Rhetoric—Study and
teaching—United States—History. 4. Creative writing (Higher education)—United
States—History. 5. Authorship—Social aspects—United States. 6. Women—Education
(Higher)—United States—History. 7. Women and literature—United States—History. I.
Title.

PS151 .A34 2001
810.9′9287′09034—dc21

                                                                                00-045055

10   9   8   7   6   5   4   3   2   1